Philosophy of Science

Andreas Beck Holm

Philosophy of Science

An Introduction for Future Knowledge Workers

2nd edition

Samfundslitteratur

Andreas Beck Holm
Philosophy of Science – An Introduction for Future Knowledge Workers
2nd edition 2018

Also published in Danish as
Videnskab i virkeligheden – en grundbog i videnskabsteori, 2. udg. 2018

Translation: Elisabeth Xiao-an Li; 2nd edition additions translated by Andreas Beck Holm
Editor: Annette Kjølby
Copy editor: Anders Juhl Gajhede
Cover: Imperiet (Annette Borsbøl, www.imperiet.dk)
Typeset: Steen Christensen, SL grafik (www.slgrafik.dk)
Print: Specialtrykkeriet Arco
ISBN: 978-87-593-3228-3

Samfundslitteratur
info@samfundslitteratur.dk
samfundslitteratur.dk

FSC
www.fsc.org
MIX
Papir fra ansvarlige kilder
FSC® C089429

Contents

Many people have contributed more or less directly to the realization of this book—more than I am able to mention here. However, I wish to thank Jan Engberg, Helle Dam-Jensen, Holm Fleischer, Nick Bo Todberg Madsen, Nikolaj Kure and, not least, Carsten Bagge Laustsen and Annette Kjølby for their comments and suggestions. A very special thanks goes to Stine for her daily patience.

Andreas Beck Holm
Aarhus, October 2013

Preface to the Second Edition

Since *Philosophy of Science* was first published in 2012, it has been used in a variety of contexts, which is very gratifying. Many educators have provided valuable feedback, detailing what works in the book, and what changes and additions they find desirable. The purpose of this second edition is to incorporate some of these suggestions. A few errors have been corrected, some chapters have been modified, and a presentation of recent cases and discussions has been added to the book. The single most important change consists in a new chapter on pragmatism. The author and the publisher hope that this update will make *Philosophy of Science* even more useful to future teachers and students.

Andreas Beck Holm
Aarhus, September 2018

Introduction

Of Science, Knowledge Societies, and Knowledge Workers

It is often said that we live in a knowledge society, and that education is a highly important raw material, but what does this mean?

Only a few decades ago the wealth of a society was determined by its ability to produce industrial goods. The larger, faster, and cheaper the production, the more substantial was the wealth of the population and the greater the power of the state.

> **Industrial Societies:** Societies whose wealth is dependent on the mass production of industrial goods.

For instance, the Allies did not win the Second World War because of better tanks, but because they mass-produced tanks faster than the Germans were able to destroy them. Of course, quick and cheap production is still important today. However, today, industrial workplaces tend to move abroad, while growth in our part of the world is mainly found in so-called knowledge-intensive companies. This is the development from an industrial society to a knowledge society.

> **Knowledge Societies:** Societies whose wealth depends on highly educated employees developing services and high technology products.

Needless to say, production also takes place in knowledge-intensive companies, but there is a great difference between producing cartons of milk and producing computer programmes. In knowledge-intensive companies the predominant part of the work process consists not of production itself, but rather of a development process where the employees' knowledge is the raw material. Thus, to an increasing extent, it is *knowledge* workers rather than *machine* workers who generate growth in companies and society.

But where does the knowledge of these workers come from, and why is it attributed such credibility and applicability? The answer to the first question is that knowledge comes from institutions of higher education, such as universities and business schools. This is where the key employees of a knowledge society are educated. The answer to the second question is science. Research-based teaching characterizes institutions of higher education. This means that the knowledge presented to students is based on scientific work.

The sciences thus figure directly in what can be called society's *knowledge dynamics*. The institutions of higher education produce new scientific knowledge. University graduates, the knowledge workers, communicate this new knowledge to the general public where it can impact discussions on politics and social conditions. Environmental and climatic issues are an example of how the sciences have influenced both the public debate and the policies pursued. The sciences are also presented through knowledge workers to the business world where the theories and technologies of science are applied in practice. Finally, in return, both the business and political world affect educational institutions. Political guidelines are laid down for the sciences, and the business world's use of scientifically based knowledge enables cooperation between businesses and educational institutions. Furthermore, the development of society and the business world places demands on the educational institutions. The knowledge acquired by students in these institutions must be relevant and credible; it must be founded on science. This entire dynamic, illustrated in the figure below, is pivotal to the growth, welfare, and progress of a knowledge society.

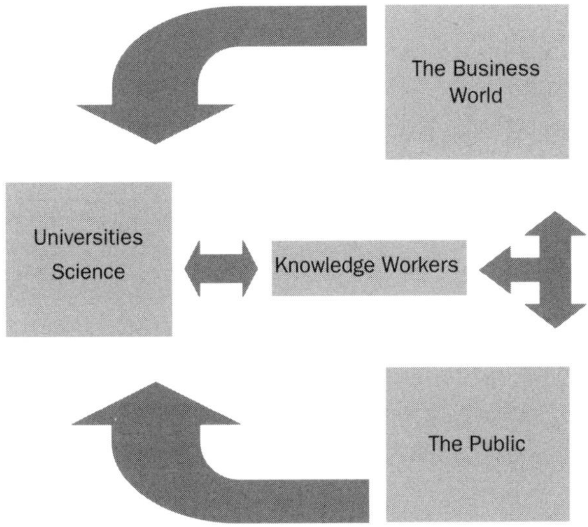

Figure 1.1. The Knowledge Dynamics of Society

This book is intended for future knowledge workers; i.e., students at institutions of higher education. As illustrated by the figure above, students play a central role in the knowledge dynamics of society because their education is based on research. To put it plainly, it is their role to communicate scientifically based knowledge to society and to the business world.

What does it mean to be a knowledge worker? The mere possession of knowledge is not the answer, although this is, of course, a prerequisite. What characterizes knowledge workers is that they *work* with knowledge rather than simply *have* knowledge. Developing this ability is an important part of higher education. Among other things, being able to work with knowledge means being capable of questioning information in a relevant and critical manner: Is it well founded? Is the argumentation sufficient, or does it run counter to well-established theories in the particular field of study? The ability to ask questions of this type is also a precondition for being able to present and defend one's knowledge when using it in the "real world" after graduation. In other words, to be a knowledge worker, you must have a critical approach to knowledge.

Being able to question and approach knowledge critically requires an understanding of the actual nature of knowledge and the sciences. For example, why is scientific knowledge in particular rated so highly in knowledge societies? When is knowledge certain? What is meant by objective knowledge, and is objectivity even possible? Can knowledge prove to be ethically or politically problematic despite being true? These are the questions that the philosophy of science is concerned with.

! **Philosophy of Science:** The systematic study of how scientific knowledge is produced, substantiated, and used in society.

This explains why philosophy of science is an important subject for students in higher education. Philosophical deliberation forms the basis for students' ability to pose relevant and critical questions to subjects and texts, as well as to the teaching they receive. Philosophy of science strengthens the students' general subject knowledge, and the insights gained from this discipline are applicable to all other subjects. In other words, philosophy of science is a prerequisite for students not just to become knowledgeable but also to become knowledge workers; thus it is also a precondition for graduates to be able to fill the central function of knowledge workers in organizations, businesses, and in society in general. For example, science plays a central part in the climate debate. You will therefore need to be aware of the importance of science if you want to make any qualified contributions to this discussion. Do scientists have definitive proof that climate change is caused by humankind? Is it a problem if scientists do not have such proof? Responding to these and similar questions requires knowledge of philosophy of science.

This very broad definition of philosophy of science not only includes philosophical issues but also issues connected with, for example, the sociology of knowledge. The reason for this broad definition is that a wide perspective is necessary to better understand the role of the sciences in the real world. Philosophy of science must, however, not be mistaken for methodology. This is partly because philosophy of science is concerned with many issues unconnected to methodology and partly because, unlike methodology, it is not associated with any specific discipline. Nevertheless, one area of philosophy of science does deal with the theoretical preconditions of different methods.

We can clarify the differences between the two approaches and at the same time illustrate the connection between philosophy of science and society, as well as the business world, by distinguishing between three different but interconnected *levels of knowledge* in society.

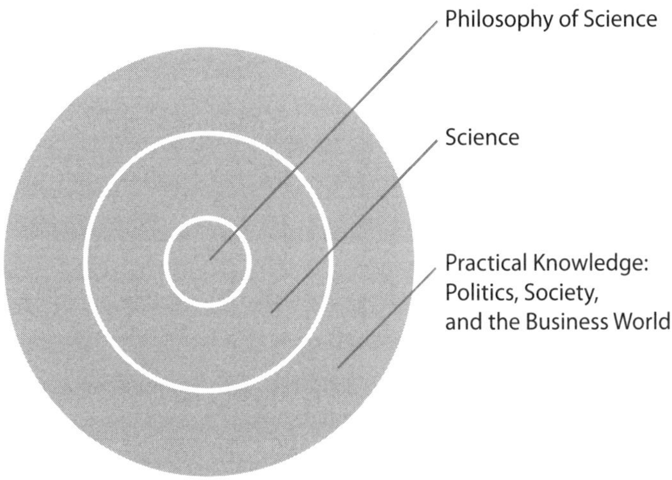

Figure 1.2. Society's Levels of Knowledge

The most *practical level of knowledge* is characteristic of the world of business and politics. In a changeable market, for example, executives want to know when it is most cost effective to buy a certain raw material for production. Here, as we have previously noted, the need for knowledge is practical. The focus is solely on a specific business's economy rather than on general laws.

These general laws are, however, a central concern at the *scientific level of knowledge*. Researchers and scientists rarely carry out their research for specifically economic reasons; instead, they attempt to detect general laws. An example could be the correlation between supply and demand on the one hand and market price on the other. Therefore, the researcher does not ask what the optimal economic disposition for a specific business is, but rather what *generally* determines the market's price development. It is at this level of knowledge we find methodology; that is, discussions of which strategy researchers should apply in their work.

Finally, the *philosophical level of knowledge* is the most general of the three. We are not concerned with the specific subject area of science, which in our example is the relation between supply, demand, and market price. Instead, the scientist's own research is questioned: What are the theoretical preconditions of this research and are they reliable? Or are the researchers in fact pursuing a mistaken line of thought when they ask whether one entity "determines" the other? They might in fact determine each other *mutually*. On this level, the relationship between the sciences and reality is discussed and so are the epistemological prerequisites for different methodologies.

The questions posed at each of the three levels of knowledge are motivated by different intentions; thus knowledge on one level is not the same as on the others. Nevertheless, the three levels of knowledge are necessarily intertwined. The business executive needs the theories of the scientist if he is to answer his practical questions. As we have seen, the knowledge worker's task is exactly to draw the scientific and business levels together; likewise, scientists are in need of philosophical reflection on their own research. This is especially evident in cases where the development of philosophy of science has directly affected the levels of both the sciences and the business world. In the next chapter we will take a look at one of the most important examples of this: positivism. On the level of science, this theory inspired, among other things, the development of scientific management. This view of management dominated the business world for several decades on the practical level of knowledge. You cannot understand scientific management—its emergence, its theoretical justification, its limitations, and its significance for corporate life—without *also* possessing knowledge on the philosophical level of knowledge.

Distinguishing between the three levels of knowledge shows how philosophy of science plays an important role in both the sciences and the business world. It is part of our reality. It also makes it clear that philosophy of science is a discipline in its own right with its own subject matter and traditions. At the end of this chapter the reader will find a number of basic questions of philosophy of science, which illustrate the range and content of this discipline. Most readers will be able to discuss these questions without previous knowledge of the subject, but as soon as the questions are considered cohesively rather than individually, answering them becomes more complex. For example, if you believe the sciences should be politically neutral (question five), simultaneously claiming that they should be controlled by a society's economic interests (question four) becomes difficult, as economic interests will always be politically defined. The answers to the different questions appear to be systematically implicated. In the course of time, this has led to the rise of a number of schools of thought, each providing greatly differing answers to these basic questions in philosophy of science, and taking these answers as the point of departure for the further development of their theories.

Although these schools of thought disagree among themselves, they complement each other and provide different, useful insights. Philosophy of science is therefore not a complete and finished theory, but rather a number of different viewpoints of the same issues. It is through the critical comparison of these perspectives, their insights and limitations, that we can learn to reflect on the basic questions common to them all. This book will therefore be based on a review of some of the most significant schools of thought in the philosophy of science.

About this Book

Although this book will hopefully be of use to students from a variety of fields, as well as anyone with a general interest in the philosophy of science, it was originally intended and written as an introduction for students in business schools. The practical examples found in the book reflect this and are drawn, for the most part, from subjects such as business communication, economics, management, and marketing.

To underline the professional integrity of the field, the different philosophies are presented in their particular theoretical context and on their own terms. Each presentation is supplemented by sub-chapters, which round off the exposition of the different positions. Here you will find examples of how philosophy of science is significant for the other levels of knowledge. Not all readers will find examples from their own subjects, since the intention has obviously not been to render independent thought superfluous. On the contrary, it is the intention that the reader, when seeing these examples from related subjects, will be able to reflect on how each position relates to his or her own field of study.

The book provides an overview. Each chapter ends with a summary and each of the book's three parts concludes with a summative chapter, which compiles the examined key concepts, discusses the differences and similarities of the various positions, and links these to the knowledge workers. These summative chapters will provide a strong foundation for later revision.

Philosophy of Science – An Introduction for Future Knowledge Workers is not intended to be an exhaustive portrayal of the enormous field that is philosophy of science. Instead, it seeks to present an accessible introduction to some of the important theorists and issues in the philosophies of the social sciences. Positions, subjects, and authors have partly been selected because of their thematic connections, but to a greater extent, because of their universality in the social sciences. Furthermore, selection is based on the principle that a thorough exposition of a few positions is more beneficial than a superficial account of many. The book is an appetizer for the philosophy of science. It will hopefully not only whet the reader's appetite for more, but also show that this discipline is neither irrelevant nor boring. It is useful not only in theory, but also in real life!

Questions

1. What characterizes science? (As opposed to, for example, astrology, numerology, and palm reading?)
2. When is knowledge certain?
3. Are there differences between the natural sciences and the social sciences? Which?
4. What role do the sciences play in society?
5. What role do the sciences play in politics?
6. What role do the sciences play in relation to ethics and morality?

Part 1

Classical Philosophy of Science

In the first part of this book we will become acquainted with positivism and three of its most significant critics. Positivism is the earliest philosophy of science, and it is the one that has had the greatest influence on science, society, and the world of business. The critique of positivism presented to us by Popper marks perhaps the most important debate to be found within classical philosophy of science. With its focus on practice, pragmatism, on the other hand, presents itself as an alternative to both positivism and Popper's critical rationalism. Part one will conclude with an introduction to Kuhn's theory of paradigms. This theory has been greatly influential in the social sciences and, moreover, throws positivism, critical rationalism, and the disagreements between these positions into relief. It simultaneously points to one of the topics in the second part of the book: social constructivism.

Positivism: The First Philosophy of Science

Naturally, a philosophy of science does not appear on its own. First and most importantly it requires a developed science that can be studied. Furthermore, before a philosophy is considered necessary, the science in question must have achieved a certain importance in society. Consequently, philosophy of science is a relatively new discipline, but it draws on a long tradition of philosophical discussions.

The Prehistory of Philosophy of Science

In the Middle Ages there was no use for a philosophy of science. The Bible was considered to reveal and express the truth about the world. Even so, scientific work was still carried out. Theologians'[1] interpretation of the Bible and the church fathers was conducted scientifically. There were other sciences, too, primarily philosophy, law, and the natural sciences; however, these were all subject to theology. For example, the studies of the natural sciences were required to substantiate the truth as established by the church and not challenge the ecclesiastical worldview. If one were to do so, the ramifications could prove brutal. In

1 The word "theology" means the study of God. It is the study of (the Christian) faith and scriptures. It was the predominant science of the Middle Ages.

the year 1600, the Italian philosopher Giordano Bruno (1548–1600) was burned at the stake, charged with heresy for insisting that the sun, and not the earth, was the centre of the solar system (Rowland 2008: 9–13).

The Catholic Church had accepted the natural philosophy of Aristotle (384–322 B.C.) as the official, true representation of the physical world, but towards the end of the Middle Ages, the flaws of this philosophy became decidedly obvious. For this reason the natural sciences began to break with the Aristotelian worldview during the Renaissance (the period from about 1400–1600). Only a few years after Bruno's death his views were reiterated by the famous Italian physicist, Galileo Galilei (1564–1642). Although the church forced Galilei to withdraw his claim, the papacy found itself so weakened that, ultimately, it was no longer able to force the sciences to work within the confines of Aristotelian thought. Instead of scientific research having to adhere to the church's view of nature, the sciences began examining nature by means of systematic observation and experiments. Observations of nature became the only authority for the new sciences, which emerged during the seventeenth century.

This shift in perspective quickly led to an impressive development in fields such as astronomy and physics. However, a question, which had been completely absent throughout the Middle Ages, was now raised: If knowledge is not divinely revealed, where does it come from?

The natural sciences seemed to provide a clear answer to this question as their progress originated from observations of nature. It became evident to the philosophers, known as *the empiricists,* that all knowledge is obtained through observation; that is, through our senses.

> ! **Empiricism:** The philosophical school of thought that claims all knowledge is acquired through sensory experience; human beings have no innate ideas; and the observations of the sciences precede and are independent from theories.

John Locke (1632–1704), one of the classical empiricists, expressed this view by stating that our mind is originally like a blank piece of paper—

clean of all ideas and concepts. All the knowledge we "write down on the paper" throughout our lives derives from our sensory experience of reality. It is, of course, this experience that the sciences systematize through observations and experiments. According to many of the empiricists, this is done by way of the *inductive* method, which means that the scientist constructs a general theory from an array of separate observations (Martin 2000: 31). For example, if you want information about the behaviour of chimpanzees, you must keep the animals under observation over a long period of time until you are finally able to establish a conclusive theory on the basis of the collected observations.

! **Induction:** The methodological view that scientific theories are solely the sum of a number of separate observations; knowledge begins with observation; and it must be possible to trace any theory back to sensory data.

Empiricism is not the only way of answering the question as to how knowledge is acquired. The rationalists, the most important representative of whom was the French philosopher René Descartes (1596–1650), held the opposite view: our senses are unreliable and we are continually mistaken in our perception of the world (Descartes 2002).

! **Rationalism:** The philosophical school of thought that claims true knowledge is acquired only through reason and not through the senses. Human beings must therefore be born with certain ideas; for example, with a disposition for logical thought.

We might think we see an oasis in the desert, but it is really a mirage. We might think our drink tastes like oranges, but in reality, the orange flavour comes from artificial additives. We are continually mistaken and thus the sciences cannot be based on sensory experience. Instead, true knowledge is obtained by applying reason. Consider geometry: Through reason we can be certain of the properties of a perfect, right-angled triangle, yet we can never draw such a triangle, even with the most advanced computer programmes; hence our understanding of what it means that something is a perfect, right-angled triangle, is not derived from our senses but purely from reason.

Rationalists believe, therefore, that deduction is the only way of procuring true knowledge. For classical rationalists deduction means—for example in mathematics—drawing conclusions from simple, general principles regarded as necessary truths (necessary in the sense that denying them leads to absurdity), to arrive at more complex claims. Logical arguments are also based on deduction.

> **!** **Deduction:** For the classical rationalists, deduction is the scientific methodological view that true knowledge is reached through logical conclusions drawn from indisputable, general principles. Deduction thus constitutes a way of obtaining knowledge, which does not require observations of reality. An example can be found in mathematics, where theorems are proven on the basis of axioms.

The example below illustrates how logic can provide true, ascertainable knowledge that is not based on our observations of reality.

> **!** **An Example of Deductive Logic:**
> Premise 1: All humans are mortal.
> Premise 2: Peter is a human.
> Conclusion: Peter is mortal.
> If the premises are true, the conclusion is also true and follows by logical necessity. In other words, what we have here is a truth we can be certain of, even though it is not based on empirical evidence.

According to the rationalists, deductive reasoning is the path to true knowledge, precisely because it is not based on uncertain observations but on rational and logical thought and reliable principles.

The dispute between empiricists and rationalists continued throughout the seventeenth and eighteenth centuries, and it is often encapsulated by the contrast between two types of knowledge: *a priori* and *a posteriori* knowledge, which respectively mean knowledge *independent of* and *from* sensory data.

> **A Priori Knowledge:** Knowledge that is not dependent on our sensory experience (as in rationalism).
> **A Posteriori Knowledge:** Knowledge based on our sensory experience (as in empiricism).

The famous German philosopher, Immanuel Kant (1724–1804), proposed a way of solving the dispute. According to Kant, we must distinguish between *das Ding an sich* (the world in itself) and *das Ding für uns* (the world as it appears to us). The difference between the two is due to the fact that we humans invariably view the world as being structured in, for example, time, space and causality. Time, space, and causality are thus not inherent properties of the world; they characterize our experience of the world. This means that we are unable to conceive of the world independent of these categories (that is, the world as it is in itself). We are, however, able to arrive at true knowledge about the world as it appears *to us*, much like the empiricists claimed. At the same time, it is obvious that we are not born as blank sheets of paper since we approach the world with expectations, for instance, of causality. The rationalists are therefore right in claiming that we possess certain concepts that are not derived from our senses, and that we can have non-sensory knowledge (Kant 2002).

Kant's solution is brilliant, yet it seems that the steam engine, rather than Kant, is what led to the end of the dispute between classical rationalism and empiricism. From the end of the eighteenth century, industrialism swept across Europe and completely transformed society. This was a social, technological, and economic revolution, the dimensions of which we can hardly imagine today. The natural sciences were the driving force of this revolution, and thus the dispute between empiricism and rationalism seemed definitively settled in favour of empiricism. The empirically based natural sciences had, in practice, proven to lead the way to both true knowledge and the development of society. It was time to put past discussions aside and reinvent philosophy as philosophy of science. At any rate, this was the aim of positivism.

Comte and Classical Positivism

In the nineteenth century, the modern concept of science began to take shape. Before this time, "the scientist" was envisaged as a learned and cultured philosopher or theologian, surrounded by thick books. Science was *spiritual science*, corresponding to what we today call the humanities. Because of its great progress, natural science had, by this time, gained an altogether novel prominence in society. The new image of the scientist became something similar to today's adverts for toothpaste: men in white laboratory coats, surrounded by glass bottles, test tubes, and an aura of authority. In this period great faith was placed in the natural sciences and their ability to not only uncover the truth about the world, but also to lead society in the right direction. This belief in progress and this scientific self-awareness were clearly displayed by the philosopher, Auguste Comte (1798–1857), who can be characterized as the founder of the first philosophy of science.

Why did Comte call his philosophy of science a *positive philosophy* and why has it come to be known as positivism? In this context, positive is not the opposite of negative; rather, positivism claims that the sciences acquire knowledge solely by investigating that about which we can be positively certain. Positive therefore means actual or concrete. In other words, a science can be said to be positivistic insofar as it examines only what actually and positively exists (Comte 1974: 19–41). Comte thus carries on the fundamental claim of classical empiricism that all knowledge is acquired through examining what can be perceived through our senses.

> **!** **Positivism:** A school of thought that is based upon classical empiricism. Scientific knowledge is acquired through the systematic gathering of empirical data and only theories derived from such data can be considered scientific.

Positivism is not a *descriptive* but rather a *normative* philosophy of science. But what does this mean? Comte does not merely aim to describe how the actual sciences proceed; on the contrary, positivism is meant to establish rules determining how the scientists need to work for their results to be considered "genuinely" scientific. Positivism thereby constitutes a set of rules for scientific conduct, and Comte greatly emphasized these rules, because, according to his understanding, the sciences are the only source of true and certain knowledge.

As mentioned previously, the first and most important criterion a theory needs to live up to in order to be considered scientific is that it must be based on concrete sensory data. This eliminates a number of theories, for example, theology and ethics. It is impossible to prove empirically that God exists or that it is wrong to kill. First and foremost, Comte wished to get rid of *metaphysics*. Metaphysics is a collective name for worldviews that are not based on empirical evidence. This applies, among other things, to the entire tradition of philosophy.

! **Metaphysics:** Worldviews that are not based on empirical observation. Examples include: ethics and morality, ideas on human nature, political ideology, and classical philosophy.

According to Comte, metaphysics and religion are unscientific and, if allowed to spread in society, impede scientific progress. When positivism puts forward rules for science, and thereby for true knowledge, the aim is therefore to subdue any theory that is not scientific.

However, Comte never explicates this objective, as he believes that the development from religion and metaphysics towards a positivistic science is an inevitable historical tendency, and that human beings will gradually grow accustomed to thinking scientifically (Comte 1974: 20). In fact, Comte believes that history has undergone three phases of development: In the first phase, human beings accounted for their existence and the world around them in theological terms. Natural disasters were considered God's punishment, not the consequence of geological or meteorological phenomena. In the second phase, theology was replaced by metaphysics. Things were no longer explained by God, but rather by abstract ideas. In Comte's time, history had finally reached its positive stage with the rise of scientific, and therefore true, explanations. Natural disasters were no longer explained by God or nature, but by geological and meteorological studies. The three stages are different, but the transition between them is seamless. The metaphysical explanations naturally built upon the observations made during the theological stage, and the same applies to positivistic science. Today, we simply have a better understanding of these observations. It therefore becomes a fundamental view in positivism that the sciences are *cumulative*, meaning that they develop evenly and without fractures as knowledge is continuously accumulated (Proctor 1991: 159).

! **Cumulative Science:** The sciences develop through the constant accumulation of knowledge, and knowledge derives from observations and experiments.

In other words, since we continually build on the knowledge of the past, the sum of scientific knowledge increases all the time. This is the foundation for positivism's greatly optimistic view of science.

But what exactly does it mean that the sciences must examine what is directly available to the senses? Moreover, how is this to be done? According to the positivists, science is characterized by inductive reasoning. A researcher first observes the phenomena he wishes to investigate. He carries out his observations thoroughly, systematically, and under different circumstances. The latter is important to ensure that the observed data is valid everywhere and is not caused by unique, locally determined conditions. Scientific theories are concerned with regularities, for example statements such as: "Every time X is observed, Y can subsequently be observed". Furthermore, it is crucial that the researcher does not let observations be distorted by prejudice or by expectations regarding the results of the observations. They must be *theory-independent* to ensure that nature "speaks for itself".

! **Theory-Independence:** Observations must not be governed by theories, but must be completely unbiased.

When sufficient material has been collected, the scientist can sum up the observations and establish a theory. This theory will subsequently be substantiated by additional observations. According to some positivists, deduction can be employed during this stage of the study to pinpoint exactly what the researcher is to look for. The purpose of these supplementary observations is to prove theories, as scientific theories are characterized by their being verifiable. In other words, the goal of the sciences, as well as their criterion of truth, is *verification* (Hanfling 1996: 193–213).

! **Verificationism:** Sciences must seek to prove their theories through observations. Scientific (i.e., true) theories are verifiable theories.

It is crucial to understand that, according to the positivists, knowledge derived from scientific observation is objectively true. A popular saying insists that one must take into consideration "the eye of the beholder", but in this case it does not apply. First of all the scientist must lay aside his prejudices when working (Kriel 1994: 14). Secondly, he is able to use scientific instruments through which to "see", making his observations more precise and leaving less trace of the observer.

Having said that, to what exactly do the sciences gain access through observation? When I look at an apple, I receive numerous sensory perceptions: the redness, the round shape, and the scent of fruit. These (and many more) perceptions constitute the sum of my observations. I can be certain of these observations, and thus they form the basis for a scientific theory of apples. I may assume that something is feeding me these sensory experiences, but all I can be sure of is the information relayed to me by my senses about the apple. As a result, the sciences are not concerned with the world, but rather with our sensory perception of it. For the positivists, the world "in itself", independent of our senses, merely constitutes a futile question of metaphysics. For how is it possible to devise scientific laws about things that cannot be observed? This view is termed *antirealism* and can be traced all the way back to the eighteenth century's classical empiricism (Hume 1985).

> ! **Antirealism:** The sciences are the systematization of sensory perceptions, not theories of a reality "underlying" sensory perceptions.

Positivism and antirealism are thereby intrinsically linked. Like the empiricists, the positivists claim that the senses are the only source of true knowledge and, needless to say, our senses do not give us access to the way things are in themselves, independent of our senses.

Understanding antirealism can be difficult, so how can we best illustrate this idea? Imagine a small, uninhabited island in the Pacific Ocean located thousands of miles from the nearest human being. Then imagine that a meteor hits the island with tremendous force. Normally, we would say the meteor came crashing down with a bang, but is this really true? Sound is a sensory perception. It occurs when sound waves hit the ear. Without ears there can be no sound, and since there are no living creatures on the island, or in close proximity, there are no ears. The positivists would contend that discussing whether the impact of the meteor produces sound is meaningless. The only sound it makes sense to discuss is the sound we perceive through our senses. This sound, on the other hand, can be made the object of scientific study.

Positivism's understanding of science can thus be summarized by the illustration below:

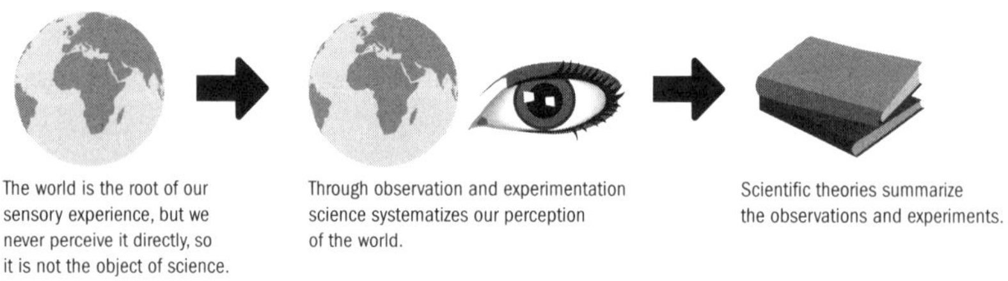

Figure 2.1. Positivism's Understanding of Science

According to the positivists, every scientist must follow this approach if his work is to be deemed scientific. This is important, as science, according to this view, is the only way to achieve true knowledge. It is obvious—certainly to Comte—that the degree to which different disciplines are able to live up to this ideal varies greatly. Astronomy, physics, and chemistry are prime examples, whereas the humanities and social sciences prove more problematic. According to Comte, this is not because the various sciences are to be considered fundamentally different; they are all moving towards the positive stage, with the humanities and social sciences simply limping behind the others. Because of this, they must adopt the empirical method, which, according to the positivists, is already fully developed in the natural sciences (Comte 1974: 25—28). Comte does, however, dismiss psychology as a pseudoscience. Psychology is based on introspection, which means that a person looks inside himself to observe his feelings and state of mind. From a positivistic perspective, it is impossible to be both the observer and the observed, as one cannot be neutral and objective in one's observations in that situation. According to Comte, psychology can therefore not result in good science.

For Comte, the sciences are the expression of an objective, politically *neutral* rationality, which can be applied in all areas and thus also to societal life.

! **The Neutrality of Science:** Science is politically, religiously, and ethically neutral. Science is objective rationality.

The industrialization that characterized Comte's age led to great social inequality and political instability. Comte sees science as the solution to these problems. The considerable disagreements in society are caused by the fact that some people think scientifically, while others still linger on in the theological and metaphysical stages. The solution is to ensure that everyone reaches the scientific stage of thinking, which in turn will ensure that everyone comprehends what is for the common good in society. According to Comte, this is achieved by reforming the educational system, which in those days had not kept up with the development in society and in the sciences (Comte 1974: 34–41).

One last question remains regarding the position of philosophy of science itself: What purpose does it serve when true knowledge can only be gained through empirical study? Comte responds that because of an inner conflict, the sciences cannot do without the theory. As mentioned previously, all sciences are defined by the empirical method; i.e. induction and verification. In principle only *one science* exists, namely the empiricist science, and this one science can be applied to all possible fields, from nuclear physics to economy and linguistics. Comte illustrates this using the image of a tree, where the separate sciences constitute the branches of the same tree and the empirical scientific method constitutes the trunk.

! **Unitary Science:** The various scientific disciplines are scientific because of the same empiricist method; therefore, in principle there is only one science, which can be applied within all the different areas of the individual scientific disciplines.

Nevertheless, as the various scientific disciplines gradually developed, the notion of a unitary science became harder to maintain. Specialization leads to different sciences moving farther away from each other with unity being lost. According to Comte, it is the task of philosophy of science to function as a special type of science; namely, the science of the scientific method itself and thus the science of what unites the separate disciplines (Comte 1974: 29–31).

Logical Positivism

As we have seen, Comte's positivism gave rise to the first formulation of a programme for the philosophy of science. Needless to say, this was groundbreaking; however, Comte's ideas also contain fundamental weaknesses. First and most importantly, distinguishing between science and metaphysics causes him problems, as his own description of science is, to a great extent, metaphysical. This applies, for instance, to his theory about history, as absolute historical laws of development cannot be observed in nature.

Because of this and similar flaws, during the first half of the twentieth century, a large number of scientists and philosophers attempted to rethink positivism and establish a stronger, more stringent version, which goes under the name *logical positivism*. This school of thought emerged in Vienna in the 1920s and established itself as the dominating trend within philosophy of science, until it started losing ground in the 1960s. Rudolf Carnap (1891–1970), Alfred Jules Ayer (1919–1989), Otto Neurath (1882–1945), and Carl Gustav Hempel (1905–1997) all represent logical positivism.

! **Logical Positivism:** The reinvention of positivism as a logically stringent theory, the central element of which is the definition of an empiricist criterion of linguistic meaningfulness: only sentences that can be traced back to simple empirical observations (which can be either true or false) are meaningful.

The logical positivists agree with Comte in most areas. They are antimetaphysical, antirealist, and, most importantly, they champion the empiricism of classical positivism. Finally, they also believe in the idea of the unity of science. The differences between the two are mainly based on the way positivism is viewed. Comte's philosophizing and historical approach proved to be yet another form of metaphysics, so the new positivism was to be based on logical analysis, hence its name.

As discussed earlier, Comte was of the opinion that objective scientific rationality should reform society and politics; the logical positivists partly agree, but also emphasize that objective facts are something entirely different than the values and appraisals found in, for instance, politics or ethics (Hempel 1965). The scientists must strictly adhere to uncovering objective facts and leave the assessment of how the results are to be applied in practice to others. The scientists are not themselves to be reformers of society. For instance, it is the task of nuclear physics to uncover the nature of elementary particles, but it is the elected politicians' decision as to whether their knowledge is to be used for nuclear power plants, nuclear weapons, or nothing at all.

According to Comte, metaphysical explanations were merely antiquated ways of thinking. The logical positivists explain why disposing of metaphysics still proves so difficult. At the same time, they want to demonstrate that metaphysics is not only obsolete, but also meaningless. They therefore put forth a criterion of meaning: a statement is only meaningful if the conditions that make it true or false can be clearly presented. This means a statement is only meaningful if it points back to simple observational statements, such as: "The thermometer shows 100 degrees". This type of statement expresses "pure" observations; i.e., they are not determined by theory or context, but purely by observation. Thereby, language points beyond itself to the simple observation. On the basis of this criterion of meaning, it becomes clear that the statement, "water boils at 100 degrees Celsius" is meaningful, while "stealing is morally wrong" is not. For whereas the statement of water's boiling point can be traced back to the simple observation statement; "the thermometer shows 100 degrees", we can never observe an action's moral qualities (Carnap 1931/1932: 221–222).

This criterion of meaning is an expression of *phenomenalism*; i.e., identifying an apple through the sensory experiences (phenomena) we have of it (Mach 1959). By means of phenomenalism the logical positivists sharpen the antirealism of classical positivism. "An apple" is nothing more than the sum of our sensory perceptions of it. In other words, when speaking of "an apple", we are speaking of nothing but the sum of the perceptions tied to it. The counterargument will naturally state that an apple must exist separately from these sensory perceptions, but what does "separately" really mean? Since we are able to describe all aspects of an apple as perception, it becomes meaningless to assume that a mysterious "essence" exists separately from sensory experience; an essence we, per definition, cannot perceive.

! **Phenomenalism:** The view that an object is the sum of our sensory perception of it. It makes no sense to talk about a hidden core underlying our perceptions.

According to the logical positivists, metaphysics has not yet been eliminated because their distinction between meaningful and meaningless sentences is not evident from everyday language. For instance, a sentence such as "Picasso is a moist, spicy colour" is undeniably meaningless, but this is not obvious from the grammatical syntax of language. The sentence is grammatically correct. The same problem applies to metaphysical statements. They appear to make sense, as they are grammatically correct, but they are nonetheless meaningless sham statements. Getting rid of metaphysics requires the development of a new, logical syntax, which can be used to make an immediate distinction between meaningful and meaningless statements. The logical positivists consider this the first task of philosophy of science. Once solved, a second project follows naturally: dissolving the whole of metaphysics by means of this logical syntax (Carnap 1931/1932: 228).

The logical positivists also argue for the implementation of the empiricist method within the areas of the human and social sciences. Many researchers have participated in this project entitled *behaviourism* (Hempel 1983), and it constitutes an ambitious attempt to realize Comte's vision of a unitary science.

! **Behaviourism:** Positivism's programme for the human and social sciences where the study of human beings becomes the study of their behaviour, not their thoughts and feelings.

As mentioned earlier, Comte rejected psychology as a pseudoscience because it was concerned with the feelings and state of mind of the individual, which cannot be observed objectively and neutrally; however, according to the behaviourists this need not be the case. Sciences such as psychology and sociology are, from their perspective, not concerned with the thoughts and feelings of human beings, but strictly with their *behaviour,* which is, of course, observable. The meaning conveyed by a statement such as, "Peter is upset", is not that "Peter is feeling upset", but rather that Peter has been observed to be crying, staring into space, and uttering statements such as "I am upset". The human and social sciences must completely ignore questions of human thought and state of mind, and instead focus exclusively on behaviour. In this way, there is essentially no difference between studying chimpanzees, human beings, or rock formations.

There are many aspects of positivism that might seem completely unreasonable when encountering them for the first time. Behaviourism is one of these aspects, for how is it possible to disregard human thought and emotional life? For many people, the claim that religion, morality, and metaphysics are meaningless constitutes another ostensible absurdity. Nonetheless, it is important not to underestimate positivism. It has been crucial to our way of thinking about and understanding the world. If you come across two people engaged in discussion and one of them believes he can win the argument by stating that his claim "has been scientifically proven", it is likely a result of a positivistic understanding of the world. The same applies to rejecting a theory solely because it "cannot be proven". Finally, many of the theories discussed in this book arise from confrontations with positivism. It is no meagre feat for a theory to have ignited so many reactions—and thereby many new and interesting philosophical reflections.

Nevertheless, owing to its many weaknesses, positivism is no longer the dominant school of thought in philosophy of science. Let us briefly look at a few of these weaknesses. Firstly, it seems obvious that the sciences in reality do not operate the way the positivists imagined. In fact, researchers do not spend all their time first gathering observations and then organizing them into provable theories. There are even examples of important scientific laws that cannot be proven by empirical data, as is required by positivism. This includes Newton's second law and Darwin's theory of evolution. Secondly, most people agree there is no such thing as "simple observational statements". Even statements such as "the thermometer shows 100 degrees" require knowledge of what a thermometer is and how temperature is measured. It can never be an expression of "pure" observation. Thirdly, it is simply erroneous to assume that only statements that can be true or false can be considered meaningful. A statement like "happy birthday" can be neither true nor false, but at a birthday party it still makes more sense than the observational statement: "It's your birthday". Finally and fourthly, it is no longer considered certain that objective and neutral observations are possible; in most cases they will, in actual fact, depend on "the eye of the beholder".

Positivism: A Summary

In this chapter we first considered the prehistory of philosophy of science. The weakening of the power of the Catholic Church during the Renaissance prompted the question: If our knowledge does not come from the Bible and Aristotle, from where does it come? Classical empiricism and classical rationalism provided us with two different answers. The rationalists believed that knowledge can only be gained through reason, while the empiricists claimed that all true knowledge is gained through sensory perception. This view was maintained by positivism.

Positivism is not only a specific way of understanding how the sciences operate; it also constitutes a set of criteria for the sciences. Its methodology continued classical empiricism's belief that induction leads to true knowledge. The sciences must first gather sufficient amounts of objective and theory-independent observations, which can then subsequently establish a single theory. Later on, through the gathering of more observations, an attempt must be made to prove the theory. All sciences, regardless of their subject matter, must apply this method. Those that do not must be reinvented and made empiricist, as was the aim of behaviourism. In other words, when all is said and done, there is only *one* science. It is not characterized by being concerned with a particular subject matter, but is defined by its empiricist approach. On the other hand, it is applicable to all areas, whether language, economics, biology, or something else entirely.

This view also entails rejecting every theory not based on concrete sensory perception. Such theories are termed metaphysics, and the positivists' anti-metaphysical understanding of the sciences explains their antirealism and phenomenalism. We should not speculate about what the "world" is, but instead be strictly concerned with the concrete sensory data we acquire through empirical observation.

Positivism expresses great optimism in the possibilities of research. Seeing that we perpetually build on past observations, the sciences develop smoothly and continuously, and we can trust that our empirically supported knowledge is true. This view hardly reflects the way things actually are, and is but one of the problems of positivism we established in closing.

However, these problems do not render positivism useless for all purposes. As a methodology it still plays an important role in many natural and social sciences, for example, statistics and economics. Many readers of this book will already be acquainted with positivistic science without knowing it. Examples of this will be given at the end of this chapter, as we proceed from philosophy of science to the social scientific level of knowledge.

Positivism in Practice

Example: Scientific Management or Taylorism

As mentioned in the introduction, scientific management is probably the best example of how positivism has impacted not only the sciences but the business world as well. The concept derives from the American engineer Frederick Winslow Taylor (1856–1915) who published the book *The Principles of Scientific Management* (Taylor 2008) in 1911. This approach is therefore also called Taylorism. In brief, scientific management is concerned with increasing the productivity of companies by optimizing individual work processes. This is done by analyzing them down to the separate movements of the individual employee working at the assembly line. The idea is that, if each employee's productivity can be raised by just a fraction, the total productivity increase of the company will be huge. The question remains why this way of thinking is considered positivistic. The keyword here is behaviourism. The Taylorist approach is based on the idea that social dynamics (e.g., the work processes within a company) must be understood as *behaviour,* which can be observed objectively and quantifiably, and can be adjusted by external influence. Increasing production is not about strengthening the psychological work environment, but purely about optimizing behaviour; thus positivism, as well as behaviourism, has left its direct mark on countless companies throughout the world. Below are some examples of its influence on the sciences.

Example: The Transmission Paradigm in Communication Science

The significance of positivism has not only been asserted in psychology and management theory, but can also be found in the research of culture and communication. The earliest attempts to understand communication scientifically were made within the so-called transmission paradigm (Frandsen, Halkier, and Johansen 2007). This term was derived from the fact that communication is not understood as dialogue, but rather as a sender impacting a recipient through the conveyance of a message. Among the classical examples are Harold Lasswell (1902–1978), Warren Weaver (1894–1978), and Claude Shannon (1916–2001). Together, the latter two developed one of the most famous and most utilized models of communication.

In what sense does the transmission paradigm reflect a positivistic line of thought? In this case, communication is understood as the generation of a particular *effect,* which can be noted in the behaviour of the recipient. Because we are dealing with *transmission* rather than *dialogue*, it is only through this behaviour that it is possible to see whether communication was successful. In this way, the transmission paradigm expresses a behaviouristic approach in which the effect of a particular *stimulus* can be observed through the *response* of the test person or message recipient. At the same time, the paradigm is positivistic insofar as interpretation and context are assumed to be unnecessary for understanding what is communicated. This reflects the fundamental positivistic assumption that if meaningful statements are expressed with sufficient clarity and precision, they are immediately comprehensible and do not require interpretation.

Example: Geert Hofstede's Theories of Intercultural Communication

A third example of positivism's influence on the social sciences is Geert Hofstede's (born 1928) theories of intercultural communication (i.e., communication across nationality and ethnicity). Here, positivism appears in several different ways. Through empirical studies of national cultures, Hofstede first of all attempts to put forth universal laws that can predict people's behaviour. At the same time, he does not view culture as a troublesome element of all communicative situations but rather as an obstacle that must be overcome. We are thus dealing with the same understanding of communication as the one found in the transmission paradigm.

Example: How You Can Work with Positivism as a Method

How would a positivist instruct a group of students writing an assignment about communication in a large company? He would tell them to begin by *observing* this communication. These observations must be thorough, systematic, and cover a wide range of situations: communication between management and employees, between colleagues, between corporation and customers, et cetera. It is important that the students remain unprejudiced throughout their study so as to avoid their work being biased by prior understanding and expectations. It is also important that they maintain a neutral position towards what they observe. Finally, it is crucial that they solely consider the observed communicative behaviour and do not resort to conjecture concerning motives, thoughts, and other unobservable properties of the test persons.

Once the students have gathered a sufficient amount of observations, they will be able to detect patterns and tendencies in the communication, and these can be summed up to establish a general scientific theory. Finally, they can attempt to prove their theory by, for example, deducing what can be expected from future observations based on the theory. If these observations further substantiate the theory, they will be able to conclude that it is true, and their project can be considered successful. If this is not the case, their data must be insufficient, and more observations are needed in order to formulate a new and verifiable theory.

Questions

1. What does induction mean?
2. What is meant by the sciences being cumulative?
3. Why is it, according to the positivists, important for observations to be theory-independent?
4. What does verification mean and what part does it play in positivism?
5. Explain the positivistic idea of a unitary science.
6. What is behaviourism?
7. Explain logical positivism.
8. What role do the sciences play in society according to the positivists?
9. Which positivistic traditions can you identify in your own field of study?
10. In your opinion, what are the strengths and weaknesses of positivism?

The Critical Rationalism of Popper

In the preceding chapter we saw how the positivists established rules for science. These rules could be summed up by the following methodology: all theories must be based on inductive research. The Austrian-British philosopher Karl Popper (1902–1994) was one of the first and most significant critics of positivism; however, his criticism is not as radical as the one voiced by later theorists. According to Popper, the positivists may have provided the wrong answers but the question they asked was the right one: What are the criteria to establish something as science?

Popper's Philosophy of Science

Popper too, considered it the task of philosophy of science to find criteria for distinguishing between science and non-science (Popper 1974: 39). This is what he termed *the problem of demarcation*. Furthermore, like the positivists, he believed that the solution to the problem was to be found in the method of science.

> **The Problem of Demarcation:** The question of how to distinguish between science and non-science.

There are, however, clear differences between positivism's and Popper's understanding of the problem of demarcation. For the positivists, the sciences were the only source of knowledge, whereas metaphysics and religion were considered meaningless. Popper completely disagrees with this. Unscientific theories can quite easily be true, just as scientific theories can prove false. Unscientific theories can even be greatly meaningful; for example, most people consider the moral prohibition against killing to make perfectly good sense. Popper goes so far as to claim that unscientific theories can develop into sciences (Popper 1974: 38); e.g., as over time astrology developed into astronomy. What cannot be ignored, however, is the fact that astrology as such is not a science. The question then is why not?

The positivists were unable to answer this question, as the theories of astrology are based on empirical observations of the stars, and astrologers are able to find plenty of "proof" of their claims. Anyone who has read his or her horoscope in a magazine will have to agree that it reflects reality to some extent. Nevertheless, no one considers astrology a science. And if a notorious pseudoscience can pass positivism's criteria for being scientific, it is a sure sign that these criteria must be flawed in some way. In other words, the fact that a theory can be proven is not enough to make it scientific.

Consequently, Popper rejects the verificationism of positivism. The problem is that proof of a theory can always be found if proof is what you are looking for (Popper 1974: 36). If someone believes in astrology, its validity can easily be proven. Furthermore, if a theory is vague or defined in general terms it becomes easier to prove. The reason why horoscopes in magazines usually seem to offer accurate predictions of so many people's lives is that their predictions are vague and imprecise. In this way anyone can make them fit his or her own situation. Popper's rejection of positivism's idea that induction is the hallmark of science is an even more crucial point. He points to this as constituting both a logical and practical problem.

From a purely logical point of view, previous observations can never reveal what future studies will show. Although biologists have never observed chimpanzees outside of Africa, this does not guarantee that one might not be found in India one day. Induction can therefore not provide us with certain knowledge. In philosophy of science, this is what is called *the problem of induction*, and it has been debated since the eighteenth century (Popper 1974: 42–46).

> **The Problem of Induction:** Even if all our observations of the world have so far yielded the same result, we can never be certain that our next observation will not produce a different result.

The practical problem consists of the fact that in reality observation is never the starting point of the sciences. Popper relates how he once conducted an experiment in front of a full auditorium at the University of Vienna (Popper 1974: 46). He asked the students to "observe" and then write down what they had seen. The students gave him a quizzical look and asked what he wanted them to observe. Of course, this was the point Popper was trying make. The "pure" observation championed by the positivists does not exist, as observation will always begin with an idea of what is to be studied. The biologist does not merely observe chimpanzees. He has a clear concept of what he wishes to observe about the animals in advance, why exactly this particular behaviour should be observed, and how the results of his observations will fit into his collective research. In other words, he has *a theory*.

In this way Popper raises considerable doubt about the two cornerstones of positivism: verification and induction. Observations cannot be used to prove a theory, and only logic and maths are able to prove propositions, precisely because these sciences are not based on observations! But do the sciences become meaningless if their theories cannot be proven? And why do researchers spend so much time on observations and experiments if these can never prove their theories? Popper's most significant contribution to the philosophy of science is found in his answers to these two questions.

Sometimes researchers are wrong. Theories that everyone believed to be true are proved wrong by new studies. Observations of reality thus serve a purpose; they can disprove theories. This forms the basis for

Popper's *asymmetry thesis*: only one observation is needed to *disprove* a scientific theory, but due to the problem of induction even endless amounts of observation could never *prove* a theory (Popper 1974: 41).

> ! **The Asymmetry Thesis:** Numerous observations can never prove a scientific theory but one observation is enough to disprove it.

The answer to the second question posed above must be that researchers spend so much time making observations of the world in order to *test* their theories; that is, to find out whether they are really valid. What consequences does this have for our understanding of science?

The first consequence is that a theory must always precede an empirical study. The afore-mentioned example of the biologist and the chimpanzees shows that observations are always planned and governed by what we expect from the results; that is, by our hypothesis. This view also imputes a new understanding of what observation is. According to the positivists, the ideal researcher is completely passive so as not to influence what is being observed. According to Popper, on the other hand, observation must necessarily be an activity; i.e., something that is undertaken actively and purposefully.

Another consequence is that the very purpose of the sciences becomes to test theories in order to disprove (falsify) them (Popper 1974: 46). This view is the reason why Popper's philosophy of science is also termed *falsificationism*.

> ! **Falsificationism:** The opposite of verificationism, this is the view that the sciences do not seek to prove but rather to disprove their theories; i.e., the sciences consist of critically testing hypotheses.

Popper's point can be hard to understand yet it makes sense on reflection. As we have seen, the scientist begins by conceiving of a theory that can provide a possible answer to a specific problem. He cannot prove the theory but he can test it to make sure it is valid. This is done by subjecting the theory to any tests that may expose its incorrectness. If the theory survives these tests, it can be considered reliable.

A common feature of unscientific theories is that they cannot be tested in reality. The astrologist's predictions are too vague and unclear to be tested properly. Should events deviate completely from his predictions, he will always be able to devise an excuse; thus it is impossible to test astrology.

Popper's criterion of demarcation can therefore be explained as follows: If a theory can be tested in reality it is scientific (Popper 1974: 37). This enables him to define quite precisely what characterizes a good, scientific theory. It should not only be based on an educated guess about the properties of reality; it should also be formulated with such precision that it is clear which observations will respectively substantiate and falsify it. Finally, it must be formulated with such a degree of universality that it can be tested in many different ways. The scientific tradition is the history of one theory replacing another; however, it is not the history of these theories, but rather of the researchers' critical attitudes. In other words, the scientific tradition is the tradition of criticizing theories (Popper 1975: 348).

It is important to note that a theory does not cease to be scientific once falsified (just like an unscientific theory does not become scientific because it is true). It ceases to be valid but continues being scientific (if it was not scientific to begin with, it would not have been falsifiable at all). The only exception are cases where proponents of a refuted theory refuse to give it up but, like the astrologer, attempt to explain away its flaws instead. In this way they succeed in rendering the theory immune to the tests that once falsified it. The consequence of this is, however, that the theory is no longer scientific (Popper 1974: 37).

Falsification holds Popper's answer to the question of what characterizes scientific method. Researchers begin by theorizing about a specific correlation; for instance, why chimpanzees only exist in Africa. On the basis of their theory, they put forward a number of hypotheses of what the subsequent studies will reveal. The hypotheses constitute the explicit expectations we have for the outcome of our study based on the theory. They also state which results are impossible according to the theory. For instance, it goes without saying, that if the biologists find chimpanzees outside Africa, their theory will be invalidated.

The reason for making hypotheses is that they can be tested directly in an experiment, unlike the theory itself. There are two possible outcomes of this type of testing: The results will be inconsistent with the theory, in which case the theory will be considered falsified or disproved, and the researcher will have to devise a better theory. Otherwise, the experiment will yield the exact results predicted by the hypotheses. In this case, the theory will be considered valid, at least until new and better ways of testing it are discovered. The scientific method is depicted below:

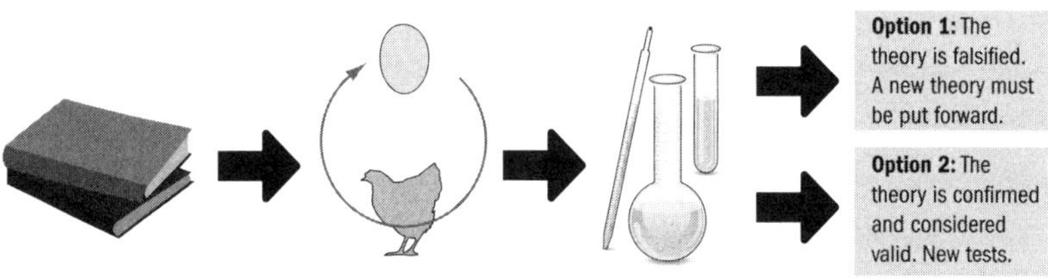

The researcher first puts forward a theory.

Specific hypotheses that can be tested in practice are deduced from the theory.

The hypotheses are tested in an experiment.

If the theory is falsified, a new one is put forward. If the theory is confirmed, it is considered valid.

Figure 3.1. Falsification

Popper's philosophy of science is also termed *critical rationalism*. It is rationalist because it makes use of deductive reasoning, although deduction in this context is understood in a slightly different manner than in the classical rationalism discussed in the previous chapter. The classical rationalists considered deduction a non-empirical way of acquiring true knowledge; however, Popper uses deduction as a method to move from theory to hypotheses (Popper 1974: 51). The point of departure for deduction is still non-empirical (the theory), but deduction is used to formulate hypotheses that are to be tested empirically. An example of this type of deduction could be the following: If we were to put forward the theory that water boils at 100 degrees Celsius, then our experiment must show that the water in the pot begins vaporizing at 100 degrees Celsius. It is this persistent empirical testing of hypotheses that makes Popper's rationalism critical.

> **!** **Critical Rationalism:** Shares with classical rationalism the idea that the point of departure of the sciences is a theory; however, it differs by requiring the theory to be tested empirically.

Popper is a rationalist in a second sense as well. As mentioned earlier, the classical rationalists believed that knowledge is acquired through reason, not through sensory perception. This means that human beings must be equipped with a number of inherent ideas since only this type of idea can be completely independent of the senses. Popper does not actually believe that we are born with particular ideas, but he must still consider this issue of classical rationalism. He may well lay claim to having solved the age-old problem of whether the chicken or egg came first. Popper answers that before the chicken there was an earlier kind of egg, and before that an earlier kind of chicken (Popper 1974: 47). In other words, a theory is preceded by an earlier observation and this observation is preceded by an even earlier theory. But where does this process begin? As theory always precedes observation, Popper must go back to before a person's birth. We are not born with ideas and concepts but rather with expectations. A baby is born into the world with expectations of care, food, and protection. Popper claims that, ever since the first childhood, human beings have continually understood their surroundings according to a "horizon of expectations" (Popper 1974: 47). Naturally, our expectations may not be fulfilled, but in that case we simply devise new expectations. In this sense, the sciences are merely a systematized, formalized, and institutionalized version of the way man finds his bearings in the world.

This is all very well, but many will still find it hard to get accustomed to Popper's claim that the sciences will never be able to prove their claims. Does this not make science a meaningless pursuit? The answer to this question reveals a third reason why Popper must be considered a rationalist, as rationalism is also characterized by being a realist position (Popper 1974: 63). Obviously realism must be understood as the opposite of antirealism (as found in positivism). While the antirealists claim that the sciences are only concerned with our perception of the world, the realists argue that the sciences are meant to examine and uncover the world in itself, which exists independently of our perception.

> **Realism:** The opposite of antirealism, this is the view that the world exists independently of our perception of it and that the sciences are meant to uncover the world in itself, and not just collect our sensory experiences.

Returning to the island struck by a meteor from the previous chapter, the realist would claim that the impact of the meteor would produce a loud crash. The fact that there are no people to hear it is completely immaterial.

How is Popper's realism related to the question of the meaningfulness of science? According to the realists, the sciences are made meaningful, not because their theories can be "proved", but because they are concerned with the world as it is in itself (and not merely with our perception of it). We can be sure of this exactly because our theories are falsified. We cannot claim whatever we want because the real world corrects us when we are mistaken. This is a crucial point because when one theory proves wrong, we never start from scratch. We learn from the flaws of the first theory and put forward a new one, which takes into account what nature previously disproved. Science is a meaningful pursuit, not because it arrives at the definitive truth but because we continue to learn more about the world (Popper 1975: 356). In other words, *better* theories— rather than theories that can be proven true— constantly replace those that are shown to be insufficient. Often a new theory will explain and correct previous theories, because it is formulated at a more general level than its predecessors.

Popper thus presents us with a different view of the development of the sciences than the one put forward by the positivists. In Popper's view, this development is not an even, unbroken, upward-sloping line. On the contrary, the line is broken every time a theory is falsified, and yet the line still moves upwards over time as we constantly draw closer to the truth about the world, although we can never be sure that we will reach it. The only thing we can be certain of is the erroneous character of our previous, but now falsified, theories.

Popper's contribution to the debates in philosophy of science constitutes a strong and original attack on positivism, yet Popper's view of science is not without problems of its own. One of them is the fact that, in practice, research is not carried out the way he envisioned it. Although it is generally accepted that a theory is required before observations of the world can be made, a theory is not simply abandoned because it is "falsified". If this were the case, the sciences would never have come so far! Many theories that scientists through the ages have considered important and necessary could be falsified. As we shall see in the next chapter, this even includes Newton's work. However, scientists do not automatically reject theories if they are inconsistent with observation. Sometimes they simply put the troublesome results aside expecting to find a better explanation at a later point.

Popper's Critical Rationalism: A Summary

As we have seen, Popper's point of departure is his criticism of positivism. When it comes to defining scientificity, positivism's notions of induction and verification are both logically and practically insufficient. Popper himself believes that his principle of demarcation provides a much better definition of what constitutes a scientific theory; namely that (contrary to pseudosciences, such as astrology) it can be tested empirically.

According to Popper, scientific studies begin with the formulation of a theory—an informed guess as to how reality can be explained. Hypotheses, which can be directly tested empirically, are deduced from the theory. As these are confirmed, the theory is considered valid. If these are disproved, the theory is falsified and a new and better theory must be put forth. This methodological view is termed falsificationism.

Popper continues classical rationalism's emphasis on deduction and the significance of scientific theory, meanwhile insisting that theories must be able to be tested in practice. Scientific progress is made through the continuous testing of theories, but we can never be sure that we have uncovered the truth about the world.

Moreover, this understanding reflects Popper's continuance of another aspect of classical rationalism—realism—which is the view that the sciences study the world as it is in itself and not just our perception of it.

We will now leave the knowledge level of philosophy of science and consider how Popper's theory is reflected by work in the social sciences.

Critical Rationalism in Practice

Popper's critical rationalism makes several methodological demands on the sciences; however, unlike positivism, it does not form the basis for a unitary science. It has therefore not inspired researchers to reinvent their disciplines as "Popperian". There are no parallels between critical rationalism and behaviourism, which was inspired by positivism. Nevertheless, it is evident that Popper and his idea of falsification touched upon something central in the way researchers work. For this reason, finding examples of "Popperian" scientific studies is not a difficult task.

Example: Falsificationism in Comparative Politics

What do we mean when we say that something is a welfare state? In comparative politics, the Danish sociologist Gøsta Esping-Andersen (born 1947) has proposed a distinction between three welfare regimes, that is, three fundamentally different ways of organizing a welfare society. Esping-Andersen discusses liberal, conservative, and social democratic regimes; however, this distinction falls short when considering countries in Southeast Asia, such as South Korea and Taiwan. Because of this, others have put forward a theory of a fourth type of welfare state existing in these countries. In an article from 2007, Yih-Jiunn Lee and Yeun-wen Ku attempted to test this theory (Lee and Ku 2007) by operationalizing it according to fifteen indicators (e.g., economic modernization and welfare costs to the state). These indicators could then be translated into hypotheses, which Lee and Ku were able to test empirically. On the basis of their tests, they were able to substantiate the theory of a fourth welfare regime characterized by low welfare costs and the importance of family as a social safety net. In this case, a theory was operationalized by hypotheses that aided in testing the theory empirically and led to its confirmation.

Example: Falsificationism and Microeconomics

In the microeconomic sciences, Eugene Fama's (born 1939) efficient markets hypothesis (EMH) has played an important role since being presented in the 1960s. Much simplified, it states that prices in the financial market reflect the information available to the market and thus the economic realities. The hypothesis has been strongly criticized in recent years. According to many people, the recent financial crisis in particular has emphasized its insufficiency, though by 1986 Lawrence H. Summers (born 1954) had already attempted to disprove it both theoretically and empirically (Summers 1986). *Theoretically,* he criticized the statistical tests used to substantiate the hypothesis. According to him, these tests were unable to identify even significant deviations from the development predicted by the hypothesis. *Empirically,* he sought to disprove the hypothesis by pointing out the many actual deviations from it in reality.

In this case, critical testing revealed a discrepancy between empirical reality and what ought to be expected according to the theory, so the theory was falsified. There are still supporters of the EMH despite Summer's (and many other's) criticism of it. This example demonstrates the weakness of Popper's philosophy of science, as discussed earlier: On the actual scientific level of knowledge, theories are very rarely either falsified *or* validated.

Example: How *You* Can Use Falsificationism

Popper's theories can, of course, be used in practical work with, for example, communication. If we consider again the example from the end of the previous chapter, Popper too would have some good advice for the students who want to study the communication in a company. First of all, it is important that they know exactly what they wish to investigate and why this particular area is interesting. Are they interested in the internal or the external communication? Do they want to study communication between management and employees, between employees, or something else entirely? What do they expect to gain from their study? The next step is to formulate a theory about their demarcated subject. The more general the theory the better, as this makes it easier to test in practice. Once the theory is in place, the students must deduce from it a number of hypotheses about the specific results they expect to get. The hypotheses must be directly comparable to the empirical observations. When this is done, the students have finished their preparation.

When the students have made their observations of the company, they must return to their theory. Did the actual results correspond to the hypotheses? If so, they can consider their theory confirmed and they will be able to conduct new critical tests. However, if their results are not consistent with the hypotheses, they will be forced to conclude that their theory is incorrect. They must put forward a new theory and new hypotheses. Fortunately they will not have to start all over again. While working with their original theory they will have gained experience, made surprising observations, and even discovered new correlations. From this, they will not only be able to put forward a better theory but also a theory that can explain the shortcomings of their previous assumptions. They will thus be one step closer to understanding the communication of the company.

Questions

1. According to Popper, what is the fundamental problem in philosophy of science?
2. According to Popper, which problems are related to positivism?
3. Explain what the asymmetry thesis is.
4. According to Popper, what is the criterion of scientificity?
5. How do the sciences work, according to Popper?
6. According to Popper, how do the sciences develop?
7. What assumptions does Popper have in common with positivism?
8. Explain how Popper continues classical rationalism.
9. What examples of falsificationism can you think of in your own field of study?
10. In your opinion, what are the strengths and weaknesses of Popper's view of science?

Pragmatism

Popper shares with the positivists the static, classical view of the world presented by the natural sciences: Science is to unearth universal and eternal laws. The assumption that such laws exist is, therefore, what makes science a meaningful enterprise. Uncovering the truth about the world is, in other words, a goal in itself.

However, not all researchers recognize in this portrayal of science a valid depiction of their own work. Theirs is a world of constant change, where the link between research and the practical level of knowledge is not only immediate, but also what makes their work meaningful. Truth is, therefore, neither eternal nor the only purpose of research. These scientists may find pragmatism a far more appealing alternative.

Science and Practice

Pragmatism emerged in the USA after the American Civil War (1861–1865), and for this reason its most important classical representatives are all American: Charles Sanders Pierce (1839–1914), William James (1842–1910), and John Dewey (1859–1952). Compared to a theory like positivism, pragmatism is a rather loose family of related theories, but what they share is the inspiration from the three theorists mentioned above.

This does not imply that Pierce, James, and Dewey agree on all matters. They do, however, share the viewpoint that the world is dynamic, that chance and chaos play a significant role in determining its development, and that for this reason it makes little sense to search for an eternal truth. This implies that instead of focusing on the alternative between induction and deduction, science should be assessed based on its societal implications. From the abstract preconditions of knowledge, we therefore turn our attention to its practical end product.

Ideally, this end product should allow us to act, to do something. It is from that fundamental principle that this philosophy of science derives its name, for 'pragmatism' comes from the Greek word *pragma*, meaning action. The abandonment of the ambition to find an absolute truth also reveals Greek inspiration, as it is a viewpoint first presented by the skeptics. Skepticism was an influential school in late antiquity whose primary message was that we are unable to uncover the truth about the world, and that finding the truth is therefore not a relevant ambition for science.

! **Skepticism:** The philosophical viewpoint that we are unable to obtain certain knowledge about the world.

In pragmatism, this inspiration is seen in the fact that research focuses on action and practical use rather than abstract notions of truth. But how exactly are we to understand this focus on action? Do the pragmatists claim that any viewpoint is adequate as long as we can make use of it? No, this is not the case. Granted, the pragmatists believe that our understanding of an absolute truth is an unobtainable ideal (Dewey 1998: 8). This does, however, not imply that all useful statements about the world have the same validity. What, then, does it imply?

William James gives us the answer. We assess a theory as true or false based on its practical consequences, not based on abstract principles. This has two specific implications.

Firstly, true theories are those that we can verify in practice. We do that, for example, by conducting experiments. This is why James claims that a theory is not simply true; truth is something that happens to it as our enquiries lead us to consider it as valid (James 1907: 142). In other words, the pragmatists still claim that we need to verify our theories, but they point out that what we really mean by "verifying a theory" is demonstrating that it works in practice.

Secondly, true theories are not interesting in themselves. Their significance is primarily due to the fact that they are far superior to false theories when it comes to facilitating our ability to act. We have, for instance, good reason to believe that our theories of aerodynamics are true, because they allow us to construct airplanes. If, on the other hand, I decide to act on the persuasion that I can fly, I will merely end up with a broken arm. It is in this practical consequence that the falsity of my conviction becomes evident.

We also consider theories true if they allow us to predict future events. It is, for instance, because meteorology allows us to forecast that tomorrow will be a rainy day that we consider it a true science. For this reason, James goes as far as to say that true ideas are to be understood as instruments of action (James 1907: 143). Just as the practical importance of a saw is that it allows us to cut wood, the practical importance of aerodynamics is to allow us to construct airplanes. So we don't call a theory true because we can use it, but we can use it because it is true. However, the importance of the theory is not so much to be found in its truth, but rather in its applicability—a true theory with no practical consequences for us would have no significance whatsoever (in fact, we probably wouldn't call it "true", or "theory" for that matter). So what makes a theory important is not that it is "mirroring reality", but that it is useful to us. This viewpoint is referred to as instrumentalism.

! **Instrumentalism:** The viewpoint that scientific theories must primarily be understood as instruments for our actions.

This does, however, not imply that scientists should only focus on areas where the applicability of their work is immediate. While context defines which ideas are useful, contexts change all the time, and scientific research therefore has to broaden its scope.

When it comes to instrumentalism, James is in agreement with Pierce, even though his perspective is slightly different. While James is interested in defining truth, Pierce wants to understand the concept of meaning. And as might be expected, he believes that the meaning of a sentence is its applicability when it comes to controlling our behavior (Pierce 1905). Experience teaches us which ideas are particularly useful for this purpose. To use our previous example, my idea about being able to fly is not particularly meaningful according to this criterion, while the opposite is true of the theories of aerodynamics.

Knowledge and Society

Having established what the pragmatists understand by such concepts as truth and meaning in a world of chance and constant change, what does it mean to possess knowledge? When do we know something about a topic? And how does scientific research practically obtain knowledge? Those are the questions that we will take a look at now.

Unsurprisingly, the pragmatist view is that our knowledge of an object is simply our perception of the practical effects produced by it. When scientists make an enquiry, they register these effects (Ormerod 2006: 898). The idea that objects, as a matter of definition, possess qualities hidden from researchers may not be meaningless, but it is certainly irrelevant to scientific research and to the question about what we can know. Basically, knowledge is what appears in the practical investigation of an object or a problem. A priori knowledge—knowledge that is not based on observations of reality—is illusory, and the same goes for strict logical definitions. The world is a messy place that requires thorough investigation rather than stringent deduction to be understood (Ormerod 2006: 904).

This, of course, sounds just like positivism. So is pragmatism really just a kind of positivism? Part of the answer to this question is found already in the introduction to this chapter: Pragmatism does not share the positivist view of the world as a stable and regulated whole, and the pragmatists have no ambition of uncovering an eternal truth. For this reason, pragmatism is not a normative theory. Furthermore, instrumentalism is incompatible with a positivist approach.

Having said that, it is not completely unjustified to draw parallels between the two approaches, as pragmatism is also a kind of empiricism. According to the pragmatists, their approach is even more thoroughly empiricist than positivism. The kinship between the two theories is expressed in their shared disdain for metaphysics, i.e. any form of knowledge not based on empirical research. This also implies that pragmatism and positivism are both critical of the western intellectual tradition. Furthermore, both theories consider the verification of theories to be not only possible, but also of decisive importance when it comes to deciding on their validity.

Yet the very question of verification also serves to highlight another difference between the two approaches. For positivism, the social, cultural, and historical context of the researcher has no role to play in science. The scientist is seen as an abstract individual who, in principle, makes the same observations, no matter who he or she is from a social perspective. As will become clear in chapter 7, this positivist idea is criticized by hermeneutical philosophers; however, pragmatism is equally critical. Research is, by necessity, a social process, and this is particularly evident when it comes to the verification of our theories.

When beginning to study a problem, scientists often focus on different aspects and explain their results in different ways. Contradictory explanations are then subjected to scrutiny. While some theories may be easily discarded, others require more thorough testing, with one eventually emerging as the strongest. After many tests of its validity, scientific consensus will emerge about this theory and its explanation of the phenomenon in question. In this sense, reality is what scientists agree on; it is a social consensus (Pierce 1878). In other words, the verification of our theories is necessarily a matter of cooperation. The positivist would obviously never agree that the social interactions of scientists play a decisive role in our determination of what is true and false, but the pragmatists here anticipate a point made by Thomas Kuhn, who is the topic of our next chapter.

Finally, pragmatism differs from both positivism and critical rationalism when it comes to understanding scientific research as a process. We already saw how the pragmatists refuse to set up rules for science—research does not begin with the application of a particular method. How, then, does it begin? According to the pragmatists, its point of departure is a phenomenon which puzzles us (Burks 1946: 303).

In our everyday interactions with the world, we do not reflect on its true nature. We act. We are focusing on practice. Only when we encounter something unexpected, something that does not really fit into our everyday life, do we pause and seek an explanation. The fact that water obeys the laws of gravity is only what we expect, but should this suddenly turn out not to be the case, we would certainly appreciate an explanation. And in this respect, scientific research is no different from our everyday lives: Enquiries begin with our surprise at the unexpected. This surprise leads us to formulate hypotheses, i.e. possible explanations of the surprising phenomenon in question. Scientific work therefore comes to consist of testing these hypotheses. This is the view of the scientific work process that pragmatists refer to as abduction.

! **Abduction:** The view that scientific research begins with the encounter of surprising phenomena, and that scientific enquiry consists in testing different hypotheses, i.e. different possible explanations of the phenomena in question.

While the pragmatists claim that this is how research actually takes place, they do not insist on either induction or deduction as a method when it comes to testing hypotheses. On the contrary, while these different approaches will typically supplement each other in the work of the scientists, it is impossible to set up rules defining when and how induction and deduction are to be applied. Just like the phenomenon that the researchers wish to understand, the enquiry itself is determined by a particular context, and so by a particular application.

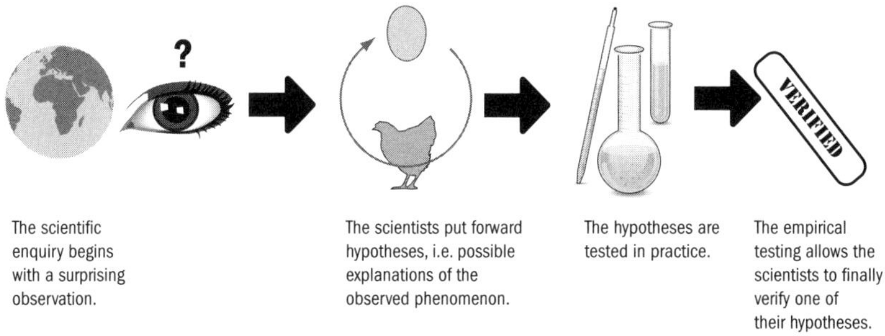

Figure 4.1. The Development of Science According to Pragmatism

This underlines what should already be evident: Pragmatism is, generally speaking, marked by a very undogmatic approach. What matters is not abstract rules, but the usefulness of what we do. This attitude also has consequences outside the realm of science, in relation to society and politics. And the pragmatists themselves, in particular John Dewey (Dewey 1998), explicitly draw these consequences. In a changing world where no truth is absolute, nobody is absolutely right or wrong; therefore, the good society must be marked by openness, pluralism, and dialogue. Everybody can contribute to the life of the community and deserves a voice. This is also the pragmatist argument for democracy: No political system is better at securing a pluralist society.

Modern Pragmatism: Richard Rorty

After Dewey's death in 1952, pragmatism lost much of its influence. It has, however, experienced a revival in recent decades, not least because of the influence of the American philosopher Richard Rorty (1931–2007). His early masterpiece, *Philosophy and the Mirror of Nature* (Rorty 1993), was published in 1979 and signaled the beginning of a period—the 1980s and 1990s—that was favorable to pragmatism. At a time when the rebellions of the late sixties had died out and the belief in a different societal order was weakening, Rorty advocated what was, in his own view, a pragmatist message of abandoning the idea of an absolute truth about the world and society. Instead, we need practical reflections on how to make life better for ourselves and others. In short, we ought to abandon philosophy of science as a discipline (Barnes 2006: 1549).

Rorty thus clearly adopts the skepticism found in classical pragmatism. Philosophy of science, in his view, has no more validity than poetry and art, and it is to be judged solely by one criterion: Does it help improve society? This is, of course, itself a philosophical viewpoint, and as such it cannot possess absolute validity. We probably cannot avoid such viewpoints – it is difficult to get rid of philosophy altogether. For Rorty, this fact implies that we should adopt an ironic distance to our own convictions. We should understand that they are contingent and determined by our concrete context. By not getting too attached to our personal convictions, we can keep focusing on what really matters, i.e. the practical implications of philosophy (Ward 2008: 292).

This may sound very benign, but Rorty was nevertheless a philosophical provocateur, and some of the objections that his work provoked may serve as an illustration of the problems that others have traditionally identified in pragmatism. Below I will mention just two.

Pragmatism: A Summary

In this chapter, we have seen how the pragmatist understanding of the sciences springs from the skepticist view that we cannot find an eternal and immutable truth about the world because the world is neither eternal nor immutable, but marked by constant change. The importance of the sciences is, however, due to the fact that they allow us to act, to do something in practice. Their value, in other words, is instrumental. Furthermore, we assess a theory's validity on its practical consequences when it is tested empirically.

Pragmatism shares this focus on empirical testing with positivism and, for that same reason, it also agrees with the criticism of theories that are not based on empirical studies. However, pragmatism differs from positivism not only because of its skepticism, but also e.g. by seeing research as an irreducibly social practice and by its view of research as a process. For in a pragmatist perspective, we do not begin simply by observing the world. Research begins with a surprise, with the encounter of unexpected phenomena. This forces us to formulate hypotheses, i.e. possible explanations of the inexplicable, and these hypotheses may then subsequently be tested in practice. As we have seen, this is the view known as abduction.

Pragmatism's undogmatic approach naturally leads to the view that all opinions should be heard and respected. This indicates that society should be open and democratic. Dewey, in particular, makes this point, but it is also articulated by a modern pragmatist such as Rorty, who also, by the way, insists on the continuing relevance of the skepticism found in classical pragmatism.

Pragmatism may in many ways appear both plausible and sympathetic, but it has also been met with criticism. For instance, in contemporary debates, Rorty's pragmatism has been accused of promoting a conservative agenda because it focuses on small improvements of contemporary society, but rejects the metanarratives that enable the formulation of visions for a fundamentally different societal order. Now, there is nothing wrong with being a conservative (and, by the way, according to Rorty himself he was a progressive rather than a conservative), but pragmatism may nevertheless have a problem if it can be demonstrated that its predominant practical (!) effect is simply to legitimize the societal status quo.

Another line of criticism elaborates on this last point: Some might claim that you cannot really make the world a better place unless you have some absolute standards of truth and of the good. And so pragmatism, in this view, undermines its own explicit ambition to improve on society by rejecting such standards.

Pragmatism in Practice

Historically, pragmatism has inspired work in a range of different areas of research, particularly in the humanities and social sciences, where scientists have easily identified with its focus on applicability. Below, we will take a look at a couple of examples.

Example: Pragmatism and Communication Theory

One of the fields in which pragmatism has been very useful is communication theory. This is unsurprising, given that research in this field is less about uncovering an absolute truth than about understanding the various ways in which we practically construct our common social world through communication.

Chris Russill (2005) demonstrates how there is a direct link from the classical formulation of pragmatism as found in James and Dewey to modern communication theory. The pragmatist tradition in this field emphasizes the necessity of, and obstacles to, communication in a contemporary pluralistic world with no common standards of how to deal with differences and disagreements.

As pointed out by Robert T. Craig (2007), different theories of communication reflect different practical contexts of communication, and the challenges connected with these contexts. For instance, in the case of linear transmission models of communication (models based on the distinction between a "sender" and a "receiver") the theories discuss the amount of information, whether the information is accurate, and what effects it might have. These theories are not the ultimate truth about communication but practical tools that may, in specific contexts, support practical communication.

Craig also summarizes what, in his view, characterizes a pragmatist understanding of communication. Just like Russill—and in accordance with classical pragmatism—he emphasizes the decisive role of communication when it comes to facilitating cooperation in social contexts characterized by pluralism and diversity. Communication, in other words, is a tool for overcoming disagreement and conflict. This is obviously a practical purpose. Just as in classical pragmatism (as well as in Rorty's philosophy), this view has greater societal implications. It promotes a democratic ideal about communication as the key to peaceful coexistence between groups with different views and opinions.

Example: Pragmatism and Geography

In geography, researchers use different concepts for space, such as landscapes, regions, climate, et cetera, but what status do such concepts have in relation to the objects investigated by the researchers? Trevor J. Barnes presents us with a pragmatist answer to this question.

In accordance with classical pragmatism, he understands the concepts as instruments. The applicability of these conceptual instruments is determined by the specific context of the scientific enquiry. This implies that the concepts need not be a part of a consistent theoretical framework, their function and justification is to make possible experiments that may lead to a better world. And we only apply them so long as they are able to contribute to this purpose. For this same reason, scientific terminology is never determined once and for all, but always preliminarily.

Concepts like "place" or "space" have, therefore, no meaning except in relation to specific contexts. They are tied to practical problems and to a particular community.

Example: How *You* Can Use Pragmatism

Based on the insights presented above, the students will already have been encouraged to adopt a pragmatist approach to their enquiry into the communication of an organization. But exactly what are they to do?

To begin with, they should form an overview of the communication of the company in question. Based on this overview, they may consider why this organization is of particular interest to them. Have they detected something about its communication that does not immediately fit in with their theories? It is precisely the unexpected that will be interesting. They can test various hypotheses, i.e. different possible explanations of the surprising phenomenon in question. In this context, they are free to choose which theories of communication are more useful when dealing with the case in question. The exact manner of comparing and examining their hypotheses will, in other words, require a concrete assessment based on the problem identified. The case itself, i.e. the practical communication under scrutiny, determines how to best conduct the enquiry. No methodological rules have absolute validity; nevertheless, the students will probably experience the need to combine induction and deduction in their work.

When they finally agree on an explanation, it must be one that works in practice. First of all, it must explain the practical observations that motivated the enquiry to begin with. Secondly, it must have practical implications. In this specific case, one would characterize the enquiry as a success if its conclusions help improve the communication of the organization. In this manner the students may live up to the pragmatist ambition to not only make us smarter, but also make the world a better place.

Questions

1. What is skepticism, and in what sense can classical pragmatism be said to be inspired by skepticism?
2. Explain in your own words how we are to understand pragmatism as a position in philosophy of science.
3. What is "truth" from a pragmatist perspective?
4. Explain the concept "instrumentalism".
5. Explain how pragmatism differs from positivism.
6. Explain the concept "abduction".
7. According to pragmatism, which role should science play in society?
8. How do you see the influence from classical pragmatism in Rorty's philosophy?
9. What examples of pragmatism can you think of in your own field of study?
10. In your opinion, what are the strengths and weaknesses of the pragmatist view of science?

Kuhn's Theory of Paradigms

The previous chapters have focused on, among other things, the differences between positivism and critical rationalism with good reason, as the differences are both numerous and significant, yet Popper and the positivists essentially view the sciences in the same way. They possess a special rationality and a particularly privileged standing in our understanding of the world. This is why outlining clear criteria for the nature of science is important. These criteria serve as rules for how studies of the world can be conducted scientifically.

However, you could also adopt a completely different approach: you could examine how the sciences really work and develop. After this you can then return to Popper and the positivists and test whether their criteria of scientificity are meaningful when seen in light of the reality of science. As we saw in the previous chapter, this is a far more pragmatic approach; however, it has also inspired theorists outside classical pragmatism. We find it in particular in the American historian of science, Thomas S. Kuhn's (1922–1996) groundbreaking work *The Structure of Scientific Revolutions* from 1962.

From Normal Science to Scientific Revolution

Although Kuhn does not seek to discover a criterion for distinguishing between science and non-science, he is naturally aware of the distinction between the two. At one point, science must have come into existence. One approach could, therefore, be to explore when it first emerged and what characterized its emergence. This is Kuhn's strategy.

To understand the rise of modern science one must go back to the Renaissance. As briefly covered in the chapter about positivism, the power of the Catholic Church, and therefore its worldview, were decidedly weakened during this period. This also applied to the Aristotelian philosophy of nature, which the church deemed a truthful representation of the world. This period witnessed a great growth in scientific studies, led by famous philosophers and scientists, such as Nicolaus Copernicus (1473–1543), Galileo Galilei (1564–1642), Tycho Brahe (1546–1601), Johannes Kepler (1571–1630), and Francis Bacon (1561-1626). According to Kuhn there is, however, something peculiar about the early natural sciences, for although the work carried out is undeniably scientific, somehow the results are less so (Kuhn 1973: 13–16). The studies point in no particular direction. They lack clearly defined criteria for determining which aspects are significant, and numerous rivalling schools of thought, with individual understandings of what is important to study, can be found within the various sciences (physics, chemistry, etc.). For Kuhn, the question of science is about how it has progressed historically from this confused mishmash to "real" science.

The answer is that one of the many rivalling schools of thought ended up defeating the others. It proved capable of yielding results that could not be matched by its competitors; for example, by finding a convincing solution to a problem that all scientists had previously unsuccessfully struggled to solve. Most people were convinced by this breakthrough, so it is of less importance that a few stubborn opponents refused to join the winning school of thought. They were quickly ignored and forgotten.

No matter how skilled the scientists from the winning school of thought were, they still could not have succeeded in answering all the scientific questions of that period. Many problems remained that could not be clearly connected to the results that won the particular school of thought acknowledgement in the first place. If this is the case, what was the decisive contribution of the winning school? According to Kuhn, the answer is a *paradigm*.

> ! **Paradigm:** A paradigm consists of exemplars and a disciplinary matrix, and is the frame of understanding that characterizes a particular scientific discipline (e.g., physics, chemistry, economics).

How is this concept to be understood? According to Kuhn, a scientific paradigm constitutes a frame of understanding, which provides sense and direction in the work of scientists. The early scientific schools of thought each worked within their own frames, but a science first becomes genuinely scientific when it is collected under one paradigm. Only upon reaching this point can all scientists move in the same direction, and only then can significant progress be made. In other words, only when all physicists and chemists view the world alike will physics and chemistry make serious scientific headway.

A paradigm contains two elements: The first is a *disciplinary matrix* (Kuhn 1977: 463). This term applies to everything that unites scientists and researchers as a social group; for example, the textbooks they have all read, the education they have all completed, and the common journals in which their work is published. Apart from this, Kuhn underlines three features of the disciplinary matrix: firstly, a shared symbolic language—typically expressed as equations and formulas—that can be employed for internal communication; secondly, agreement upon a number of scientific principles and basic laws; and thirdly, a number of shared values, for instance, the value of precise measurement and statements. Although the individual researchers will never have an identical understanding of these values, they will all endorse them.

> ! **Disciplinary Matrix:** The rules, conventions, and common principles that unite the members of a specific scientific community.

The second element of a paradigm consists of *exemplars* (Kuhn 1977: 471). These are the particularly pedagogical examples of the paradigm's ability to explain the world, which can be found in any textbook. Their purpose is to make sure students view the world in the way validated by established research within the paradigm.

> **!** **Exemplars:** These are fundamental examples of the validity of the paradigm. By encountering exemplars in textbooks and teaching, students are taught to view the world in the same way as established research within the paradigm.

Kuhn even compares exemplars to the *Where's Waldo?* children's books. Just like a child must learn to spot Waldo, students must learn to discern the scientific content in the examples they are presented with. Much like the child, who, when viewing the same illustration again, will immediately be able to find Waldo, the idea is that by training with exemplars the student likewise becomes accustomed to immediately being able to identify what paradigmatic research dictates as being relevant. In this way, young researchers are assimilated into the professional community, the disciplinary matrix. Consider medical science. To the untrained eye, two x-rays look completely identical; however, the doctor will immediately notice the tiny spot on one of the x-rays, indicating a malignant dysplasia. Because of many years of training with exemplars, he intuitively sees what everyone else would miss, but what is crucial as defined by the established paradigm of his specific field.

When Kuhn speaks of paradigms shaping what we see, it must be understood literally. This may sound strange. One could be led to believe that a paradigm simply provides a few rules on how to view the world, and so it does, yet shared rules are not enough to ensure that the paradigmatic science will establish a cohesive research tradition. Reaching this point first of all requires that two colleagues *see* the same thing, for example, when looking at an x-ray (Kuhn 1977: 472).

The paradigm thus ensures the fundamental consensus among researchers, which is the secret behind the astounding efficiency of modern science. Once the fundamental aspects are agreed upon, it becomes easier to approach more specialized issues. As mentioned, there will be plenty of problems, although the paradigm instils hope in the scientist that solutions can be found. The paradigm is like a large puzzle with the edges already laid out. It leaves the scientists with the vast job of filling in the frame (Kuhn 1973: 36). In some areas, it may be difficult to get the pieces to fit. In these cases great creativity must be shown in order to force nature into the framework of the paradigm. A large part of the scientists' work can therefore be characterized as scientific uncluttering. This task is characteristic of *normal science*; i.e., research within the boundaries of a paradigm acknowledged by everyone within a given scientific field (which is the opposite of a science divided by competing schools of thought).

! **Normal Science:** Research carried out within the framework of a commonly acknowledged paradigm.

Kuhn mentions three tasks that provide an exhaustive portrayal of normal science (Kuhn 1973: 29–35). First of all, ambiguity in the paradigm must be reduced and any gaps in its worldview (the puzzle) must be filled. Secondly, a paradigm will typically include some central observations, some facts that are of crucial importance to its explanatory power. Part of normal scientific work is to provide more precise measurements of these facts. Finally, the third task of normal science is to find new areas in which the paradigm can be applied. As it has proven so productive in solving one type of problem, it must be tested to see if it can be applied to other fields as well.

Note what normal science, according to Kuhn, does *not* do. It does not put new theories forward and it does not attempt to "prove" the paradigm. At the most, normal science can lead the paradigm into a state of crisis, but it cannot put forth a new one. Normal science is fully occupied with finishing the puzzle of the paradigm and for this reason scientists will often be skeptical of colleagues who present new theories. The overall purpose of normal science is solely to strengthen the paradigm and its applicability.

In the puzzle of science, the solution—the paradigm—is known beforehand. Furthermore, scientists must abide by a number of rules. First and foremost they must apply the scientific rules the paradigm is based on. They must utilize the instruments typically employed in the specific scientific environment, and they must, more or less explicitly, endorse the values and worldview of this environment (or what the positivists would term metaphysics) (Kuhn 1973: 40–42).

Now, one might think that Kuhn has given us a comprehensive account of science and of scientific development. And one might think that this development is an even and undramatic process where each scientist places his few pieces in the great puzzle; that one day we will be able to place the last piece, finally reaching the truth about the world. Unfortunately, it is not that simple, as paradigms do not last forever. Instead, they replace each other through what Kuhn describes as *scientific revolutions* (Kuhn 1973: 111–135).

! **Scientific Revolution:** The transition from one paradigm to a new one, which is characterized by scientists suddenly viewing the world differently after the old paradigm has been thrown into a state of crisis.

A scientific revolution is heralded by a crisis in normal science. The puzzle simply cannot be solved and the scientists are unable to explain or excuse the anomalies. In the end, normal science falls apart and the scientists lose the framework for their work. The question becomes: How do the scientists get themselves through such a crisis? Or one could ask: How does a new paradigm replace the old one?

In the middle of the crisis, a scientist or a group of scientists will discover an entirely new pattern in the problematic data. You could say that they suddenly discover Waldo somewhere completely different from where they expected to find him in the old paradigm. It can also be illustrated by Kuhn's own example, derived from pictures such as the one below.

Figure 5.1. A Vase or Two Faces?

In the old paradigm, all scientists saw a vase when looking at the picture. After a period of crisis, one scientist suddenly discovers that "really" it is not a picture of a vase but of two faces. He literally *sees* something in the picture, which has not previously been noticed (Kuhn 1973: 111–112). We have all experienced this (on a smaller scale) when battling a problem we do not understand. Suddenly we realize what the solution is and we view the problem with "fresh eyes". This is called a gestalt-switch. The transition from one paradigm to another is therefore not a rational process; instead, it is something as irrational as one talented scientist's "aha" experience.

Once the scientific community has reached agreement regarding the validity of the new paradigm, normal science starts over. Even experienced scientists must, like first year students, learn to view the world according to this new scientific worldview. Large amounts of data and observations, significant in the old paradigm, will now appear meaningless or irrelevant. Although the instruments as a rule will be the same, the scientists will employ them for new types of observations.

Is it an exaggeration to say that we see the world differently after a paradigm shift? Do we not always see the same, although we might interpret what we see differently? Not according to Kuhn (Kuhn 1973: 121). Certainly much interpretation goes on in the sciences but, like all interpretation, it is dependent on a framework—a context constituted by the paradigm. A paradigm is thus the condition for interpretation and not the result of interpretation. This is why the paradigm determines what we observe, whether we see a vase or two faces.

The claim Kuhn is making and asking us to accept is extremely radical. Because a paradigm decides what we see and because the transition from one paradigm to another constitutes a gestalt-shift, the paradigms become *incommensurable*. In other words, comparing two paradigms to determine which is most correct is impossible, as there are no paradigm-independent facts against which this can be measured (Kuhn 1973: 113–127). Newtonian studies substantiate Newton's paradigm, while Aristotelian studies confirm Aristotle's worldview. The latter may well have ended up collapsing, but so far this has been the fate of all paradigms, Newton's included. Moreover, there is no reason to assume that the paradigms within which scientists work today constitute the final and conclusive truth about the world.

! **The Incommensurability of Paradigms:** Two paradigms cannot be compared, and one cannot be said to be truer than another.

In other words, we are as far from the worldview of positivism and Popper as is humanly possible. The work and development of the sciences is not a governed and rational process and we cannot be certain that it brings us closer to the truth about reality. Normal science is characterized by a number of practical tasks and by a community (the disciplinary matrix), but not a particular method. Furthermore, the sciences do not possess a specific rationality, which makes them a better or more accurate way of constructing theories. The question of criteria for demarcation, which is the fundamental issue for Popper as well as the positivists, is thus, in Kuhn's view, completely meaningless.

In addition, Kuhn would object to Popper's view by arguing that the validity of a scientific theory cannot, in practice, be determined by its consistency with observed facts. Several of Newton's theories could never be proven more than approximately consistent with the empirical data because his theories did not consider, for example, air resistance or the mutual attraction between planets, yet these theories were of great significance to the sciences (Kuhn 1973: 32). Even theories that are consistent with empirical data are often only relatable to nature in very few areas. For example, according to Kuhn, there are only three ways of testing Einstein's general theory of relativity empirically. With that he states that Popper was wrong to believe that theories of a more general nature are always easier to test.

The positivists were wrong as well. Scientific observations are never independent and objective, and they never aim at proving theories. Evidently, what is seen does not necessarily depend on "the eye of the beholder" but it always depends on the paradigm, which determines what the eye sees. Scientists do not seek to prove their paradigms. On the contrary, they work from the assumption that they are true, or else they would not spend time exploring them. Finally, scientific development is not cumulative. Although it progresses evenly, it only develops within the paradigmatic framework, and consequently only for as long as the particular paradigm is considered valid.

Unlike Popper and the positivists, Kuhn does not provide any methodological precepts; however, his account of the *actual* development of science can be illustrated as below:

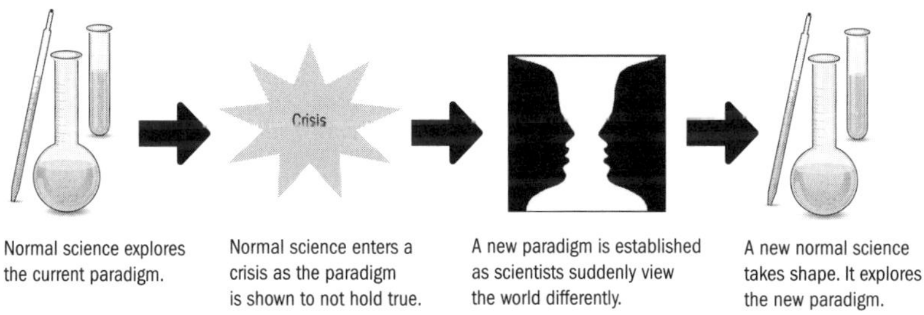

Figure 5.2. Science According to Kuhn

As we have seen, Kuhn can be considered a critic of Popper and positivism's classical theories of science; however, can Kuhn himself be criticized? If the sciences develop through revolutions and if the paradigms are incommensurable, will science not become a meaningless pursuit? Will we not merely end up with pure *relativism*, where one paradigm might do just as well as another?

> ! **Relativism:** The view that claims can only possess validity in a specific and limited context; thus, no truth is absolute.

Naturally, these objections have been raised against Kuhn. Of course, some theorists see no problems in relativism. The Austrian-American philosopher Paul K. Feyerabend (1924–1994), for instance, advocates what he himself calls epistemological anarchism (Feyerabend 1994). He claims both that research is neither characterized by a specific method, nor even by a specific rationality, and that science for this very reason is no more rational than poetry or astrology. This is, obviously, an extreme position. Kuhn, on the other hand, would not have considered himself a relativist, and there are several good reasons for agreeing with him on this point. First of all, not everything changes in a paradigm shift. The sciences will, for instance, still be characterized by the same values and norms that set the standards for good science. These are what ensure that the entire scientific community does not crumble during the crisis. Secondly, there is in fact a qualitative difference between the different paradigms. Modern physics can be *used* for much more than Aristotle's natural philosophy. Moreover, if a paradigm enables us to fly to the moon or put an end to polio, is it not less important that we can never be certain of reaching the truth about the world within the current paradigmatic framework? Finally, Kuhn argues that paradigms actually do collide with reality. Although the paradigm determines what we see, it is not immune to the observations and experiments that end up causing its crisis. We can be certain that we are working towards an improved understanding of reality because reality "resists" our paradigms when these are incorrect. As a result our claims about the world are not without significance.

With Kuhn, philosophy of science has come a long way since its origins in Comte's positivism, and the most striking difference between the theory of paradigms and its predecessors is what we, in this chapter, have paid the least amount of attention to. There is a crucial shift in focus, as Kuhn does not consider it the task of philosophy of science to lay down rules determining what "true science" is, but rather to describe actual science. According to Kuhn, science first of all constitutes a community characterized by shared norms and training. If he were asked to specify what characterizes "true science", he would probably answer that it is a social practice. You engage in it with others. His view of science therefore forms a natural transition to the next section of the book, in which selected traditions within the philosophy of the social sciences will be presented.

Between Popper and Kuhn: Imre Lakatos

As previously stated, Kuhn's theory may be seen as a critical alternative to positivism and to Popper's critical rationalism. Is it, however, necessarily the case that we have to choose between these alternatives? Or is it conceivable that there may be a middle ground between the two that does not (as pragmatism) force us to abandon the ambition to know the truth about the world? One may say that the Hungarian philosopher Imre Lakatos presents us with just such an alternative.

According to Lakatos, scientific work always takes place within so-called research programmes. A research programme is characterized by, among other things, common theories and examples (Lakatos 1970: 99), but it does not shape our perceptions in the way Kuhn's paradigms do, and, moreover, more research programmes may coexist at any given time. A scientist will stick to his or her programme as long as it progresses, and will not be held back by observations that appear to contradict their theories. It is only when the research programme stagnates and begins to degenerate that these anomalies become a problem. Eventually, this process will lead to the formulation of alternative research programmes. What then follows is what Lakatos refers to as a "war of attrition" (Lakatos 1970: 102) between the programme in crisis and its new competitor, until further research has revealed which one of them is more efficient at generating scientific progress.

Lakatos thus rejects Popper's principle of falsification as far too crude, but at the same time he adheres to the idea that it is through falsification (of research programmes, not of singular theories) that science progresses. And he distances himself from Kuhn, among others, by insisting on the idea that science possesses a specific rationality and that we can therefore be confident that it makes progress (Lakatos 1970: 116–118).

Kuhn's Theory of Paradigms: A Summary

Contrary to the theories of the positivists and Popper, Kuhn's theory is not normative; i.e., it does not set up criteria of scientificity. The theory of paradigms is descriptive, as Kuhn examines actual sciences to uncover how they work in practice. He finds that a particular frame of understanding characterizes them all: a paradigm. Historically, this emerges when a conquering school of thought outmatches its opponents and imparts its particular worldview upon the science in question. Through the disciplinary matrix and exemplars, the paradigm provides modern science with a common frame of understanding, as well as a social context, which enables its great progress. Kuhn calls this normal science, and it is the task of normal science to explore the paradigm, which all scientists are convinced is valid.

But paradigms do not last forever. At one point they will enter a period of crisis, which will affect the entire discipline in question. The crisis results in a scientific revolution, in which a researcher or a group of researchers come to view the world in a different light. This gestalt-switch forms the basis for a new normal science and the exploration of a new paradigm.

Kuhn's theory marks a sharp break with both positivism's and Popper's philosophies of science. According to Kuhn, their methodological precepts have nothing to do with the actual work of scientists. In practice, science is first of all a social activity and the paradigm constitutes a social consensus.

The Theory of Paradigms in Practice

There is no doubt that the natural sciences are Kuhn's primary frame of reference. This does not mean he did not find the social sciences interesting. Examples of the significance of the theory of paradigms permeate these sciences, both in research and on the practical level of knowledge. There is, however, a significant difference between the paradigms in these two branches of science. While one paradigm replaces another in the natural sciences, it is normal for several paradigms to coexist in the social sciences.

Example: The Paradigms of Transmission and Interaction in Communication Theory

One example includes the paradigms of transmission and interaction found in communication theory (Frandsen, Halkier, and Johansen 2007). In the paradigm of transmission, communication is viewed as a message being conveyed from sender to recipient. In the paradigm of interaction, communication is viewed as dialogue.

The models found within each of the two paradigms show different things, so it is impossible to consider one more correct than the other.

Why, then, does it make sense to speak of two *paradigms*? The answer is that different things will be visible depending on which model is used. In the paradigm of transmission focus is on how the message reaches the recipient, which medium is used, and which obstacles will be encountered when transferring the message. In the paradigm of interaction, people see something other than a message needing to be conveyed. Communication is rather a social process in which mutual generation of meaning takes place.

The two different perspectives govern what the researchers see, which problems they discuss, and even what the concept "communication" means to them. In this sense they function as paradigms.

Example: Neoclassical Economics and Information Economics: Two Paradigms in the Economic Sciences

In the economic sciences, neoclassical economics constituted the dominant paradigm throughout the twentieth century. The neoclassical economists maintain, among other things, Adam Smith's (1723–1790) belief in the effective self-regulation of the free market. With time this paradigm has been challenged from different sides, inspired explicitly by Kuhn's theory of paradigms.

The 2001, Nobel Prize Winner, Joseph E. Stiglitz (born 1943), believes that information economics constitutes a paradigm shift in relation to neoclassical economics (Stiglitz 2002). The old paradigm possessed a certain explanatory force but it also had significant limitations, which are demonstrated by its inability to explain, for example, unemployment and poverty. Stiglitz wished to explore these limitations. According to him, the crucial point was that neoclassical economics did not take into account the important role played by information and, not least, by the unequal distribution of information in the market. In the neoclassical paradigm, used-car salesmen and their buyers hold the same amount of knowledge, but, as many car buyers will attest, in practice this is not the case. Information economics, on the other hand, is motivated by the desire to understand how economic decisions, and thus the development of the market, are affected by the non-transparency of the market. According to Stiglitz, its emergence as a new paradigm should be considered evidence of a fundamental crisis in the old neoclassical paradigm.

Example: Corporate Social Responsibility and the Need for a New Economic Paradigm

According to Jouni Korhonen, neoclassical economics is also at the root of what he refers to as the dominating social paradigm in modern societal life (Korhonen 2002). The problem with this paradigm is that it is incompatible with newer theories about the social responsibility and sustainability of businesses. For example, globalization and specialization are two elements of the dominating social paradigm; however, the combination of regional specialization and the global circulation of goods and services is not unproblematic in relation to obtaining a sustainable product (the transport sector is one of the largest sources of pollution), nor when it comes to combating poverty and aiding social development (poor regions are kept in their role as manufacturers of raw materials). Social responsibility requires the development of a new paradigm, one that emphasizes diversity and balance, as in natural ecosystems. Korhonen not only applies the concept of paradigms to a specific scientific frame of understanding, but also to the self-understanding of an entire society. Although inspired by it, this particular use of the paradigm concept therefore differs strongly from Kuhn's philosophy of science.

Example: How You Can Use Kuhn's Theory of Paradigms

What would Kuhn say to our, by now, somewhat confused students who are still waiting to get started on their study of communication in a large company? Which methodological precepts would he prescribe, and how are they to work with paradigms in their study? Kuhn would answer the first question by stating that scientific work cannot be defined by methodological precepts. Each separate science holds a number of conventions about how to carry out studies and, as long as these conventions are complied with, one's work can be considered science. Conventions are, however, not the same as precepts. His answer to the second question would be that it is impossible not to work within a paradigm. Because of the conventions (the disciplinary matrix) the students have been trained in since their first day of study, and because of the examples (exemplars) through which they have learned to work with communication, they will intuitively know what to look for when studying communication in a company. However, it is important that the students are aware of which paradigm they are working in, as this will strengthen their understanding of their own work. How does the paradigm govern the questions they ask and the answers they find? Once they understand this, they are able to critically reflect on the paradigm.

Questions

1. According to Kuhn, when does a science become "real" science and why?
2. What characterizes "normal science" and how are we to understand the concept "paradigm"?
3. Explain the concept "disciplinary matrix".
4. Explain the concept "exemplars".
5. Why do crises appear in the sciences and what is a "scientific revolution"?
6. In your own words, explain how the transition from one paradigm to another takes place.
7. How does Kuhn's concept of scientific revolutions relate to positivism's and Popper's philosophy of science?
8. Give three examples of paradigms from your own field of study.
9. Consider a previous assignment or exam paper. Which elements of the three philosophies of science discussed so far (positivism, critical theory, theory of paradigms), can be applied to shed light on your work?

10. In your opinion, what are the strengths and weaknesses of Kuhn's theory of paradigms?

A Summary of the Classical Philosophies of Science

Which Key Concepts Have We Examined?

In the first part of the book, we considered the classical philosophies of science. However, to begin with, we examined two metaphysical schools of thought: *empiricism* and *rationalism*. Empiricism is characterized by its belief that empirical studies of the world serve as a means to knowledge, whereas rationalism claims knowledge is acquired through logical, rational thought. They therefore also adhere to different methodologies. The empiricists believe in *induction*, the method of extracting a general law from a variety of single observations. The method of the rationalists is *deduction*, which means drawing theorems from axioms, or drawing conclusions from logical premises. The difference between the two can be summed up by the distinction between *a priori* and *a posteriori* knowledge, respectively knowledge independent of and derived from our sensory perception of the world.

We saw how *positivism* continued the empiricist approach in a philosophy of science context. By emphasizing the fact that only empirical observations are a source of true knowledge, positivism constitutes a critique of classical *metaphysics* (all worldviews not based on empirical data). The positivists imagine scientific development to be even and unbroken because it continuously accumulates knowledge about the world. This is the basis for the idea of *cumulative science*. This idea requires that observations are *theory-independent*, which means they must not be biased by what the scientists expect from their results. *Verificationism* states that the aim of science is to prove theories and that only theories that can be proven are scientific. Furthermore, like empiricism, positivism is a type of *antirealism*, where science is concerned with systematizing our perceptions in order to discover regularities in the way in which they appear. Science is not about a "world that lies behind sensory perceptions". In relation to society, positivists consider *science as neutral* rationality, unaffected by, for example, political ideology or religious preference. In addition they believe that all sciences are scientific in the same way. This means that the human, social, and medical sciences, for example, are all components of one *unitary science*. *Logical positivism* attempted to reinvent positivism as a philosophy of language. Its overriding point is that only statements that can be traced back to simple sensory perceptions are meaningful. This view led to *behaviourism,* which constitutes the positivist research programme for the humanities and social sciences. To be truly scientific, these sciences must base their studies of people and society on empirical observation, using the same method as in the natural sciences. This means that the human and social sciences should only study behaviour. The logical positivists also strengthened the antirealism of classical positivism by championing a form of *phenomenalism*, which is the view that an object is the sum of our perceptions of it. It makes no sense to speak of an object's inherent properties that "underlie" sensory perceptions.

The positivists and Popper agree that philosophy of science is about finding a solution to *the problem of demarcation*, the question of how to distinguish between science and non-science. Apart from this, however, they disagree about most things. Popper rejects the verificationism of positivism for several reasons, firstly, because of *the problem of induction*. Even though all our observations have yielded the same results up until now, we can never be sure that future studies will yield the same results as past studies. Popper puts forth *the asymmetry thesis*; that is, no amount of observation is able to prove a theory, but only one observation is needed to disprove it. This insight led him to *falsificationism*, the view that science does not consist of proving but rather critically testing theories. Popper's understanding of science can also be termed *critical rationalism.* He carries on the ideas of classical rationalism insofar as he believes that theory always precedes the scientists' research; however, his rationalism is *critical*, seeing that theories must be tested empirically. Furthermore, Popper can also be considered a rationalist insofar as he is a proponent of *realism.* Contrary to antirealism, he believes the world exists independent of our perception of it, and it is the task of science to uncover the world in itself, not only our experience of it.

Pragmatism, on the other hand, takes as its point of departure the rejection of the view shared by Popper and the positivists, i.e. the view that the aim of science is to find the absolute truth about the world. This rejection makes it clear that pragmatism is inspired by classical *skepticism*: The philosophical view that we are unable to uncover the objective truth about the world. Instead, scientific theories and scientific terminology are to be understood as instruments for our actions—the view summarized under the concept *instrumentalism.* For this reason, the pragmatists also refrain from insisting on a specific methodology as the thing defining scientific research, as such. Instead, they claim that research in reality begins with a surprising observation that the scientists then have to formulate hypotheses to explain. This view is referred to as *abduction.*

According to Kuhn, science takes place within the boundaries of a *paradigm*, which can be understood as the scientists' framework for understanding the world. A paradigm partly consists of a *disciplinary matrix,* which joins together the members of a particular scientific community as a social unity, and partly of *exemplars,* which are fundamental examples of the validity of the paradigm, by means of which students are trained to view the world in the same way as established science. Research within a generally accepted paradigm is termed *normal science.* But this is not the only type of science. When the examination of a paradigm exposes its limitations, science experiences a crisis, which results in a *scientific revolution* marking the transition from one paradigm to another. Researchers look upon the world differently and the old paradigm appears outdated. This radical shift explains the *incommensurability of paradigms* (i.e., their incomparability). Nevertheless, Kuhn would not consider his theory to be an expression of *relativ-*

ism, which is the view that statements can only be valid in specific and limited contexts.

Some Themes in Classical Philosophy of Science

When considering these positions from a broader perspective, a number of themes recur. One is the question of whether philosophy of science ought to be normative or descriptive; that is, whether it is meant to prescribe rules for scientific work or merely describe how science functions in practice. The first view is held by positivism and Popper, the second by Kuhn and pragmatism.

Another fundamental difference between the four positions concerns the question of what it means to "observe the world", or more specifically, to conduct empirical studies. According to the positivists, ideally the scientist must objectively and neutrally register what he observes, much like a camera. Nature must speak for itself, and the scientist must be but a passive onlooker. According to Popper, however, because observation is meant to test theories, it must be a planned, goal-oriented, and selective activity. Finally, according to Kuhn and the pragmatists, speaking of an "objectively true picture of the world" makes no sense at all. According to the pragmatist, the specific case and the specific purpose of our enquiry determine our choice of theory, and therefore also what we see. Kuhn would point out that two people can observe the same object and see widely different things if they view it through different paradigms. Observation may well be planned and focused, but the paradigm defines the goal of these observations.

In other words, we are dealing with different perceptions of the relationship between theory and observation. Is observation theory-independent; i.e., free of prejudice and expectations? According to the positivists, it must be to be considered scientific. According to Popper and Kuhn, it is necessary that observation is theory-dependant. In Popper's view, the theory you wish to test determines what you study but not what you see; however, according to Kuhn, the paradigm determines what you see when observing the world. As we have seen, the pragmatists advocate yet a third alternative: Observations depend not on theory, but on their contexts.

This difference is relevant for another disagreement pertaining to the question of whether we can achieve true knowledge about the world. The positivists are verificationists and thus wholly believe that the claims of science can be proved. Neither Popper nor Kuhn share this belief, but they do not consider themselves relativists either, as theories (or paradigms) can, in their view, be refuted by studying the world. The pragmatists are led by their skepticism to agree with Popper and Kuhn on this point, and they would not accept being labelled as relativists either. We may be unable to obtain certain knowledge about the world, but we can obtain the knowledge that we need in practice.

These differing philosophies of science also present diverging views of humanity. The positivists and Popper both view the scientist as an objective observer who, rationally and without consideration for personal interests, political views, personal and cultural background, or social aspects, attempts to uncover truths about the world. The scientist's status as an individual is thus disregarded. According to Kuhn, the scientist is, first of all, a human being and thereby a member of a community with norms, traditions, and conventions. His science cannot be understood isolated from the community. As we have seen, the pragmatists agree with him on this point.

This leads us to the last difference between these four positions, one that relates to the fundamental question: What is science? According to the positivists and Popper, science is characterized by a particular rationality, which because of its method is an especially suitable tool for studying the world. For the pragmatists, science is an instrument that allows us to make the world a better place. And according to Kuhn, science is first of all a social activity. It is neither more nor less rational than any other social activities, and it is defined by conventions, not by a particular method.

The Knowledge Worker and Classical Philosophy of Science

How can the knowledge worker make use of classical philosophy of science? First of all, by means of positivism and critical rationalism, he can consider different work strategies on his own level of knowledge. For example, in connection with preparing a consultancy report, should he start by gathering material for the report as prescribed by positivism? Or should he, as the critical rationalist, begin by putting forward a theory of the expected correlations, and then let this theory guide his research?

Naturally, knowledge workers focus on practice. This is why the pragmatist approach will often appeal to them. While positivism and critical rationalism may stimulate reflections on methodology, pragmatism emphasizes the importance of the specific problem under scrutiny as well as the importance of the practical usefulness of knowledge work.

The knowledge worker can also learn from the way researchers, on the scientific level of knowledge, have attempted to combine positivism and critical rationalism in methodology. Ingeman Arbnor and Björn Bjerke (Arbnor and Bjerke 2009) called this the analytical method. It constitutes the prevailing approach in sciences like microeconomics and statistics. According to the analytical method, empirical material is first collected inductively. Subsequently, a theory is put forward, and from this the researcher is able to deduce a number of predictions that can be used to verify the theory empirically. Note how, in methodology, it is possible to combine positivism and critical rationalism on the scientific level of knowledge. Furthermore, note the fact that the analytical method can only be understood if we possess insight into the philosophies of science on which it is based.

Like science, a business is a social system held together by norms and conventions that define the employees' frame of understanding; therefore, a company's culture functions as a paradigm. For this reason, the knowledge worker can profitably make use of Kuhn when considering the strengths and weaknesses of an organization: Which elements make up the paradigm of the organization? What are its strengths, and how does this paradigm limit progress within the organization? Is it possible that the knowledge worker is working within a different paradigm, and which problems can this discrepancy create?

Questions

1. What are the characteristics of a scientific theory? What, for example, is the difference between astrology and astronomy?
2. Are we able to conduct unbiased studies of the world? What happens if we are unable to do so?
3. Select an (imaginary or real) exam question from your own field of study. Explain how you would approach the assignment depending on whether you adopt a positivistic, critical rationalist, pragmatic, or paradigmatic theory.
4. Give suggestions as to how you imagine you would be able to apply positivism, critical rationalism, pragmatism, and Kuhn's theory of paradigms in your future life as a knowledge worker.
5. Return to the questions in chapter 1. Discuss them again, but this time in light of the four chapters about classical philosophy of science. How would each position respond to the different questions?

Part 2

Philosophies of the Social Sciences

Positivism and critical rationalism are not the only schools of thought that offer precepts on how the social sciences should operate. In the second part of this book we will begin by focusing on hermeneutics, as this is the oldest philosophy of the human and social sciences and because it constitutes a break with positivism. Following this, we will examine structuralism, not only because of its great significance, but also because it forms a clear opposition to hermeneutics. Finally, we will explore social constructivism, which continues the inspiration from Kuhn, and has gained great prevalence in a large number of sciences.

Hermeneutics

Of the four philosophies of science examined in the first part of this book, positivism is the most important one. This is seen indirectly in the fact that both Popper, the pragmatists, and Kuhn find their point of departure in the criticism of positivism, and it is further supported by the fact that the positivistic approach to science dominates many actual sciences, as well as much of the work carried out at the practical level of knowledge. This also applies to the social sciences. As we have seen in chapter 2, these must be behaviourist (i.e., based on the observation of behaviour).

Positivism and classical as well as critical rationalism share the view that the researcher is an objective and neutral observer without cultural or historical prejudice; however, humanist researchers have always opposed the claim that this view applies to all sciences. They argue that approaching the human and social sciences based on the idea of an observer without culture or history is impossible, as these sciences are precisely concerned with culture and history. The prerequisite for understanding culture is being a cultural being; thus it becomes necessary to draw a sharp distinction between the natural sciences and what was known as *Geisteswissenschaft*, literally, "spiritual science". Demonstrating this difference is the concern of the German historian, Wilhelm Dilthey (1833–1911).

Schleiermacher and Dilthey: Classical Hermeneutics

In Dilthey's view, spirit and nature are fundamentally different. Because of this, the sciences cannot explore them in the same way (Dilthey 1999: 87). The natural sciences observe physical phenomena to derive universally valid regularities. Their intention is to *explain* what happens when a magnet attracts iron filings or when a chemical compound changes colour. Of course, it is possible to adopt the same view when approaching the human and social sciences; for example, when studying what takes place when a writer writes his novel, when a business communicates, or when the stock market plunges. However, if you do so, you have not truly grasped what it means to work scientifically with issues of people and society. The interesting question here is *why* does the writer write in this exact way? *Why* do businesses communicate the way they do and *why* are the investors selling their shares? The human and social sciences are not about *explaining*, but about *understanding*. The task of these sciences is not to discover causal relations, but to *interpret* expressions of human activity.

This distinction fundamentally characterizes hermeneutics as a position in philosophy of science. It constitutes a shift in perspective compared to the theories we examined in the first part of the book. The question is no longer What is science? because science can be many different things depending on its subject matter. The fundamental question of hermeneutics is What is understanding? because, in this view, the human and social sciences aim at achieving understanding. This chapter is concerned with this particular question.

! **Spiritual Sciences and Natural Sciences:** Dilthey's fundamental distinction between human and social sciences (concerned with human life and activity) and the natural sciences (concerned with the regularities of the physical world).

As the examples above indicate, hermeneutics is relevant for understanding all types of human activity and all forms of cultural products: architecture, literature, archaeology, economics, marketing, et cetera. For the purpose of clarification, we will predominantly employ the example of textual understanding in this chapter. First of all, this is the original concern of hermeneutics and secondly, textual analysis is a common characteristic of many human and social sciences.

Hermeneutics has a long history in the human and social sciences. It is considerably older than both positivism and Dilthey. People were already working with hermeneutics in the Middle Ages, as it was the task of the theologians to understand the Bible in the correct way or, more specifically, to understand it in accordance with the doctrines of the Catholic Church. Classical philology worked with texts handed down from the Greek and Latin tradition, while students of law were concerned with understanding legal texts. Hermeneutics thus has a very long tradition in these three sciences; however, it had not yet developed into a philosophy of science but was rather a collection of methodological precepts.

Dilthey's direct source of inspiration is the German theologian Friedrich Schleiermacher (1768–1834). For him, hermeneutics is more than a methodology of theology and philology. It is a general discipline, and its validity surpasses the individual sciences and pertains to all types of understanding. However, interpreting texts is still Schleiermacher's primary focus. For example, his distinction between two different types of analysis is, first of all, made in relation to textual understanding. *Grammatical* interpretation presents a work in light of contemporary texts within the same cultural area, while *psychological* interpretation seeks to understand the work on the basis of the author's thought and ideas (Schleiermacher 1999: 59). When these two types of analysis form a synthesis, we understand a text; we even understand it better than the author himself, and this is the purpose of the hermeneutic operation. Schleiermacher's overtaking and developing of the concept of the *hermeneutic circle* is, however, even more important as it becomes a crucial element of the hermeneutic tradition (Schleiermacher 1999: 64–79).

! **The Hermeneutic Circle:** This is the view that all understanding is contextual; i.e., we understand the whole on the basis of its constituent parts, but at the same time we understand the parts because they are elements of this whole.

How are we to understand the concept of the hermeneutic circle? When reading a book, for example, we may be reading individual words and sentences, but we understand these because we know of the greater context which they are part of. Depending on whether they appear in fiction or academic literature these same words and sentences can have very different meanings.

At the same time, we obviously understand the book as a whole on the basis of its parts: its words and sentences. Understanding is therefore circular. We understand the entirety of a text because of its words and we understand the words because of the text in its entirety. Considering a book in isolation may, however, not be enough. If we truly wish to gain an understanding of it, we must acquaint ourselves with the author's personality and his other works. Here too, understanding is circular. We understand the work and the author based on the parts—the individual books—while the individual books first become fully comprehensible in light of the whole: the work and the person. We can even go one step further and claim that complete understanding requires insight into the greater whole of which author and work are a part; that is, the society and historical period in which the author lived. For instance, Shakespeare can only be understood in light of sixteenth-century England, which constituted the frame for his authorship, yet we can only gain an understanding of sixteenth-century England by means of the texts handed down from this period—among these, the texts of Shakespeare. In other words, the hermeneutic circle expresses a general view that all understanding is circular; that is, that all understanding consists of the constituent parts being explained by the whole and the whole being explained by the parts.

There are many different opinions of what hermeneutics is and ought to be, and thus many different interpretations of the hermeneutic circle can be found; however, viewing understanding as a circular process is an especially consistent feature of hermeneutic theory. A graphic portrayal of the core of the hermeneutic view of the sciences must therefore necessarily be in the shape of a circle:

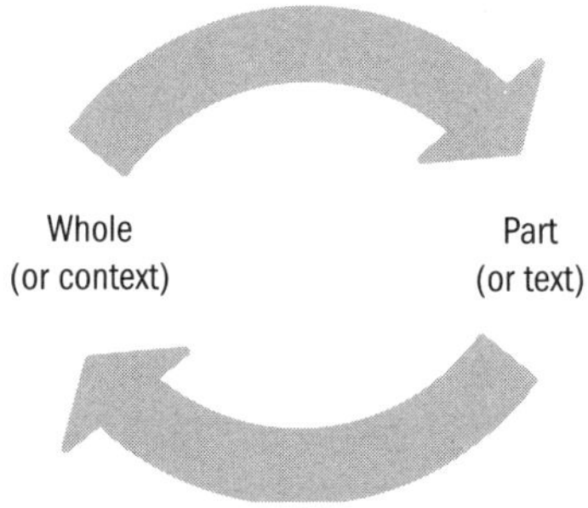

Figure 7.1. The Hermeneutic Circle

Nevertheless, it is important to be aware that we are none the wiser at this point because the hermeneutic circle raises at least as many questions as it answers. Above all, there are three particularly pressing questions: Firstly, if understanding is circular, where does the process of understanding end? When can we claim to have reached "true" understanding? Secondly, what is the specific object of our understanding? Is it the intention of the author, his social context, or something else entirely? Finally, how do we even enter the circle; that is, how do we begin to understand a text when we initially have no context to view it against? Hermeneutics is especially concerned with these particular questions.

Schleiermacher's answer to the latter question consists in a distinction between two different methods of textual interpretation. Viewing the parts and the whole in relation to each other (i.e., moving around the hermeneutic circle) constitutes the *comparative* method. A second approach, the *divinatory* method, involves making a qualified guess of the text's whole and, thus, the right understanding of it, to enter the hermeneutic circle (Schleiermacher 1999: 58–59). This conjecture can then later be corrected as one gradually delves deeper and deeper into the text by means of the comparative method.

Dilthey's answer is slightly different and more advanced. To understand it, we must take as our point of departure the question of why Dilthey uses the term *spiritual science* instead of *human and social sciences*. It is not just because of his old-fashioned vocabulary. Instead, we must ask what these sciences are concerned with. They encompass many disciplines, everything from art, literature, languages, communication and cultural theory to psychology, architecture, law, economics, and archaeology. Do these disciplines have anything in common? According to Dilthey, they do. All human and social sciences deal with expressions of human thought, action, will, belief, fear, and aspirations. This is why these sciences do not operate in the same way as the natural sciences. A bridge is not merely a physical structure with measurable properties. It is an expression of desire to cross a river. A stock market plunge is not a natural disaster. It expresses people's fear of losing money. Dilthey summarizes this by stating that the object of all these sciences is the lived experience of human beings, i.e., manifestations of the life of mankind. Unlike animal expressions of life, human life is characterized by language, thought, intentions, beliefs, et cetera, which was previously termed "spirit". The object of these sciences is therefore spirit objectified or *objective spirit*; that is, the tangible expressions of human life in the shape of texts, buildings, music, and so on (Dilthey 1999: 96).

! **Objective Spirit:** According to Dilthey, the object of the human and social sciences is the lived experience of human beings, which can be found objectified in the social sphere in shape of, for instance, texts, buildings, or music.

The reason why we are able to discern that a bridge is an expression of human will (an expression of life) and not merely a part of the landscape is because we are human. When we, to use another of Dilthey's terms, ponder and reflect on our lives—considering our past and future—we think like the bridge builder or author, whose work we seek to understand (Dilthey 1999: 93). By drawing parallels to our own life, we are able to deduce the meaning of the bridge or the novel. "Entering" the hermeneutic circle is therefore no longer a problem. We enter it by drawing parallels to our own existence.

The second question mentioned above pertains to what understanding means. According to Schleiermacher, the answer is that a text has been understood once we have grasped the author's intention with it. In other words, the meaning of a text is what the author wished to express (Schleiermacher 1999: 50). However, what if the intention of the author makes no sense to us; for instance, if it is tied to a distant past with norms and thoughts, which no longer mean anything to us? What once was considered a revolutionary and provoking message will seem trivial and immaterial to us, although we are able to correctly summarize what the author says. Today the critique of religion put forth by eighteenth-century Enlightenment philosophers seems rather tame, but back then it was extremely provoking. Have we "understood" Voltaire's attack on the Catholic Church if we are able to cite his message, yet are strangers to the era against which it was aimed? According to Dilthey, the answer is no. To properly understand Voltaire, it is necessary that we acquaint ourselves with eighteenth-century France, the author's background, the power of the king and the Catholic Church, et cetera. Understanding is first complete when we are able to put ourselves in the author's place and view the world as he does. The goal of hermeneutic interpretation is this *re-experience,* which fuses the frames of understanding of the interpreter and author. This is true understanding (Dilthey 1999: 102–105).

! **Re-experience:** To put oneself in the place of the author, viewing the world through his eyes. According to Dilthey, this characterizes true understanding.

Dilthey hereby puts forward a rather demanding proposal as to what it means to, for example, understand a text. The question now becomes how re-experience can be attained. Is there a specific method for reaching this goal? The hermeneuticians do not agree on the answer to this question. Schleiermacher, whose point of departure was the methodical hermeneutics of theology and philology, has no problem in offering methodological precepts. Dilthey's views are slightly more ambiguous. On the one hand, he claims that hermeneutics, like the natural sciences, applies induction and deduction—terms that go well with the hermeneutic circle's movement from the parts to the whole and from the whole to the parts. His concept of interpretation views understanding as a particular technique (Dilthey 1999: 105–109). On the other hand, the concept of re-experience implies that, unlike the natural sciences, the human and social sciences cannot be encapsulated by a specific method. Understanding cannot, like explanation, be proved, and if understanding is viewed as re-experience, it will never be completely rational. A third way of considering this question is presented by the German philosopher, Hans-Georg Gadamer (1900–2002). He rejects the view that hermeneutics is a method and, at the same time, criticizes Dilthey's view of understanding as re-experience.

Modern Hermeneutics: Gadamer

Why does Gadamer dislike the understanding of hermeneutics as a method? His dislike stems from the fact that viewing the sciences as method entails the idea of the rational and distanced scientist, which we earlier ascribed to positivism and rationalism and which hermeneutics opposes. This scientist considers the world as something alien (an object), which he himself is not a part of, but which he can come to understand through reason. If we attempt to transfer this perspective to the human and social sciences, we are certain to run into problems. We will then have to ask, like Schleiermacher, how we can even begin to understand. It may, for instance, become necessary to invent an artifice, such as Schleiermacher's idea of *divination,* to be able to even enter the hermeneutic circle at all. However, according to Gadamer, Schleiermacher's concept is a pseudo-solution to a pseudo-problem. We do not have to find a way into the hermeneutic circle; we are already inside of it. We are not alienated and distanced from the culture we are attempting to understand; we are already a part of it. We constantly understand our interaction with the world because we are part of a particular tradition (Gadamer 1999: 139–147).

According to Gadamer, this tradition means that we never start from scratch when attempting to understand something. If a person wishes to read Shakespeare or Voltaire, there are more introductions, commentaries, analyses, and discussions available than can be read in a lifetime. Even if we never manage to read any of these works, we will already have a natural pre-understanding of the authors, because their works have become the common property of western culture. For instance, Shakespeare can be encountered everywhere, from films, books, and theatre to the television show, The Simpsons. Understanding, according to Gadamer, is thereby understood as a bequest, since the past is constantly communicated to the present.

Most people will probably be able to agree with Gadamer's emphasis on the significance of tradition in textual understanding. However, his view that our *prejudices* are not only favourable to, but also a prerequisite for, all understanding may require closer scrutiny. How can anyone make such a claim? For a start, Gadamer would turn the question upside down and examine why the concept "prejudice" has such negative connotations today. Once again, positivism's and rationalism's view of human nature is to blame. According to these perspectives, the scientist must be rational and completely without prejudice; however, as we have noted earlier, such a person, if he existed, would not be able to understand culture and social life. Our prejudices come from belonging to a cultural tradition (Gadamer 1999: 139–147). The handing down of prejudices is what makes understanding possible. For instance, many people have an idea (a prejudice) of what *Hamlet* is about, even though they have never read or seen the play. In itself prejudice is therefore not a bad thing, but it is, of course, crucial to be aware of personal prejudices when working with a text, and to correct them when they turn out to be wrong.

! **Prejudices:** The ideas we have of, for example, a book, which are a result of cultural and historical tradition. In our reading we test our prejudices and are therefore able to acquire true understanding; however, prejudice is a precondition for this process.

Interpretation is thus not about approaching a text "neutrally" or "without bias" because we are never neutral or unbiased. On the contrary, interpretation is about dealing with the meeting between prejudices and texts. In other words, understanding is when text and interpreter enter into dialogue, and neither party enters a dialogue without prerequisites. They instead make an effort to approach each other.

This is where some of the crucial differences between Dilthey's and Gadamer's hermeneutics become visible, the most significant pertaining to historicity. All hermeneutic knowledge and all understanding is concerned with the past. The creation of any text, any piece of music, any building, or any economic development must necessarily come *before* their interpretation. Even the simultaneous interpreter can only translate what has already *been* said, although he does have the advantage of being almost concurrent with the speaker. He thus shares the speaker's context and understands his intentions. However, this is not the case when considering texts by Shakespeare or Voltaire. Dilthey considers this temporal distance a problem, which is why understanding means re-experience in his view. Gadamer believes the opposite to be true. Temporal distance does not constitute an obstacle but allows for a more rational assessment of texts since they have already been thoroughly discussed. Its removal should not be sought. On the contrary, there is a favourable possibility for understanding because we are familiar with the influence that the text has had (Gadamer 1999: 163–171). For instance, assessing Hitler's *Mein Kampf* is much easier today than when it was first published in 1925, because today we know the history of the text's impact. Gadamer believes, therefore, that to understand a text, one must not seek to abolish but rather to be receptive to its alien nature.

If understanding does not consist of adopting the author's point of view but, on the contrary, is enabled by distancing oneself from this point of view, what then is the goal of interpretation? Gadamer sums up his view with the concept of *fusion of horizons*; however, this seems to beg a new question: Which horizons are we dealing with, and how are they fused?

People always find themselves in the midst of the world, in the middle of a tradition and at a certain historical point in time. This is the precondition for understanding, and it is on this condition that our understanding is shaped. The world is viewed differently today than it was during the thirteenth century, when illness was considered God's punishment, and where the strict hierarchical structure of society was seen as the natural order. Our *horizon of understanding* is different today because we live in a different time. In this way, present time always constitutes a horizon of understanding. It could be said that it determines our worldview.

Now one might think that a fusion of horizons means cancelling out the difference between two horizons of understanding. It is slightly more complex than this according to Gadamer's view. Although the horizons differ from each other, they are not sharply separated. Our modern horizon of understanding is also formed by tradition, which connects us to the past. This means history is part of our present worldview. In addition, the horizon of understanding of the past is not a stable entity. This is partly because our work is always characterized by our prejudices about it, which are handed down to us by tradition, and partly because the historical text is "read into" a contemporary context, where it will necessarily convey something different from what was originally intended by the author (Gadamer 1999: 159). For example, Voltaire's critique of religion, which was aimed at the Catholic Church in the eighteenth century, means something completely different to people who today believe that "Islam" poses a real problem. These people will use Voltaire's arguments to persecute Muslims even though this was never the author's intention. In this way, the altered historical context supplies texts with new meaning.

So what does fusion of horizons of understanding mean? It is in fact a dual process. On the one side, when encountering a text of the past, the interpreter experiences the tension between his own horizon of understanding and the past, whose horizon will always differ from that of the present. This tension is genuine, and therefore the interpreter must consciously relate to the unfamiliarity of the text. In other words, we will never quite be able to understand how people were thinking in the thirteenth century. On the other side, understanding is achieved as the interpreter works with the text and makes it part of his own horizon of understanding, thus altering his horizon. In other words, what he learns from his encounter with the text of the past changes his world-view (Gadamer 1999: 170).

! **Fusion of Horizons:** The dual process, which characterizes understanding according to Gadamer. First of all, the foreignness of the text handed down from the past is acknowledged; hereafter, the textual work itself creates a new horizon of understanding in which the text's past horizon and the interpreter's contemporary horizon form a synthesis.

The fusion is not the reduction of the author's or interpreter's horizon of understanding (unlike Dilthey's view that the interpreter must attempt to completely adopt the worldview of the text); rather, it consists in the creation of a new understanding, in which the knowledge of the foreignness of the text is preserved, while the text simultaneously acquires new meaning. The fusion does, therefore, not mean that both horizons disappear, or that one is swallowed up by the other. The fusion results in the preservation of both original horizons since they form a synthesis– a joint horizon. In other words, the understanding of the text reaches a peak as it becomes *applicable* to a contemporary context (Gadamer 1999: 176).

Gadamer's emphasis of the aspect of application in interpretative work means that, to him, understanding is not about the *reproduction* of meaning (e.g., reproducing the author's original intent), but rather about *producing* new meaning (What does the text convey to us today?). He therefore views the hermeneutic tradition before Schleiermacher and Dilthey favourably; that is, hermeneutics as a tool for subjects such as theology, philology, and law. Although he does not believe that hermeneutics can be reduced to a method, he acknowledges the way in which understanding and application are one and the same process in these disciplines. The law student does not study the law for its own sake but with a view to applying it in a specific case. The task of the interpreter is to make sense of what is translated in the context in which it is translated. The hermeneutics of these individual sciences can thus provide a better understanding of what hermeneutics must be as a philosophy of science.

Hermeneutics: A Summary

Hermeneutics is about understanding, and hermeneuticians agree that understanding is attained through the hermeneutic circle. The parts of, for example, a text can be interpreted by relating them to the whole of which they are a part, while the whole can likewise be understood by looking at the constituent parts. You could say that hermeneutic science bases its understanding of *the general* (e.g., a historical epoch) on the interpretation of *the particular* (e.g., written sources from this particular epoch) and vice versa.

However, as we have seen, there are perceptible differences between Dilthey's and Gadamer's approaches to hermeneutics. These differences firstly appertain to the question of what "understanding" actually means. Dilthey claims that understanding is about putting oneself in the place of the author, while Gadamer believes that the challenge is rather to create a new horizon of understanding on the basis of the horizons of the text and interpreter. He thus rejects Dilthey's fundamental issue (How can we understand a text if its horizon of understanding is alien to us?), because, according to Gadamer, the foreignness of a text is not a problem and does therefore not need to be removed.

Nevertheless, we are able to discern a clear continuity in the hermeneutic tradition. From Dilthey to Gadamer, the hermeneutic project is formulated in opposition to the positivists' generalization of what they considered the methodology of the natural sciences. For this reason, hermeneutics is based on the clear contrast between the natural sciences and the human and social sciences. While the natural sciences are aimed at a particular target—the complete comprehension of their different areas—the interpretative work of the human and social sciences in principle constitutes a never-ending process. Complete understanding will never be reached; however, this is not the aim of interpretation. To be more precise, the illustration of the hermeneutic circle should therefore be shaped as a spiral rather than a circle. Hermeneutic interpretation continually delves deeper into the understanding of the object of study, and this immersion simultaneously expands the area of these studies.

According to the hermeneuticians, there is also a great difference between the prerequisites of these different branches of science. The natural sciences require the scientist to be as unprejudiced and unbound by tradition as possible; however, the human and social sciences must work within the framework of a particular tradition. Hermeneutic science has more characteristics in common with dialogue than with experiments and observation.

This idea of a sharp contrast between the different branches of science can, however, be criticized. Hermeneuticians consider the natural sciences to be identical to positivism's understanding of science and they formulate their own theory as an opposition to this, though, as we have seen in the previous chapters, the natural sciences differ considerably from the positivistic view of them. Consequently, it seems doubtful that the social and natural sciences are as different as the hermeneuticians believe them to be.

The positivists could voice further criticism: If work within the hermeneutic circle is an eternal process that never reaches truths of an absolute nature, will it not result in relativism, where one interpretation is as good as the next? The hermeneutician would have several answers to this. First of all, the positivists are alone in believing that the sciences can lead to such a thing as "absolute truth". Secondly, when working with human beings, the basic premise is that there are no correct answers. Thirdly, hermeneutics does not lead to relativism. Not all interpretations are equally good, and by comparing part with whole, text with context, we are constantly working towards better and improved interpretations.

Hermeneutic Research in Practice

As mentioned before, all expressions of human life are the object of hermeneutics. Although hermeneutics has, in practice, primarily been aimed at the interpretation of texts, it can also be applied to everything, from communication theory to economics. Below, we will consider some examples from the scientific level of knowledge.

Example: Schramm's Third Model of Communication

The first example is Wilbur Schramm's third model of communication. It defines communication as the interaction between two parties, as in dialogue (Frandsen, Halkier, and Johansen 2007: 75). Each participant decodes and interprets the other's messages separately while simultaneously sending his own. Here, the positivistic division of sender and recipient has been foregone and replaced by two equal interpreters who both send simultaneously. In other words, the messages are no longer *delivered* but *interpreted.* Schramm's model can be considered a communication theoretical version of the hermeneutic circle. Through their dialogue, the participants continue to gain a better understanding of each other as they constantly compare what is communicated, partly with what has been said earlier and partly with the context of the communication.

Example: Intercultural Communication

Intercultural communication is a discipline that is concerned with the particular challenges that arise in communication across national, ethnic, and cultural borders. We are, in other words, dealing with communication across different horizons of understanding. The work conducted in this area will always involve the hermeneutic challenge of interpreting the behaviour of the interlocutor correctly. This applies to the translation of texts and to occasions when an interpreter must provide simultaneous translation in a negotiation. In both cases, the challenge is to understand the interlocutor according to his own context while simultaneously ensuring that the message has meaning in one's own. This is a concrete example of the applicability of Gadamer's concept of the fusion of horizons.

Example: Hermeneutics and Consumer Behaviour

We have made use of literary and historical texts to demonstrate the strength of the hermeneutical approach in our account of it; however, texts can be many different things, such as interviews with consumers. This is exactly what William Locander, Howard Pollio, and Craig Thompson (1994) work with. The purpose of their interviews is to map out consumption patterns by viewing them hermeneutically. For an article published in 1994, they interviewed three different types of consumers. One type is more concerned with price, the other with quality, and the third is very sceptical of advertising, "as it rarely keeps its promises". These types are familiar to us all. The point made by the researchers is that the viewpoints of the three interviewees do not reflect distinctly individual values. They are expressions of different, but very ingrained traditions of western culture, even though the interviewees are not aware of this. To understand their statements, they must be interpreted in light of these traditions.

The price-conscious consumer reflects a very rational understanding of economics, which is rooted in the thought of Adam Smith. The quality-conscious consumer is sceptical of the value of products, which can be bought in today's "throwaway society" and expresses nostalgia for the past, where products were of quality craftsmanship. This nostalgia can be traced back to the cultural-historical trend, German romanticism, from the beginning of the nineteenth century. Finally, the views of the interviewee sceptical of marketing ploys are based on the contrast between *false* marketing and the *genuine* recommendations provided by friends and family.

What can these insights be used for in practice? The point is not merely that it is necessary to understand the cultural tradition and context of the consumer if one is to make sense of his behaviour, although this is naturally important. When knowing the values and thoughts on which the marketing-critical consumer bases his opinions, it also becomes easier to create campaigns, which are not at odds with his mindset; for example, by using viral marketing, where the contrast between false and genuine is not as evident as in a traditional advert. In this way, the hermeneutic analysis also results in concrete strategic recommendations, directly applicable on the corporate world's practical level of knowledge.

Example: How *You* Can Make Use of Hermeneutics

Finally, let us return to our students. How can they approach their assignment about corporate communication hermeneutically? This naturally depends on which theory they choose to work with. They may begin in a divinatory way (like Schleiermacher), by making a qualified guess as to how communication in this particular organization functions, or they might (as Gadamer would) consider their prejudices about the business and its communication. These prejudices will vary widely depending on whether an entertainment park say, or a large bank, is the object of their study. Next, they can collect examples of communication and consider these examples in relation to their prejudices and assumptions. Do they really match their expectations? Most likely not, and the students will have to revise their assumptions; however, this will enable them to see the actual communication in a different light. Furthermore, they must constantly seek to explain the communication by looking at the company's context in the broad sense of the term: What is the history and culture of the organization? What is the composition of its employees? At the same time, studying the communication will obviously change their view of the company.

The students could also choose an approach inspired by Dilthey. In this case, they will try to familiarize themselves with the mindset of the people they are studying by asking, for example: What makes the manager communicate to the employees in a particular way? Does it have anything to do with the fact that he was trained in a different corporate culture? Considering the context is also important when gaining an understanding of the communicating parties' mindset.

Regardless of which hermeneutic approach the students select, they will never reach the absolute truth about the communication they are studying. Through continuous work within the hermeneutic circle, they will, however, gain a greater understanding of it and expand their own horizons of understanding.

Questions

1. According to hermeneutics, what is the difference between the human and social sciences on the one hand, and the natural sciences on the other?
2. Explain Schleiermacher's distinction between the comparative and divinatory hermeneutic approaches.
3. What is "the hermeneutic circle"?
4. What does "re-experience" mean?
5. According to Gadamer, what is the precondition for knowledge?
6. What does "fusion of horizons" mean?
7. Explain the difference between Dilthey's and Gadamer's approach to hermeneutics.
8. Give examples of hermeneutic issues from your own field of study.
9. Explain how you can approach assignments and exam papers hermeneutically.
10. In your opinion, what are the strengths and weaknesses of hermeneutics?

Structuralism

If we were to sum up hermeneutics under a single heading it could be this: understanding a text is to interpret it on its own terms. According to Dilthey, this means assuming the perspective of the author, and according to Gadamer, a fusion of horizons can only take place when respecting the text's own horizon of understanding.

However, should a scientific approach really be characterized by a respect for the perspective of the text or author? Shouldn't the sciences problematize and question this perspective? Is it not the strength of scientific analysis that it is unbound by the author's prejudice and can go behind it to see what explains and determines this prejudice? This is the claim of one of the most significant philosophies of social science in the twentieth century: structuralism.

By citing this claim, we have already established the dichotomy between structuralism and hermeneutics; however, the conflict between them in fact goes even deeper than this, namely, to the question of the object of science. What should the sciences study? For the positivists, determining the object of science was no problem. They believed it to be the world as it is immediately available to us through our sensory perceptions. Hermeneuticians may disagree with positivism on nearly every count, but they too fail to problematize the object of their science; if the topic is Shakespeare, then your object of study must necessarily be his collected works. According to structuralism, however, it is not quite that simple. The object of any science is never given beforehand, but must be *constructed*. This is the first task of the scientist.

These two fundamental views are shared by all authors normally considered to be structuralists. These authors also share three sources of inspiration, namely, Karl Marx (1818–1883), Sigmund Freud (1856–1939), and Ferdinand de Saussure (1857–1913). Roughly speaking, the differences between the separate, structuralist authors can be explained by their different emphases on each of the different sources. Marx will be examined in the next part of the book. We will not consider Freud further, although the above already gives an indication of how his theories serve as a source of inspiration in this context. Freud's psychoanalysis views the person's self-presentation as a symptom of unconscious, underlying structures. Similarly, the focus of structuralism is also the structures, of which the author is unconscious, for example, in a text.

However, the most important source of inspiration for most structuralists is neither Marx nor Freud, but the Swiss linguist, Ferdinand de Saussure. So, we will begin by taking a closer look at his work.

Saussure's Structural Linguistics

There is nothing as intuitively intelligible to us as human beings as our language. We all know what language is, and we use it constantly. At a glance it may therefore seem strange to base structuralism on linguistics. There is no reason to "construct" an object in this case; it is literally found at the tip of one's tongue. In fact, this view also seems to have characterized the approach to linguistic science in the nineteenth century. At any rate, researchers in those days made no attempt to systematically demarcate the object of their studies before carrying out their research. This resulted in a veritable disarray of different approaches, such as grammar, philology, and comparative philology. All these different sciences were concerned with "language", but at the same time they were concerned with widely different things. Although we may all think we know what language is, this intuition does not necessarily prove useful in linguistics. Saussure arrived at the same conclusion when he surveyed the disorder left by his predecessors. He concluded that since language in its immediate form does not constitute a usable object for scientific study, these studies must begin by constructing their object. This is the first task he set himself.

According to Saussure, we must first distinguish between two levels of language. Firstly, there is everyday language. This is how we all use language when speaking and writing, but "underlying" this level, we find all the *rules* (grammatical, syntactical, and phonetic) that make language work. When speaking in one's mother tongue these rules will be employed unconsciously. Saussure expresses this distinction between two levels of language in his concepts *langue* and *parole* (Saussure 2000: 11–13). Langue is language as a system, while parole is the practical use of language. According to Saussure, the system—la langue—is the object of science.

! **Langue and Parole:** The two levels of language according to Saussure. Language as a (grammatical) system is termed langue, whereas language in its practical usage is termed parole. Language as a system, or langue, is the object of linguistics.

Another fundamental demarcation concerns the question of whether linguistics should operate historically or systematically. The development of language can be studied and the system of language, as it appears at a given time, can be analyzed. Since it is not possible to do both at the same time, the question of where the sciences should focus their efforts arises. According to Saussure, the systematic approach is more important (Saussure 2000: 89). One must acquire an understanding of the system before being able to comment on its development. Saussure summarizes this distinction in his contrasting of the *diachronic* (historical) and the *synchronic* (systematic) perspectives of language.

! **Diachrony and Synchrony:** Saussure's distinction between the historical and systematic research of linguistics. The synchronic, or systematic, is the primary perspective.

At this point, we are already far removed from our starting point in language as we immediately perceive it and as it "exists in reality". But what we have gained is a precise definition of the scientists' object of study: the fundamental structures of language as they appear at a particular point in time. In this respect, the object of the sciences and our common concept of language are two separate things. In other words, the object of the sciences is a construction.

Language naturally consists of words, and words function as signs. This means they point away from themselves and express something else. They "signal to us". The word "baker" signals that you can buy bread here. The system of language is thus characterized by being a structure of signs, a system of words. How do words actually manage to "show beyond themselves"? According to Saussure, a linguistic sign is the fusion of a concept and a specific sound pattern (Saussure 2000: 66 fig.). For example, when a person tells someone that he wants a horse, this statement is understandable because the interlocutor immediately connects the sounds coming from the other person's mouth with the specific concept of the animal that these sounds refer to. This illustrates the relationship between the two entities that make up a sign. The sound pattern *refers* to the concept. Saussure calls these two entities *signifiant* (the signifier) and *signifié* (the signified), respectively.

! **Signifier (Signifiant) and Signified (Signifié):** The signifier is the sound pattern of language and the signified is the concept the sound refers to. The unity of the signifier and the signified characterizes the linguistic sign, and language is a system of these signs.

The combination of signifier and signified is arbitrary; i.e., coincidental. This does not mean we can choose to replace "horse" with another word to refer to the same concept just because we feel like it. On the contrary, language is outside of our conscious control. Language determines what we think, not the other way round. The unity of the sign is arbitrary, in the sense that there is no law of nature that determines a "horse" must be called a horse. It could also be called *Pferd* or *cheval*. Whenever we deal with foreign languages, we experience how arbitrary the linguistic sign is. This arbitrariness also constitutes the premise for the development of language. If "horse" were the *only* possible term for the particular animal, any changes to the word would be impossible. But why does language not develop more than it does? If the unity of signifier and signified is coincidental, why is it not "horse" on Mondays and *fnask* on Fridays? Obviously a development that chaotic would be impractical, yet there is a more fundamental explanation of the relative stability of language. The individual signs are held together by language as a collective system (Saussure 2000: 113). "Horse" functions in language as a whole, whereas *fnask* does not. The language system decides that "horse" is the right word.

What does it mean to "function" in a system of language, and why is it the system that determines the words? Seeing that the sign is arbitrary, its meaning is not self-evident. The word "horse" cannot be explained by it being the *only* term for the corresponding concept as this precisely is not the case. On the contrary, the sign is meaningful and, thereby, functional in language, because it *differs* from other words (Saussure 2000: 115). When someone utters the sentence: "I want a horse", it makes sense to us because we are effortlessly able to distinguish "horse" from "pig", "sheep", "panther", or "tractor". However, it is not always this simple. If a person says: "I want a bat" it could refer to the small flying animal or the piece of equipment used in sports, such as cricket and baseball. Because the sign itself does not directly reveal its meaning, help must be sought from the context. The meaning made visible by the context is the *difference* between the two signs: *bat*, as in "creature" and *bat* as in "equipment". This applies to all the signs that make up our language. They are not meaningful because of their own fusion of sound and concept, but because they differ from other signs. Language viewed as a whole is thus a *system of differences*. In other words, the identity of the individual sign is negative. "Horse" does not have any linguistic meaning in itself, but rather indicates everything it is not.

> **Language as a System of Differences:** Because the linguistic sign is arbitrary, it acquires meaning through its distinction from other signs. Language is the sum of linguistic signs and thus the system of differences provides individual signs with meaning.

In this sense, the individual signs amount to nothing at all. Imagine if archaeologists discovered an old culture but only found a single written word. They would never be able to interpret it, as words only acquire meaning because of their distinction from other words. Language is, on the one hand, the sum of all linguistic signs, while on the other hand, this linguistic whole is what gives meaning to the individual sign.

This, therefore, constitutes Saussure's manifesto for linguistics: Researchers are not to examine everyday language. They must focus on the cohesive system of language, which forms the foundation of our everyday language use, although we are not commonly aware of it. This system consists of words functioning as signs; i.e., as the fusion of sounds and concepts. The signs acquire meaning through their mutual differences, which makes the system of language as a whole a system of differences.

This may all be very interesting to a linguist, but what makes Saussure significant to the philosophy of science? Language is just one amongst many types of human interaction. We communicate meaning in all the different ways in which we interact. For instance, marketing experts know everything about the way images communicate. Most people are also aware of the signals they send with their clothing; thus it seems reasonable that Saussure's structural linguistics can be used as a model for studies in how not just language, but other social conventions function. The task then becomes to analyze the unconscious systems that enable our conscious social life by studying their sign structures. This is structuralism. In the following, we will take a closer look at which sign structures can be found in social conventions. We will examine this with assistance from the most significant theorist of structuralism, Claude Lévi-Strauss (1908–2009).

Lévi-Strauss's Structural Anthropology

Lévi-Strauss adopts Saussure's view of science. Its first task is to construct an object, which must then be studied systematically (synchronically), not historically. Most importantly, by considering forms of social practice to be governed by sign systems, Lévi-Strauss continued Saussure's fundamental perspective. We communicate through the way our social practices are organized (Lévi-Strauss 1958: 58). In his view, the structural approach is therefore not only valid in the area of linguistics, but also in his own field of study: anthropology.

In other words, both anthropology and linguistics are concerned with semiotic structures (i.e., sign systems). Naturally, there are differences between the two disciplines, yet Lévi-Strauss primarily demarcates his studies from the science of history. Anthropology and history are closely related, even inseparable. The historian attempts to understand the societies from which he is separated by time, while the anthropologist aims at understanding the social contexts from which he is separated by his not being part of them. Both aim at presenting their studies of social life so that these are intelligible to people who are not part of the particular society studied.

According to Lévi-Strauss, the crucial difference between history and anthropology is the fact that historians examine the *conscious* expressions of societal life (Lévi-Strauss 1958: 25). Their material is written sources, and it goes without saying that authors are conscious of what they write. Anthropologists, on the other hand, attempt to understand the *unconscious* conditions for social life (Lévi-Strauss 1958: 25). How should we understand this? The answer is, that under the surface of conscious societal life, Lévi-Strauss identifies deep structures that make our everyday life function, but of which we are usually unaware. It is these structures that the sciences must study.

As mentioned in the introduction to this chapter, this is far removed from the hermeneutic perspective. We are no longer concerned with understanding people's conscious intentions, but rather with discovering the unconscious structural foundation of these intentions. We can summarize the contrast between these two ways of thinking by saying that hermeneutics explains manifestations of culture, for example a text, according to the consciousness "underlying" the text, while structuralism is concerned with explaining this consciousness itself. Whereas hermeneutics considers the individual process (What was the author thinking, when he wrote the book?), structuralism focuses on the collective structure (Which form of society is reflected in the text?). For example, we do not understand *Hamlet* by explaining what Shakespeare intended to *convey* through the play. Instead, we understand *Hamlet* by studying the societal structures of Shakespeare's time—structures of which he was probably unaware but which nevertheless influenced him to communicate this exact message. In other words, in structuralism "human beings" and "consciousness" are not explanatory concepts, but concepts that need to be explained. This view can be summed up by the term *theoretical anti-humanism* (Lévi-Strauss 1994: 247).

! **Theoretical Anti-Humanism:** The structuralist view that "human beings" and "consciousness" cannot be used as explanatory concepts in human and social sciences, as the purpose of these sciences is to explain human beings and their consciousness.

In the previous section we have already seen how Lévi-Strauss first of all constructs the object of anthropology in contrast to the science of history. Furthermore, we have seen how he defines this object as the underlying, unconscious structures, which enable our conscious societal life. What does this mean in practice?

Lévi-Strauss studied the substructures of different societies, for example: the way Amazonian Indian tribes organize their villages; the differences between French and British cuisine; and the structure of kinship relations in indigenous populations. He does not claim that one single structure underlies the whole of social life, and herein lies the difference between linguistics and anthropology (Lévi-Strauss 1958: 95–100). However, all of these different substructures share two crucial common features. First of all, they constitute ways of creating order. Successful communication is dependent on the world being orderly and organized, and this is what the substructures of society bring about. For instance, our traffic system would break down if it were not for the simple basic structure made up of the traffic lights' three colours. Secondly, society's basic structures are all organized according to the same principle: *classification through opposition*. For example, the kinship relations that Lévi-Strauss studied are divided into positive and negative relations, and this same division into binary opposites applies to, among other things, the western European way of categorizing taste (e.g., sweet-sour, salty-fresh, etc.).

> **! Classification through Opposition:** According to Lévi-Strauss, all people in a society understand the world by classifying it according to binary oppositions; such as, for example, forbidden-permitted, abstract-concrete, sweet-sour, up-down, et cetera.

These different binary oppositions arrange themselves on two logical axes, one vertical and one horizontal (Lévi-Strauss 1994: 153–169). The vertical axis indicates the contrast between abstract and concrete, whereas the horizontal axis indicates the contrast between positive and negative. In connection with food, for instance, some might be permitted and some forbidden. In our culture, insects, dogs, and rats lie on the "forbidden" side of this axis, while beef, fish, and pork are placed on the "permitted" side. These two axes ensure the inner cohesion of the system of classification and simultaneously enable it to integrate new elements. For instance, we do not change our entire food culture because new herbs become available at the local grocery store—the new elements are simply adapted into the existing system of classification.

City planning, cooking, and traffic are just three examples of social interactions structured by systems of oppositions (differences), even though we are unaware of this. This structuring is the reason why our collective everyday life functions without us having to constantly deliberate on our behaviour. We do not need to speculate long to know whether or not serving dog or rat to our guests is a good idea. This question has been answered in advance by the system of classification that regulates our food culture. It ensures that our behaviour matches our guests' expectations of us, and that social interaction occurs without friction. The system communicates to us by means of its differences, and we abide by this communication without ever being aware of it.

Let us consider an example, albeit not one of Lévi-Strauss's own, that illustrates his point. Consider the picture below:

Figure 8.1. Signs that Control Our Behaviour

We are all familiar with these images and encounter them constantly in everyday life without giving them a second thought, yet these are in fact three signs that control our behaviour in the public sphere. They tell us what is socially acceptable, and thus which type of behaviour is to be expected of us by those around us. The three signs signal which person may enter which space. How are they capable of this? The signs operate by means of their mutual differences. If there were no distinction between the three pictures, they would not be able to function as signs. As mentioned, we comply with them daily without thinking about it, and without it being necessary to interpret them. We first become aware of the function of the signs if someone acts contrary to their orders.

These three pictures are not merely lavatory signs. They constitute a simple semiotic system structured by the binary opposites, "man versus woman" and "permitted versus prohibited behaviour". The system regulates our behaviour through these opposites. Sign-systems such as this one permeate our everyday life. To understand human behaviour one must therefore study these systems. As previously mentioned, this is the basic point made by structuralism.

However, according to Lévi-Strauss, the structuralist approach does not simply illuminate our social conventions, but also shows us the common features of different societies and cultures.

For example, what do a New Yorker and an Amazonian Indian have in common? Most of us would be tempted to answer: almost nothing. On the one side, we find a modern, rational, metropolitan human being living in the midst of a world of science and technology. On the other side, we find a primitive Indian who offers sacrifices to gods in trees and rivers. Throughout the nineteenth and twentieth centuries, this contrast constituted a significant part of western self-understanding; however, Lévi-Strauss breaks with this self-understanding because it turns out that, in spite of the many differences, the New Yorker and the Amazonian Indian actually approach the world in the same way. Both create order in the universe by classifying the world according to vertical and horizontal differences, as we covered earlier. If we think again of the food example, both the New Yorker and the Indian will consider some foods permissible and others forbidden on the horizontal axis. Although one eats burgers and the other eats beetles, their way of categorizing the world according to "edible" and "inedible" is completely identical.

Based on this, Lévi-Strauss is able to draw striking parallels between, for example, the lifestyle of Australian Aboriginals in the early twentieth century and the lifestyle of the rural population of nineteenth-century Europe (Lévi-Strauss 1994: 216–223). Furthermore, it is only when we understand their fundamental similarity that we can truly appreciate the differences between the New Yorker and the Indian. Naturally, there are countless differences, for although we classify in the same way, the things we classify vary. In other words, different societies have different "content", while their form, their ways of structuring social life, is fundamentally the same.

Science is one of the crucial differences between "developed" and "primitive" societies. "We" have science and "they" have magic. "We" have *observation* and "they" *interact* with nature (Lévi-Strauss 1994: 27–29). Science and magic are, however, not opposites. They indicate different ways of ordering and structuring the surrounding world; i.e., different systems of classification. The two approaches are capable of different things. Magic is used to create a world we can feel at home in, because it is full of creatures (gods, demons, etc.) like ourselves who we must respect, the way we respect other tribe members. Science, however, alienates us from the world. It considers our surroundings inanimate objects that we can manipulate and "observe". But through the application of science we can reach the moon and use electricity. This does not mean science is "better" than magic; it is simply different. And when considering a problem like global warming, one might say that we must think like a scientist to solve it, but we ought to have thought like an Indian to have avoided the problem in the first place.

One of the prejudices surrounding "primitive" societies is that they lack history. Lévi-Strauss refutes this. All societies are part of history; they simply relate to this fact differently. And when it comes to understanding the world, westerners are actually the ones without history because science is a synchronic model of explanation, which lacks historicity (scientific knowledge is supposedly universally valid), while the indigenous populations' mythical model of explanation is diachronic. They explain nature through narratives; i.e., through a course of events (Lévi-Strauss 1994: 32).

There is, therefore, a clear continuity between Saussure and Lévi-Strauss. Both view our societal life as regulated by semiotic structures, by sign structures that function because of their differences. When studying language, we are dealing with deep linguistic structures. In anthropology the structures in question are substructures, regulating everything from eating habits to city planning, or using the toilet. As sign structures, the systems communicate to us, and we obey this communication even though we aren't aware of it. When the sciences wish to understand individual behaviour or the organization of a society, the scientists must study these sign structures. As we have seen, such studies are able to demonstrate differences and similarities in the ways different cultures organize themselves.

As already noted, Lévi-Strauss is the most significant representative of structuralism, but he is not the only one. We will conclude the presentation of this theory by examining an author who, in spite of refusing to be called a structuralist or, for that matter, a philosopher of science, has still been of great importance to both structuralism and philosophy of science: Louis Althusser.

Althusser's Symptomal Reading

The French philosopher, Louis Althusser (1918–1990) is a good example of how structuralism's different sources of inspiration can lead to very different views, and even to a rejection of the concept of structuralism altogether. Althusser is not primarily a structuralist philosopher of science, but rather a political philosopher, as he was concerned with questions of power, the role of the state in society, and political ideologies. The reason for this focus is that Marx and (to a lesser extent) Freud, rather than Saussure, inspired him. He is, however, still important to a chapter on structuralism as a philosophy of science because of his concept of *symptomal reading*. This section will therefore account only for this particular aspect and not his entire work.

Althusser shares a number of common features with structuralism. These common features are the reason he is often associated with structuralism, although he rejects the concept. First of all, he operates with a similar distinction between two "levels" in society: on the one side we find our conscious, social interaction with one another, and on the other are the structures that form the foundation of our conscious life and of which we are not necessarily conscious. According to his perspective, binary oppositions also characterize this underlying structure; however, contrary to Saussure and Lévi-Strauss, Althusser does not consider these to be semiotic (i.e., constituting a sign structure). Instead, he believes we are dealing with conflicts of interest that result from the fundamental economic inequality of society (Althusser 1996b: 219). The division of society into different levels thus both explains Althusser's connection to structuralism and his rejection of it.

As we saw above, Lévi-Strauss believes the difference between history and anthropology to be related precisely to the question of these two levels. According to him, the field of historians is conscious, societal life, because written sources constitute the material they work with. Althusser would say, however, that this demarcation is based on the superficial assumption that a text is simply the product of consciousness. This assumption is wrong, for although producing a text is naturally a conscious action, the text—like its author—is part of society. It cannot therefore be reduced to just a single level, "conscious life", but must contain the same fundamental duality as all other social phenomena. How does this affect our way of reading texts?

No text is explicit about all its premises. When you speak, you always presuppose something else which remains unsaid and which you may not even be conscious of. In this sense all texts include unspoken premises, the most important among these being the text's societal context. Every text thus reflects the society in which it was formulated, regardless of whether this relationship is clear to the author himself or finds expression in the text. We are therefore dealing with two different levels: a conscious level and a structural level.

Nevertheless, a work can reflect society in different ways, and its explicit expression can be more or less in accordance with the actual social realities. When text and reality conflict, this discrepancy finds expression in the work as paradoxes, contradictions, and loose ends. Althusser speaks of the text being "ideological" because its inner conflict is a symptom of a "suppression" of society's conflicts.

Here Freud's influence on Althusser becomes evident. In his psychoanalysis, Freud unravels a patients' conscious sense of self by pursuing minor contradictions and slips of the tongue that expose this sense of self as an unconscious suppression of conflicts. Similarly, the purpose of symptomal reading is to pursue minor contradictions to demonstrate how they point to suppressed social conflicts of which the author himself was unaware (Althusser 1996: 14–25). One could say that Althusser "psychoanalyzes" texts, and that, according to him, the task of the sciences is to criticize the ideological elements of texts.

! **Symptomal Reading:** Althusser's strategy of reading, which treats the text's minor contradictions and obscurities as symptoms of the text's suppression of the fundamental conflicts in society. When this suppression has been revealed, the text can be reconstructed to avoid its previous contradictions.

Althusser's goal is, however, not simply to dismantle texts but to reconstruct them. Symptomal reading thus consists of two procedures: First of all, one must identify the cracks in the surface of the text. Secondly, one must then reconstruct the text in such a way that its contradictions are dissolved (Althusser 1996: 16).

In conclusion, it can be said that Althusser's symptomal reading is structuralist, insofar as it uncovers the way in which the structures of society find expression in the texts that seek to suppress these same structures; however, if a criterion of structuralism is that the uncovered structure must be semiotic (a sign system), Althusser cannot be considered part of this school of thought.

Poststructuralism

As we have just seen, from a structuralist perspective, meaning is determined in classificatory systems based on oppositions; however, where do these systems come from? This question may be said to open up the field of poststructuralism. Where structuralism focuses on structures and has a synchronic perspective, poststructuralism is interested in examining the processes that constitute the structures.

Poststructuralism is a loose collection of modern, predominantly French thinkers, including Gilles Deleuze (1925–1995), Jacques Derrida (1930–2004), and Michel Foucault (1926–1984). It is not clearly delimited, and in some presentations a theorist like Althusser will also be categorized as belonging to this group. It is thus far from clear where structuralism ends and poststructuralism begins. This is also apparent from the fact that many of the same themes are shared by both approaches, e.g. theoretical antihumanism.

Yet there definitely is a difference between the two approaches, and this difference becomes particularly striking when one compares the poststructural theorists with Saussure. We have seen how, from his perspective, the meaning of a sign is determined by its difference from other signs in a semiotic system. In one of the most important poststructuralist works, *De la grammatologie* (Derrida 1992), Derrida draws a conclusion from this view that is no longer structuralist but poststructuralist. For when the meaning of a sign is found exclusively in its difference from other signs, this meaning can never be determined once and for all. One sign refers to another, which refers to yet a third one, and this process, in principle, goes on forever. "Meaning" here becomes something that is eternally displaced or delayed. Before we can even go on to talk about semiotic structures, there is a process without any content, and with no end in sight. "Meaning" thus ends up being an empty concept.

The implications for philosophy of science are seen clearly in the reading strategy that Derrida develops under inspiration from Althusser, and that he refers to as deconstruction. Every text is communication of meaning. For instance, a text on philosophy of science will explain a position such as positivism by explaining how it is different from positions like critical rationalism and paradigm theory. This is obviously a logic that is quite consistent with the structuralist principle of classification through oppositions; however, if it is the case that meaning can never be determined, the text will be unable to communicate its message unequivocally. It will by necessity contain obscurities, contradictions, and ambiguities. To deconstruct a text means to submit it to minute scrutiny in order to dissolve it and demonstrate how it is really meaningless; however, unlike Althusser's symptomal reading, the aim is not to reconstruct the text but to reject the philosophical understanding of meaning—and, by doing that, the entire western intellectual tradition as a whole.

! **Deconstruction:** Derrida's poststructuralist reading strategy, which aims to demonstrate how every text contains contradictions and ambiguities that render it meaningless.

Poststructuralism thus heralds what the French philosopher Jean-François Lyotard (1924–1998) labelled postmodernism (Lyotard 1988). Postmodern culture is characterized not only by an ironic distance to the cultural and intellectual tradition, but also by the refusal to present an alternative to this tradition. Derrida's deconstruction has, however, also inspired contemporary discourse theory as seen in the philosophies of Ernesto Laclau (1935–2014) and Chantal Mouffe (1943) (Laclau and Mouffe 2001). Here deconstruction is used to better understand the formation of political identities. Political positions are always based on a discourse that contrasts "them" and "us"—for instance "Danes" and "Muslims". Just as Derrida deconstructs such contrasts in texts, Laclau and Mouffe demonstrate how political identities can never be "pure". They always presuppose what they exclude (as in the example above, where the idea about what it means to be "Danish" presupposes and thus cannot do without an idea about what it means to be a "Muslim"). This implies that the negation of a given position is present as a repressed, but constitutive element in this position itself (Mouffe 2000: 21). According to Laclau and Mouffe, this is the reason why political identities and oppositions are always preliminary, unstable, and unclear.

Structuralism: A Summary

The authors we have considered in this chapter all testify to the strength of the fundamental structuralist principles. These find their clearest and most classical formulation in Saussure's work. We have seen how the various structuralists agree that the object of the sciences is not determined by nature but must be constructed, and that the sciences must adopt a synchronous perspective on their areas of study; i.e., they must focus on structures rather than development. The most significant point made by structuralism is, however, shared by Saussure, Marx, and Freud, and can therefore be found in the works of all the structuralist authors: it is the view that neither mankind nor society can be understood on the basis of their immediate appearance. The surface level of societal life functions because of deep structures, which are not immediately visible. These organize the social world according to systems of difference and opposition. It is these characteristics that have proven fruitful in many disciplines within the social sciences and which, in this chapter, are first of all illustrated by linguistics and anthropology. Finally, we have briefly discussed how poststructuralism develops from structuralism, but draws far more radical conclusions.

The strength of the structuralist analysis is that it is capable of uncovering correlations and patterns, which we are not aware of. Lévi-Strauss's demonstration of the strikingly common features between the most divergent of cultures is an especially impressive feat of structuralism. Structuralist analysis enables us to see new connections and to revise our division of the world into, for example, "primitive" and "developed" societies.

Structuralism's relevance for philosophy of science is dual. First of all, it presents what could be called a programme for philosophy of science, which is summarized by the above-mentioned principles. As we have seen, this programme is in stark contrast to that of hermeneutics. Secondly, Lévi-Strauss, for instance, presents us with an assessment of what science really is and what part it plays in society. In the western world, science is one of our most important tools for classification with which we bring order and cohesion to the universe. In this sense, science is not "better" or more valuable than, for instance, myth, music, or religion. They all bring order to our worldview and they each possess different qualities.

Despite the many merits of structuralism, some people may still ask: So what? What use can we make of our knowledge of consistent fundamental structures in our way of organizing society? Is disregarding the content of what is studied in favour of its structure not just a form of empty formalism? It is even worse with poststructuralism, for how does the knowledge that any message can be deconstructed help us in any way? This criticism has often been levelled at structuralism and is exactly one of the reasons why Althusser would not accept this label; however, his own concept of symptomal reading demonstrates how structural analysis is both useful and beneficial in textual criticism. In the following we will see more examples of how a structuralist approach on the scientific level of knowledge can expand our knowledge of society and ourselves.

Structuralist Research in Practice

Example: Structuralist Economics

In the economic sciences, Celso Furtado (1920–2004) and Raúl Prebisch (1901–1986) are the best known representatives of the school known as structuralist economics (Jameson 1986). Similar to the study of language and culture, economic sciences are about distinguishing between the deep structures of society and its surface phenomena. The world market, which would appear to be formed by exchanges between equal parties, buyers, and sellers, serves as an example. Classical economics deals with this reality. On the other hand, from a structuralist perspective, the equality of parties merely seems to exist. In reality, the market is governed by a deep structure characterized by the inequality between the centre and the periphery of the world economy; i.e., the industrialized world and Third World countries. This opposition determines and explains other significant structural inequalities; for example, development versus underdevelopment, industry versus agriculture, and particularly, high- versus low-standards of living. This deep structure of oppositions must be mapped out in order to gain an understanding of the economic development of individual countries. National circumstances and decisions do not determine a country's economic development; they are "surface phenomena". The crucial aspect is whether the country is placed within the centre or the periphery of the world economic structure. This determines whether the country's role in the world economy will be that of supplying raw materials or that of (post-) industrial production, and so this also determines the wealth of the country.

Many of the elements found in Saussure's, Lévi-Strauss's and Althusser's writings can also be found in structuralist economics. Economic life is governed by a fundamental structure that we are not aware of, but that still regulates the economic development of society. Furthermore, it is a structure of binary oppositions, the primary contrast being between centre and periphery.

Example: Structuralist Analysis in Management Theory

The Spanish sociologist Carlos Rodríguez has applied a structuralist approach to critically evaluate popular management literature (Rodríguez 2005). These books are typically about a successful business manager or a new revolutionizing principle of leadership. Rodríguez seeks to examine whether common traits can be found in the different works, and this proves to be the case as he discovers that the structure of these apparently diverse portraits of successful managers is completely identical. First of all, they include the same seven characters: the managerial hero, the villain, the manager's assistant, et cetera. Secondly, they all follow the same course of events: the manager arrives at a crisis-ridden company, presents a completely new approach to management, defeats any opposition, and turns the company's failings into success. Thirdly, they are all structured by the same fundamental contrast between the old and flawed theory of management on the one side, and the new and successful theory of management represented by the managerial hero on the other.

It is, of course, interesting that even apparently different books of this genre are basically variations of the exact same fundamental structure; however, Rodríguez believes his study has uncovered a problem. For the books also have the same function. They are all dogmatic and picture-perfect portrayals of the ideal leader. In that sense they function exactly like the Catholic Church's educational portrayals of saints from the Middle Ages—portrayals that were also based upon a fixed template. Furthermore, these two literary genres serve the same purpose: to render undogmatic and critical discussion impossible.

Rodríguez thus identifies a fundamental structure that governs the different variations of popular management literature, and that is structured by binary oppositions. Similarly to the way Lévi-Strauss pointed out common features between the New Yorker and the Amazon Indian, identifying a fundamental structure enables Rodríguez to perceive crucial common features between this form of literature and what might appear to be a completely different genre—the saint portrayals of the Middle Ages.

Example: How *You* Can Work with Structuralism

How can our students make use of the structuralist approach in their study of communication in a large company? If they were to ask Lévi-Strauss, he would recommend that they begin by collecting examples of the written and oral communication in the company. After this, they would be able to examine the material to identify the binary oppositions that structure the communication (e.g., internal versus external, and management versus employee). By placing these different oppositions on the two logical axes (respectively: good-bad and abstract-concrete), they can make the structure of the company's communication visible. When this has been done, they can begin to put the analysis into perspective by drawing parallels to other contexts of communication. For example, according to the company's self-understanding, its communication differs significantly from that of its competitor. However is it possible that the communication of the two companies is really structured in the same way?

Althusser would recommend that the students follow a different strategy. According to him, they ought to look for contradictions and inaccuracies in the communication of the company. The firm may commend itself on its non-hierarchical structure, but how does its self-image harmonize with its communication? Does the company produce hierarchies in its way of communicating? Any contradictions the students might find in the collected material can be treated as symptoms of the real conflicts of interests within the company and the surrounding society.

Questions

1. Explain the differences between hermeneutics and structuralism.
2. Explain the concepts langue and parole. Which role does the distinction between the two play in structuralism?
3. Explain structuralism's distinction between diachrony and synchrony.
4. According to Saussure, what characterizes a sign?
5. In what sense is language a "system of differences" according to Saussure?
6. What is "theoretical anti-humanism"?
7. According to Lévi-Strauss, what characterizes the unconscious structures that organize conscious, societal life in different societies?
8. Explain "symptomal reading".
9. How would you make use of a structuralist approach in a written assignment?
10. In your opinion, what are the weaknesses and strengths of the structuralist approach?

Social Constructivism

We all know what money is. Money is said to "make the world go round", and it certainly plays a huge part in all people's lives. All over the world, people get up every single morning to go to work and earn money. Many are tempted to steal, rob, or even kill to get their hands on it. But what is it about money that makes it so important? What wondrous qualities does it possess that make people willing to do anything to get it? It is certainly not because of its physical features, as it is merely worthless pieces of metal and small pieces of coloured paper with a watermark. So where does money's value come from? Well, money is valuable because we *agree* that it is valuable. Because everyone acts *as if* money has value, it actually becomes valuable. We do not think about this in our everyday life as money's importance is not something we have decided upon. It is a convention; something we accept naturally and without asking questions. Although it *seems* natural, the importance of money is, however, constantly created and maintained by our collective behaviour. Money is a *social construction.*

This example is not picked at random. Analyzing money as a convention is perhaps the most classic example of how social constructivism dissolves what is "natural" by showing that it is socially constructed. According to the most consistent proponents of the theory, both our surroundings and our own selves are constructions, much like money. The question becomes, what are the philosophical implications of this approach? The following chapter will provide an answer.

The American social constructivist, Kenneth Gergen, distinguishes between five different types of theories, each dealing with the question of the world as a social construction in different ways: constructivism, radical constructivism, social constructionism, social constructivism, and sociological constructionism (Gergen 1999: 59–60). To maintain a sense of perspective, we will disregard this distinction and instead paint a more general picture of the social constructivist position. This general account will then be further supplemented by two concrete examples: the French sociologists and philosophers, Bruno Latour and Pierre Bourdieu.

Social Constructivism's Sources of Inspiration

One of the many common features of the various constructivist schools of thought is that they draw inspiration from Kuhn and Ludwig Wittgenstein (1889–1951). We examined Kuhn in chapter 5, where it was hinted that his philosophy of science is pertinent to the social sciences. According to Kuhn, science must first of all be understood as a community held together by the disciplinary matrix (Kuhn 1977: 463). The social ties between scientists determine what they see and thus what is acknowledged as "true science". Consequently, the sciences are a social construction as well.

As mentioned before, another source of inspiration is Wittgenstein, the famous Austrian-British philosopher. The logical positivists' criterion of meaning from the 1920s (a statement is meaningful if it can be determined to be right or wrong) was inspired by Wittgenstein's early, major work *Tractatus Logico-Philosophicus* from 1921. He personally did not publish much more than this one book, but the posthumous publication of the manuscript *Philosophical Investigations* in 1953 revealed that he had moved away from positivism in the years that followed, finally adopting the completely opposite view: words and sentences acquire meaning from the way we *use* them, not by means of their (true or false) reference to "reality".

Wittgenstein uses the concept *language games* to explain how what we say acquires meaning. The concept refers to the different contexts in which we use language (Wittgenstein 1994: 44). Each of these many contexts are regulated by rules, hence the game metaphor. For instance, language is used differently when flirting with a fellow student, presenting political arguments, or asking directions from a passer-by. These different games are what provide language with meaning, not the words in themselves (they may recur in each of the three contexts).

> ! **Language Games:** Wittgenstein's term for different linguistic contexts of usage that provide words and sentences with meaning. Flirting with a fellow student is one type of language game; presenting political arguments is another; and making small talk at a party is yet a third one.

We are constantly moving from one language game to another. One might say, therefore, that we live through these games. Wittgenstein expresses this by means of his concept *life-form*: the games we partake in determine how we live. Language and life cannot be separated as we shape our lives through our usage of language (Wittgenstein 1994: 44). For example, without language we are incapable of thinking a single thought, and so we are incapable of hoping, believing, and expressing emotions in general.

> ! **Life-form:** We shape our way of living through the language games we partake in, resulting in different forms of life.

It is easy to see the inspiration from Kuhn and Wittgenstein in social constructivism. As in Kuhn's philosophy not only scientific research, but reality in general is socially constructed. And as in Wittgenstein's philosophy, this construction is seen as taking place in and through language. Based on this view, Gergen presents four claims which, according to him, form the theoretical core of social constructivism (Gergen 1999: 47–50):

1. *There is no necessary correlation between the world and our concepts of the world.* The reason for this view is that language is not considered to be a picture of the world (as the positivists believed), but as a social convention.
2. *Our descriptions of reality originate from our social relations.* In other words, we create our worldview collectively, together with others.
3. *We shape our future through our understanding of the world.* Our collective understanding of the world determines what we can and cannot do.
4. *Reflecting on our understanding of the world is vital for our future well-being.* By problematizing oppressive ideas about others, we are capable of improving society.

These four basic assumptions will be further explained in this chapter; however, it should already be clear that they affect the assessment of both the object of the sciences (society, nature, etc.) and scientific work itself. We will start by considering the first of these two topics, the question of what world the sciences explore according to the social constructivists.

The World as a Social Construction

How can one possibly claim that there is no necessary correlation between the world and our concepts of it? The positivistic theory of meaning may perhaps be wrong, but are not the social constructivists drawing slightly extreme conclusions on the basis of this admission? Most of us will find it difficult to accept their view of language as a closed system. When I, for instance, point to the table and say "There's a radio", it must mean that a radio and not a goat is placed on the table. Let us begin by taking a closer look at the arguments for the first of Gergen's four basic assumptions (Gergen 1999: 62–89).

There is no necessary correlation between the world and our concepts of the world

According to the social constructivists, language is an excellent tool for communication; however, it is completely incapable of mirroring the world "in itself", because *language is metaphorical* (Gergen 1999: 65). As we know, a metaphor is a linguistic turn of phrase expressing something other than what is stated. Normally, a distinction is made between literal and metaphorical statements. "I am angry" is a literal phrase. It refers directly to reality; however, "I am boiling with anger" is a metaphor. It is a linguistic image, which refers indirectly to reality, as the person who made the statement is not really boiling. We can only gain understanding of what it refers to in reality by "translating" it into literal meaning.

! **The Metaphoricity of Language:** According to the social constructivists, language is metaphorical because it does not reflect the world but expresses something other than the world "in itself".

According to the social constructivists there is, however, no such thing as "literal meaning"; thus, language does not refer to reality (Gergen 1999: 65). It is, in other words, purely metaphorical. For how can "I am angry" be an accurate portrayal of a state of mind? Words and feelings are two distinct entities. To say that one "reflects" the other would be nothing more than a metaphor. We understand each other because of our common language games, not because of words' reference to a non-linguistic reality. "I am angry" is no more literal than "I am boiling with anger". The difference between the two is determined by our social conventions.

Returning to the radio on the table, identifying an object as "a radio" requires cultural background knowledge of what a radio is, and what its function is. An Amazonian Indian would undoubtedly view the object on the table very differently. He might call it "a magic box" but definitely not "a radio". The statement "There's a radio" does not point to "the object in itself"; instead, it points back to our socially constructed background knowledge.

The world we live in is the sum of all our "language games". We create it collectively through communication. In this world we love, hate, work, think, mourn, and fight through language. This is the world that makes sense to us. To put it briefly, *this* is the "real world"; thus, the metaphoricity of language does not pose a problem to the social constructivists. It is not necessary to improve language's ability to reflect the world, for example, by getting rid of the word "money" and using "pieces of paper" and "pieces of metal" instead. Metaphoricity is not about the individual words but rather about the way language functions in general. And it functions well; it just does not refer to anything outside of language.

This rejection of any non-linguistic reality may sound like the antirealism of the positivists; i.e., the view that the object of the sciences is not the world in itself (which is unavailable to us) but rather our perception of the world. However, these two positions differ greatly from each other. Antirealism is based on empiricism, social constructivism is not. This means that the antirealists partly believe that a world we cannot perceive underlies our sensory experience, and partly claim that all knowledge is acquired through sensory perception. According to the social constructivists, the only world that exists is the one we construct in collaboration with others through our language games. "Sensory perception" is of no particular importance to knowledge, but understanding the way in which our language functions is crucial.

Our descriptions of reality originate from the social relations we are part of

As mentioned before, we create our worldview in collaboration with other people. The point of Gergen's second basic assumption, in other words, is that our understanding and description of the world is not individual but collective (Gergen 1999: 48). This is a natural consequence of the importance ascribed to language, because language is shared by us all. It is what unites us.

This point is illustrated by the money example: Money is only valuable because we all ascribe it value in the language games we play with each other. The idea of the properties of money is sustained because we continue to play the same language games; thus, the world is simply our constant collective, linguistic reproduction of the world. The examples of the social nature of reality are unending. Without a collective understanding of the authority of the police force, it is just a troop of people wearing the same clothes. Without a common understanding of libraries, they are just buildings containing an awful lot of paper.

The first two basic assumptions constitute the core of social constructivism, and they not only mark a break with earlier philosophies of science, but also with our entire traditional way of viewing the world. Let us consider some examples.

Normally we consider a statement to be true if it is consistent with reality; however, if our statements are what create "reality", will not the idea of truth cease to make sense? Will we not end up with a form of relativism where no truth has absolute validity? To begin with, a theory should not be rejected just because it leads to relativism. Perhaps the relativists put forward the best arguments. In fact, some social constructivists actually embrace the relativistic implications of their position, and therefore they attempt to avoid using the concept of truth. On the other hand, some consider this to be completely misguided: the concept of truth should not be eliminated any more than we should abolish our concept of money or, in general, change our language. We must instead change the way we understand the concept. Rather than being understood as the correspondence between language and a non-linguistic world, "truth" should be understood as a special language game, which, like all other language games, is bound by specific rules (Gergen 1999: 35–37).

Our distinction between "true" and "false" merely constitutes one example of how we ordinarily understand the world and ourselves according to a number of binary oppositions rooted in history. For instance, our "inner" self is private in contrast to the "outer" world, which is publically accessible. Our thoughts, emotions, and so forth differ completely from the physical world; however, according to social constructivism both "thoughts" and "the physical world" are made from the same material: language, so there is no division between the two (Gergen 1999: 47). For this same reason, our "inner" self is not especially private because even the most intimate thoughts and emotions are expressed and understood by means of collective concepts. When it comes to our identity, it is impossible to distinguish between public and private. When telling others who we are, we typically talk about where we grew up, where we went to school, and our plans for the future. We shape our sense of self on the basis of recognized social conventions determining how a narrative is constructed. Without being aware of it, we construct our identity on the same basic, narrative structures found in films and books (Gergen 1999: 70–72). There is, in short, nothing "private" about our personality. Here, too, social constructivism reduces the traditional ideas we have of ourselves and the world to linguistic constructions.

We shape our future through our understanding of the world

Of course, not all social constructivists are the same. Some emphasize the fact that we are not aware of the social construction of the world and ourselves, as exemplified by the narrative construction of personal identity. When our identity is unconsciously constructed according to a conventional pattern, it becomes nearly impossible to change anything. In other words, we are entrapped by the collective structure we help to uphold. Others emphasize what the criticism of old prejudice demonstrates; namely, that by reflecting critically on our language, we are able to change it, and thereby change the world. This is the point of departure of Gergen's last two basic assumptions (Gergen 1999: 42–46).

Let us consider how a social constructivist would approach a concrete and relevant issue according to this view. Today, many people are of the opinion that prostitution should be prohibited because it "oppresses women". This is presented as a fact, although some prostitutes are of a different opinion. The social constructivist would seek to dismantle this "fact" of oppression. He would aim to demonstrate how the idea that prostitution oppresses women originates from the traditionalist and moralist view of women as passive and helpless victims of men's active and aggressive sexuality. Furthermore, he would aim to show how this stereotypical distinction between masculine and feminine sexuality is a fundamental element of the most traditionalist chauvinistic discourses; thus, it is those who oppose prostitution and insist on their "facts" who oppress prostitutes, rather than prostitution itself. In other words, what preserves the low social status of prostitutes is the continued discursive construction of prostitutes as helpless victims. The social constructivist's conclusion, therefore, would be diametrically opposed to the premise taken for granted in the conventional debate. It is those who oppose prostitution, rather than prostitution itself, that oppress women.

This example demonstrates how different articulations of the same problem lead to widely diverse horizons of understanding, and so to completely different views of what one can and ought to do. But the example shows even more than this.

Reflecting on our understanding of the world is vital for our future well-being

First and foremost, the example illustrates how this type of analysis can serve as a basis for articulating a new social reality in which prostitutes are no longer considered oppressed, but strong modern women who are in control of their own sexuality and who use it as they want. The analysis therefore also exemplifies the idea of *identity politics*, which, especially in the US, has been greatly inspired by social constructivism. Identity politics is concerned with changing the way that oppressed groups are talked about in society, because their oppression is reproduced in our way of speaking about them. For instance, if prostitutes are always depicted as victims, or if Muslims are always equated with fundamentalism, the social marginalization of these groups is reproduced. The idea is that by changing our language, we can strengthen the life conditions and self-respect of oppressed groups by increasing the surrounding society's respect for them. This point is made in the last of Gergen's basic assumptions (Gergen 1999: 63).

! **Identity Politics:** The attempt to improve the conditions of oppressed social groups by problematizing the way in which oppression is reproduced in our way of speaking about these groups.

Identity politics also demonstrates the biggest strength of social constructivist science. It makes us critical of the different ways that our linguistic interaction with one another creates and sustains a common social reality. This is the first step towards discussing how society can be improved; however, like social constructivism, identity politics is controversial because it claims that social marginalization can fundamentally be explained by the way we discursively construct groups and not, for instance, by economic differences.

Social constructivism makes sense as long as we are dealing with the objects of social science. Can one seriously claim, however, that the natural sciences are social constructions as well? In this field, scientists work with entities that can be weighed and measured, which surely means they must be independent of our language, right? The French sociologist and philosopher Bruno Latour (born 1947) offers his opinions on this.

Natural Science as the Construction of Facts: Bruno Latour

From 1975 to 1977, Latour worked in a biological laboratory in the US. It was one of the best in its field, and during Latour's stay, one of the scientists working there was awarded the Nobel Prize in medicine. Latour was, however, not there to study biology but to study the scientists. He sought to make an anthropological study of life in the laboratory. In other words, he wanted to observe and analyze the behaviour of the scientists in the same way that anthropologists study the natives in an African village. The result of Latour's study was a much-debated book, *Laboratory Life*, which was published in 1979 in collaboration with Steve Woolgar (born 1950).

Latour identified some striking paradoxes in scientific practice. On the one hand, it was clearly a social activity. The scientists worked together. They thought out, carried out, and evaluated their experiments collectively. On the other hand, when a scientist was able to establish something as fact, the entire social development process was forgotten. All research was suddenly concerned with "the discovery", "the good idea", or "the logical deduction" of a formula. In retrospect, science became something other than a social community: it became more "rational" and "stringent" (Latour and Woolgar 1986: 23).

According to Latour, the lab first of all functioned as a factory, where scientific papers were the finished product. The production process took place through inscriptions. Measuring apparatus and computers recorded miles of data. The scientists began by writing down the readings of these data and later the finished articles (Latour and Woolgar 1986: 52), but after presenting their "discoveries", this material aspect of the scientists' activities was forgotten too. In other words, Latour was able to assert that the mythical view of science as an especially "rational and systematic" study of "reality" was, in fact, based on the suppression of scientific work as a primarily social dynamic. Furthermore, he was able to track how the scientists themselves collectively constructed this myth. The primary question became, which social dynamic specifically characterizes science?

Latour did not just view the lab as a factory producing papers. He also regarded the individual scientists as participants in an economic system in which the currency is *credibility.* The scientist invests his credibility in a paper hoping it will return increased credibility. This leads to him being awarded more research funds, which in turn can be invested in new papers. The "cycle of credibility" functions because there is a market for scientific results. Scientists seek out the fields in which the demand for results is highest, and where their investments are most certain to pay off. The faster a scientist moves through the cycle of credibility, the better the returns on his investment (Latour and Woolgar 1986: 200–201). The driving force of research is thus not the exploration of reality, but the social demand of doing well in the cycle of credibility.

The laboratory is a factory and the scientists are investors. In practice, science does not differ from the surrounding society. Based on this analysis it is therefore not surprising that Latour is able to conclude that discussion in laboratories is neither more rational nor more focused than everyday conversations and negotiations. Logical deliberations are merely part of a type of communication, which to a similar extent is marked by negotiations, changing evaluations, and unconscious or institutionalized actions (Latour and Woolgar 1986: 152–159). In other words, the difference between scientific and non-scientific interpretational logic is not based on scientific practice, but rather on science's own self understanding of being an activity concerned with "hypotheses", "proofs", and "deduction".

At the same time, science is not like a typical factory, as it does not produce just anything; it produces facts. By means of examples drawn from research projects, Latour shows how scientists do not "discover" the truth but, on the contrary, negotiate it in a game where social relationships are crucial (Latour and Woolgar 1986: 136). For instance, the economically strong laboratories outmatch the economically weak ones, and younger scientists place greater trust in older, more acknowledged colleagues than in their own equipment. Even the thoughts, deliberations, and ideas of the scientists are no more than a recapitulation of the social life of the laboratory (institutional requirements, group traditions, seminars, suggestions, discussions, etc.).

The scientists thus produce the object of their knowledge through social interaction. This construction takes places in a network, which, apart from the scientists, also includes the branches of science that develop laboratory equipment, as well as the industry that produces it. The facts constructed by science only exist in these networks. To most people, the objects found in a laboratory are just white powders or clear liquids. These only become something else, something more "scientific", because of the specialized language game of scientists.

Latour is therefore also able to refute the argument that the sciences must "uncover" facts "in reality" because their theories "work" in practice; for example, when a "discovery" of the lab is used in the pharmaceutical industry. In fact, the only thing that can be seen is that everyone in the network (i.e., all the places where the same instruments, apparatus, and discourses are used as in the lab) constructs the world in the same way (Latour and Woolgar 1986: 182). This is, of course, not surprising. Latour does not claim that the objects of science do not exist. The point is that they do not exist independently of the network of social practices and language games that enable their existence. The relationship between knowledge and world is thus turned upside down: a thing is first deemed true, once the scientists have agreed that it is so.

Latour's anthropological study shows that science constructs its facts, and that it is a social network, which does not differ significantly from other social networks; therefore, not only our social world but also the world of the natural sciences is a construction. Latour and Woolgar are aware that their own study is not exempt from this view. Their account of science is no more correct than the scientists' account of their activities. Both are forms of fiction (Latour and Woolgar 1986: 282).

Laboratory Life is a classic in social constructivism. It compellingly argues that the "hard facts" of science are as constructed as the value of money. Obviously this analysis must be regarded as a criticism of science's self-understanding. The authors demonstrate how this self-understanding hides the actual developmental process of science; however, Latour and Woolgar are not the only theorists who discuss science as a social construction.

Science as a Field: Pierre Bourdieu

Another French philosopher and sociologist, Pierre Bourdieu (1930–2002) disagrees completely with Latour and Woolgar's approach (Bourdieu 2004: 26–31). According to Bourdieu, the sciences cannot be understood by studying a single laboratory, because it is only a smaller part of a much larger network of laboratories, universities, journals, research councils, et cetera. Bourdieu discusses how the sciences (like politics, art, and the business world) constitute a particular *field* in society, one that has its own rules, social conventions, and worldview (Bourdieu 2004: 32–35).

> **Field:** Bourdieu's concept for the different social systems in society (e.g., science and politics), which, among other things, are characterized by different types of symbolic capital.

In each field of society there are different sources of acknowledgement, respect, and, therefore, also power. In Bourdieu's terms, there are different types of *symbolic capital* in each individual field.

Furthermore, he distinguishes between economic, social, and cultural capital, which are provided by property, network, and knowledge respectively.

> **Symbolic Capital:** Symbolic capital is what provides recognition, respect, and, thereby, social status within each of the separate fields. For instance, the symbolic capital of politics is power, whereas in the sciences it is a doctorate.

In politics, ministerial and chairperson positions lead to recognition, whereas in research, scientific results, doctorates, and being published in prestigious journals yield acknowledgment. We are therefore dealing with different types of symbolic capital. In all fields of society, a continuous fight for what yields recognition in different contexts is taking place. In the world of research, the individual actors are constantly fighting for scientific capital.

The sciences may be built on theoretical intelligence, but the everyday work of scientists must be considered a craft that is based on experience, intuition, and skill. It is an example of what Bourdieu calls *habitus* (Bourdieu 2004: 36–40). This is a practical, bodily knowledge, which enables direct and unreflective interaction between researchers. Naturally, we are physically present in the social world, but the social world is also present in our bodies and in our way of acting; this is how we find our bearings in the world in general, not just in the sciences.

> **Habitus:** The unreflective, bodily knowledge of the norms, values, social conventions, and practices of a field that enables us to be part of that field.

Why is Bourdieu's view an example of social constructivism? According to him the social world does not exist separately from our social practices. On the contrary, it is divided into fields that are constituted by these practices and everything they entail, such as norms, bodily knowledge (habitus), and (the fight for) capital. We reproduce these fields collectively through our daily interaction with each other.

According to this perspective, the "truth" that the sciences uncover neither corresponds to a non-social objectivity nor (as in Latour's and Woolgar's view) is it the simple result of negotiations. Scientists may construct the truth, but its validity goes beyond this construction because of the scientific field. The competition for scientific capital, which characterizes the field, also means that all new theories will be subject to thorough and highly qualified criticism. The theories that survive testing are deemed true (Bourdieu 2004: 72–73). Using concepts such as truth and rationality makes sense because the sciences are *social* constructions.

However, society's unequal distribution of, not least, cultural capital poses a problem for the sciences. It means that some social groups have easier access to education than others and, thereby, easier access to the field of research. The consequence of this imbalance is that the sciences end up reflecting what Bourdieu terms the scholastic prejudices of these privileged groups (Bourdieu 2003: 49–85).

Researchers unconsciously project their own socially determined view of reality on to what, or who, they are currently studying. This becomes visible when they claim to understand people and society according to rational, logical terms and abstract concepts. They forget that human behaviour is not primarily rational and logical, but habitus

(Bourdieu 2003: 137–142). In other words, the researchers neglect the fact that knowledge primarily comes from what one learns by heart and not from studying thick books.

Bourdieu mentions several concrete examples of the consequences of this oversight, one example being opinion surveys. Researchers assume that all people have a "personal opinion" about, for example, politics; however, this idea stems from the researchers' own middle-class backgrounds. They have been raised as individuals who, independently and critically, take a stand and are skeptical of authorities. This does not characterize all social classes, and "personal opinion" is therefore not equally available to all. It requires cultural capital. Surveys are thus based on an elitist prejudice that all people think like the researchers and the privileged social classes the researchers are recruited from. This prejudice is routinely expressed by the fact that the less cultural capital the survey participants possess, the more questions they answer with "don't know" (Bourdieu 2003: 67–68).

The social sciences are especially sensitive to the prejudices of researchers, and for this reason Bourdieu emphasizes the importance of what he calls *the double objectification* in relation to these sciences.

> **The Double Objectification:** Scientists and researchers objectify society in their attempt to understand it; however, at the same time, they ought to make their own social and personal background the object of study to clarify how this background affects their work. Only then will they be able to avoid being controlled by their prejudices.

The researcher makes society the object of his studies. At the same time, he is part of society and is not able to step outside of it as an impartial and neutral observer. If he attempts to play this part, his prejudices will control his studies. He can, however, make himself the object of study and thus create an overview of his prejudices, where they stem from, and how significant they are. In this way he is able to prevent them from ruining his research. Bourdieu subjects himself to this double objectification as well (Bourdieu 2004: 94–114)

Social Constructivism: A Summary

The core of social constructivism is the idea that "reality" is something we create collectively through our interactions and ways of speaking about the world. If we were to attempt to illustrate this point it could be done by showing how the world, according to this perspective, must be understood solely on the basis of the language games through which it is articulated. On the one hand it differs depending on the discourse (or field) in question; for instance, the astrophysicist and the poet do not see the same thing when looking at the starry night sky. On the other hand, "the world in itself" is no more than the sum of the different discourses of the world. In other words: "the world" or "reality" has no existence outside, or independent of, our discursive construction of the world and reality. This is illustrated below:

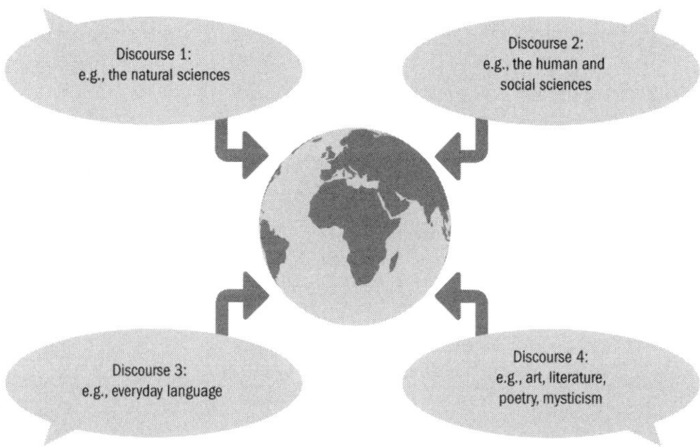

Figure 9.1. The World as the Sum of Our Discourse about the World

What are the strengths and weaknesses of social constructivism? Clearly, among its strengths is its ability to question everything we consider "natural". This invites us to critically review our conventions and prejudices. Previously we have seen examples of how what appears to be self-evident can be problematized by a social constructivist analysis.

This can provide us with insight into society and ourselves, and social constructivism can thus be a strong analytical instrument.

As hinted at above, social constructivism is often accused of being relativistic; however, this is not a particularly good argument if the reason why relativism is a problem is not simultaneously explained. In a world where a cartoon is considered a simple caricature in one country, but causes deadly offence in the next, relativism may not be an altogether implausible position. However, as we have already discussed, not all social constructivists believe that their views lead to relativism. Bourdieu is an example of this.

A more serious objection against social constructivism is that it has difficulties explaining how the sciences progress. How do new discoveries enable us to do more things, if these "discoveries" are merely new ways of talking about the world? For example, it seems difficult to argue that the moon landing should be considered a social construction. One can claim that the theory functions best when applied to the areas of social science, and some social constructivists believe the theory is only valid in this field; however, the question is whether this claim poses more problems than solutions, since we still only have access to the world of the natural sciences through our language. So what exactly is the difference between the physical and the social?

Most serious is perhaps the criticism of social constructivism for its idealism. Social constructivism states that the world is something we construct through our language, and thus in our ideas. One could, however, protest that this is merely a typical intellectualist prejudice and that people outside the universities are perfectly aware that our social world is not something we construct. Instead, we *produce* it by getting up and going to work every day. In chapter 11, we will take a look at the most important source of inspiration for exactly this objection; namely, Marx.

Social Constructivist Research in Practice

In the previous section, we noted how sociologists and anthropologists use social constructivism to understand the sciences and society; however, many other disciplines on the scientific level of knowledge have adopted this approach.

Example: Social Constructivism in Business Studies

An example can be found in the Danish researcher Hans Skytte's report *Know Yourself and Your Surroundings – A Tool for the Danish Meat Industry (Kend dig selv og dine omgivelse – et værktøj for danske slagteriselskaber)* from 2005. As the title indicates, this report was commissioned by the Danish meat industry. In recent years, this particular line of business has undergone significant changes towards becoming increasingly export-oriented and concentrated in few, but very large companies. How do these changes affect the industry's self-understanding, and how do they affect the consumers' opinions of it? The report seeks to answer these questions. According to a social constructivist point of view, this is an important issue because the development of the industry is determined by its construction of its own identity. For instance, if management regards the business as export-oriented, high priority will be given to strengthening its position abroad. The corporation, is, therefore, a social construction, and the stakeholders' collective discursive construction of it determines its development. But why did the Danish meat industry request the report?

The problem is that the industry does not construct its own private reality. Consumers and retailers form their own opinion of the development of this line of business. To ensure the future of the industry, it is crucial that its self-understanding is not opposed to the way in which retailers and consumers view it. Should this be the case, the parties will lose their common understanding, and this in turn will lead to losses in market shares.

For this reason, Hans Skytte examines both the retailers' and the industry's views of the business through a series of interviews. On this basis, he is able to provide a number of recommendations for how the business's self-understanding can approximate the view of its surroundings. For instance, the companies can broaden the educational profile of their employees. This would provide more diverse perspectives on the industry, creating a more nuanced self-understanding as well as a better understanding of how the surrounding society perceives this particular line of business.

Example: Social Constructivism and Business Strategy

Another example is Joseph Porac, Charles Baden-Fuller, and Howard Thomas's article "Competitive Groups as Cognitive Communities: The Case of Scottish Knitwear Manufacturers" from 1986. The article is about the small, Scottish knitwear industry. It is a geographically concentrated industry with a few firms that, from their own viewpoint, produce knitwear of the finest quality in the world. The high prices of the products mean that their market segment consists only of the top 2–5% of income groups worldwide.

Interestingly, the researchers discover that the framework conditions of the industry are not defined by objective economic conditions. On the contrary, the collectively constructed self-understanding of the industry has defined both its market and the competitive situation in which it finds itself. For instance, since all the companies have adopted the view that they only produce for the wealthiest consumers, they see no need to invest in new machines that could boost their productivity, and they do not consider the manufacturers of cheap knitwear to be competitors.

The analysis thus turns the traditional view of the business world upside down: economic realities are social constructions, not hard, objective facts of life. Another point is that the identity of the Scottish firms creates not only possibilities, but also obstacles. The industry is fixed in its particular way of thinking, which may keep it from bankruptcy, but also renders growth on a larger scale impossible. Studies such as this one can therefore make firms aware of the way in which their self-understanding directly influences their possibilities for development and expansion. Just as identity politics intends to change the way we act by changing our use of language, the social constructivist analysis of businesses creates new possibilities by making inappropriate mindsets visible and by pointing to better alternatives. It is thus directly applicable to the practical level of knowledge.

Example: How *You* Can Work with Social Constructivism

In conclusion, let us consider how our students can be inspired by social constructivism in connection with their study of communication in a large company. All organizations have an identity, a history—in brief, a narrative about themselves. For students adopting a social constructivist view, it is crucial that they understand how this narrative is constructed through the different practices and communicative contexts of the company. This would be Latour's approach, and he would also tell the students what this approach requires of them. They must first create an overview of what the narrative is about, and then they must minutely analyze the practices and the communication in the company in order to see how the narrative is reproduced in the social dynamics of the employees. The students can supplement this analysis by applying Bourdieu's concepts of capital and habitus. Which practices are shared among the employees even though they are not aware of this (cf., the concept of habitus)? How are these shown indirectly through communication? How is the fact that different types of capital are not distributed equally among employees expressed in the internal communication of the company? At the same time, it is important that the students undertake a double objectification of themselves as "researchers". What is their social background? What prejudices do they hold and how will they ensure that their studies do not reflect these prejudices?

Perhaps the students will find that the narrative and the practice of the business contradict each other. Furthermore, they will doubtlessly criticize much of what the employees consider to be simple, indisputable facts; thus, their analysis may also yield new perspectives on the firm and its employees.

Questions

1. What are the fundamental points made by social constructivism?
2. How have Kuhn and Wittgenstein influenced social constructivism?
3. Explain the concepts "language game" and "life-form".
4. What do the social constructivists mean when they claim that language is metaphorical?
5. What is identity politics, and how is it connected to social constructivism?
6. What is the point of Latour's and Woolgar's analysis of the scientific laboratory?
7. Explain the concepts "field" and "symbolic capital".
8. How are we to understand the concept "habitus"?
9. Give examples of issues that could be considered from a social constructivist point of view.
10. In your opinion, what are the strengths and weaknesses of social constructivism?

Which Key Concepts Have We Examined?

In the second part of the book, we have examined some of the most important traditions in the philosophy of the social sciences. We began by looking at hermeneutics, which stems from the contrast between *the human sciences* and *the natural sciences.* The latter attempt to explain the physical world, while the human sciences are concerned with understanding people's lived experience. Understanding is attained through work in *the hermeneutic circle.* The idea is that we understand the components of a text from the context they are a part of, but at the same time we only understand the whole of the text on the basis of its constituent parts. Hermeneutics does not, however, merely apply to the understanding of texts. Its object of study is any material expression of human thought; e.g., architecture, literature, art, or law. Dilthey encapsulates all these manifestations of human activity in his concept *objective spirit.* What does it mean to "understand" a text, for instance? According to Dilthey, *re-experience* is the answer. The interpreter gains understanding by putting himself in the place of the author and viewing the world through his eyes. According to Gadamer, however, we must not attempt to look past our *prejudices* about the thing we seek to understand. Our prejudices are based on tradition and are, in fact, a precondition for our being able to interpret a handed-down product of culture. Interpretation is about testing our prejudices. According to Gadamer, the goal is therefore not re-experience but a *fusion of horizons.* Although the text's horizon of understanding must be acknowledged for its foreignness, working with the text will simultaneously elevate the understanding of both author and interpreter, thus forming a new and enhanced synthesis.

According to the structuralists, the objects of the sciences are never directly available. They must be constructed. In the field of linguistics, Saussure does this by distinguishing between *diachrony* and *synchrony*; i.e., between an historical and a structural perspective on language respectively, and by emphasizing that the sciences should primarily be synchronic studies. Saussure also believed that the object of the sciences is not the conscious expression of mankind's social life but rather the structures underlying conscious social conventions. In linguistics, this results in his distinction between *langue* and *parole*; language as structure (grammatical and phonetic rules, etc.) and as practical language use. Language as structure is the object of science, and it consists of signs. A sign is the combination of a sound pattern and the concept the sound pattern refers to. In Saussure's terminology it is a combination of *signifiant* (the signifier) and *signifié* (the signified). This unity is not inherent, but arbitrary. For this reason, the sign has no intrinsic meaning but acquires meaning on the basis of its distinctiveness from all other signs. In this way, *language* is a *system of differences*, which gives the individual signs meaning.

Lévi-Strauss applies Saussure's approach to anthropology. According to him, the task of this science is to explore how human consciousness is shaped by the fundamental structures of society. This view is termed *theoretical anti-humanism.* Lévi-Strauss uncovers the structures that regulate our interactions. In doing this, he demonstrates how even greatly differing societies organize social life similarly by *classification through opposition,* that is, by organizing the world according to binary opposites.

Althusser represents a third structuralist approach. In his view, texts express the duality of the conscious expression of the author and the societal structures to which they also belong. Althusser's *symptomal reading* treats the contradictions in the texts as symptoms of the texts' suppression of fundamental economic conflicts in society. With his *deconstruction*, Derrida further develops this reading strategy not to reconstruct texts, but to demonstrate how every text contains contradictions that render it meaningless.

Social constructivism is inspired by Kuhn and, not least, by Wittgenstein's concepts of language game and life-form. With the term *language game,* Wittgenstein refers to the different contexts of usage, which provide our words and sentences with meaning. The view that we live our lives through language games, can be summarized by his concept, *life-form.*

Language does not function by means of its reference to a non-linguistic reality but is metaphorical, hence the social constructivist idea of *the metaphoricity of language.* Seeing that we construct the world through language, the key to understanding the oppression of minorities, for instance, can be found in the way we speak about them. *Identity politics* is an attempt to improve the conditions of marginalized social groups by problematizing the way in which oppression is reproduced in the dominant discursive construction of these groups.

After considering how Bruno Latour's anthropological study of a biology laboratory leads him to conclude that the "hard facts" of the natural sciences are also constructions, we examined Pierre Bourdieu's criticism of science. In his view, social life is divided into a number of different *fields,* for example the sciences, with different types of *symbolic capital* (what gives individuals acknowledgment and respect—in short, social status—in the separate fields). The field governs how we behave without us having to think about it, and Bourdieu calls this unreflective, bodily knowledge about the practices of the field, *habitus.* Finally, we considered how he applied these concepts to criticize science: it is not just a social construction, but also a construction that reflects and thus reproduces the social inequality of society. As a consequence, the social sciences especially must attempt a *double objectifica-*

tion. Researchers must not only study the object of their science, but also consider their own backgrounds to become aware of their personal prejudices. This is the only way to ensure that these prejudices do not influence their research.

Some Themes in the Philosophies of the Social Sciences

A number of the most significant differences between the three schools of thought can be summarized in four headlines.

Firstly, they disagree as to whether the social sciences differ from the natural sciences. As we have seen, this distinction is fundamental to the hermeneuticians. The natural sciences *explain* and the human and social sciences *interpret* in order to reach understanding. The structuralists and poststructuralists are partly in agreement. They (Althusser being the exception) study the semiotic structures of society—sign systems—which are manmade; therefore, the object of study differs in the natural and social sciences. At the same time, the structuralists would claim that the contrast of these two branches of science in hermeneutics goes too far. The difference of their object does not imply that the goals of the human and social sciences must be "understanding" in the hermeneutic sense. Structuralism, for example, offers a different approach to this same area of study. On the other hand, this criticism has led prominent hermeneuticians to accuse structuralists of applying the approach of the natural sciences to the subject matter of the social sciences. Finally, we have seen how the borders between the natural and social sciences are completely erased according to some social constructivists, for example Latour. The difference between the two disciplines is something we construct in our language, as are these disciplines themselves. "Nature" and "culture" are only distinguishable within the frame of our common discursive construction of reality. To overstate this, one could say that social constructivists abolish the distinction between these two forms of science by dissolving them both in language. There is thus really only social science, as our ideas of "nature" are social constructions.

Secondly, each of the three schools of thought views the question of the object of the sciences differently. According to the hermeneuticians, the researchers must attempt to understand the products of culture; e.g., texts, on their own terms. The thoughts, intentions and horizon of understanding of the author must be respected. Without this respect the text is abused and "over-interpreted". However, the structuralists and poststructuralists completely disagree that the object of scientific studies is the author's consciousness. On the contrary, they believe the researcher must aim at uncovering the unconscious structures that shape this consciousness. The text is not explained by the author's person but rather by the societal structures that influence the author and thereby the text. Finally, social constructivism differs from both these positions. It claims that both author and structures are linguistic constructions and that neither possesses greater scientific validity than the other. We can, however, be critical of how these perspectives affect our way of understanding the world and each other. Whichever narrative we choose, whether it is consciousness, structures or something else entirely, determines how we shape our collective life in society. Choosing between different approaches is more about their practical consequences than their truth-value.

Thirdly, we are dealing with different understandings of language. According to the hermeneuticians, language is important and meaningful because it expresses human thought. According to the structuralists, "language" is an imprecise concept. We must instead distinguish between language as usage (parole) and as system (langue). Language acquires meaning through the signs' system of difference. Finally, the social constructivists would claim that the meaning of words is not acquired from an "inner" process of thought or from a semiotic structure, but instead from our daily interaction with one another in different language games. Using language practically in a number of different contexts of application is what provides meaning, not the thought or structure "underlying" this application.

Fourthly, the three schools of thought disagree about the status and purpose of the sciences themselves. The hermeneuticians believe that the sciences have a special part to play in acquiring knowledge, although their goal can never be absolute truth. An interpretation will never be definite; instead, it is governed by a context, which in time will change and make reinterpretation necessary. At the same time, Gadamer rejects what many have considered to be a key element of science: the use of a specific method. According to his perspective, being fixated on a particular method hinders true understanding of the object of study. Contrary to this, the structuralists believe that the sciences are capable of uncovering truth about the fundamental structures of human society (interestingly, in this matter they disagree with the post-structuralists, who aim to deconstruct any "truth"). Lévi-Strauss also admits that science is merely one of many ways of viewing the world. It should not be considered "better" or more valuable than the mythical explanations of indigenous peoples. Different narratives have different functions and qualities. Structuralists do not see any problem in providing methodological precepts, yet these do not determine what is and is not science. What characterizes the sciences is the construction of a well-defined object and not a specific method. Finally, many social constructivists would agree with Lévi-Strauss that science is merely one of many narratives. They would, however, add that it therefore makes no sense to claim that science uncovers an "objective truth". The concept of truth only makes sense in the scientific language game that constructs "truth". The ambition of the social constructivist researchers is thus not to "uncover the world as it actually is", because even their own results are only valid in the language games that engender them. Instead, their ambition is to make us more aware of, and to question, the ways in which we normally speak about the world. This might in turn enable a change in the language games that maintain, for example, the discrimination or oppression of certain social groups. The hermeneuticians and the structuralists would, however, agree that many social constructivists place too much emphasis on language. Although it is a central element in both societal life and the life of the individual, language is still just one among many other elements.

The Knowledge Worker and the Philosophies of the Social Sciences

Similar to positivism and critical rationalism, the philosophies of science examined in the second part of this book have left their mark on the methodologies of the business sciences. Structuralism can be rediscovered in the methodology that Arbnor and Bjerke term *the system's view* (Arbnor and Bjerke 2009: 273–297). Contrary to the analytical method, this approach focuses on the contextual understanding of complex structures (e.g., organizations); thus, these are not to be analyzed by being broken down into their constituent parts. Social constructivism, on the other hand, can be found in the *actor's view*, which focuses on how we collectively construct our social reality (Arbnor and Bjerke 2009: 273–297; 298321).

The knowledge worker does not, however, need to study methodology to recognize the significance of the three theories presented in this part of the book. As these are directed at the social sciences, they have an immediate relevance to the understanding of the way in which we interact in social contexts; for example, in an organization.

Human beings will always interpret each other's behaviour spontaneously whenever interacting. Why does the contract include this particular clause? Why does management use this particular phrase when describing the challenges of the firm? The knowledge worker who is familiar with hermeneutics will have acquired tools that enable him to ask these types of questions systematically and thoroughly, and naturally this will strengthen his understanding. For instance, he will not merely stand by, puzzled by the language of management, but instead he will examine the context with the aim of understanding the underlying intent.

If an organization is dysfunctional, it is often because of structural problems. These have nothing to do with the individual staff members, and one can therefore not make them disappear by dismissing a number of employees. The problems lie in the social dynamics of the organization, and these dynamics in turn can only be understood by looking at the organization's structure. Perhaps the division of responsibilities and tasks among the employees is inappropriate and contributes to creating a poor working environment or low productivity. The knowledge worker acquainted with structuralism will be well equipped to solve the difficulties in an organization, because he will look for structural problems rather than waste his time searching for a scapegoat among the employees.

It is universally acknowledged that the way we discursively construct our common reality is of great significance. The employees of an organization react differently to "efficiency improvement" than to "cut-backs" despite their results being identical. The significance that our social construction of reality has for an organization goes, however, beyond the mere manipulation of employees. A management tool such as *appreciative inquiry* is clearly inspired by social constructivism. Among other things, it recommends that the focus of employees be directed at what already functions well in the company, which in turn can be further built upon when aiming to make even greater improvements. On this basis, organizational change can then be set into motion through the articulation of the visions one hopes to realize. If employees can be made to collectively think and talk about the future appearance of the organization and the means of change, then change is already underway.

Questions

1. In your opinion, what should the social sciences focus on when trying to understand society: human thought, social structures, or our collective construction of reality?
2. Which views of human nature are implied by the three philosophies of science discussed here?
3. Select an (real or imaginary) assignment from your own field of study. Explain how you would solve the question differently, depending on whether you approach it according to hermeneutics, structuralism, or social constructivism.

4. Give suggestions on the different ways in which you could imagine using hermeneutics, structuralism, and social constructivism in your future life as a knowledge worker.
5. Return to the questions in chapter 1. Discuss them again, but this time in light of the chapters about the philosophies of the social sciences. How would each of the different positions answer the questions?

Part 3
Selected Themes in the Philosophy of the Social Sciences

Unlike the first two parts, the third part of the book does not consider individual positions in philosophy of science. It deals instead with three issues that are all concerned with the role of research in society. But what is society? We will consider this question first, and we will do so by examining three authors considered the founders of sociology (i.e., the science of the social). Then we will take a look at the institutional basis for science—the universities—and at the relationship between research and politics. More specifically, we will focus on the question of whether scientists ought to consider the societal consequences of their research; i.e., whether the sciences should be political. Finally, we will consider the ethical aspects of the sciences. This question is not only relevant in relation to the way in which scientific studies are carried out, but also when assessing the consequences that scientific results may have for our way of living together as human beings.

The object of all the social sciences is obviously society; however, what is society really? What constitutes it? This is the topic dealt with by sociology, which means "the study of the social" (i.e., the science of how humans live together and interact with one another). For this reason it is relevant to anyone concerned with social science.

In this chapter, we will take a closer look at three classical views of what characterizes society and the science concerning it. These three points of view are put forward by authors who are considered to be the founders of sociology: Émile Durkheim, Karl Marx, and Max Weber. Their positions form the basis for some of the most influential traditions in sociology.

Despite their differences, the three authors agree on a number of fundamental issues. They all seek to understand what characterizes a society and how the social sciences should operate. These questions are of special interest to the philosophy of the social sciences and will therefore be a central consideration here.

Émile Durkheim and the Inspiration from Positivism

Many would say that we must examine separate individuals to understand the community they belong to, because surely society is nothing more than a large group of individuals. As a matter of fact, the Frenchman Émile Durkheim (1858–1917) wished to be rid of this exact preconception. Society is full of institutions that are not based on the individual, yet they regulate individual behaviour. For example, the morals of society cannot be reduced to the morals of a person or group, yet they regulate the way human beings behave. No one "controls" morals, but we are all controlled by them, also if we choose to break with them. The same applies to, for example, religion.

According to Durkheim, morals and religion demonstrate that society is something other and more than the sum of the individuals, which are a part of it (Durkheim 1972: 96). These phenomena are *social facts,* which constitute the object of sociology.

> **!** **Social Facts:** According to Durkheim, social facts are behavioural patterns and conventions in society that coerce the individual, although they exist independently of every individual.

Durkheim also considers religion and morality to be *institutions.* Because of this, he is able to characterize sociology as the science of institutions (Durkheim 1972: 3–18). This raises the question of how this science is to study its object.

Durkheim is inspired by his fellow countryman Comte, and thus by positivism and its idea of a unitary science, with the natural sciences acting as the model. He believes, therefore, that society must be examined according to the same principles that, according to the positivists, apply to physics and chemistry (Durkheim 1972: 43). Sociology must be the study of facts and the sociologist must refrain from making value judgments. He is not to raise moral questions such as: What characterizes the good society? Working scientifically means to observe and describe society objectively and neutrally similarly to the way a physiologist regards and describes the human body.

Observations must reveal causal relations in social life in the same way the physicist discovers causal relations in nature, and this causality must also be social. In other words, social life must be explained by reference to social, but not individual, facts (Durkheim 1972: 101). The explanation must uncover the cause and function of societal phenomena.

Since the goal is to uncover causal relations, the sociologist must focus on what is normal and regular in his observations of society and not consider the aspects that deviate from normalcy—what Durkheim refers to as the pathological (the sickly). Normalcy is what characterizes the members of a species in general, while pathological phenomena characterize only a few members and are often temporary. According to Durkheim, the normal is also considered the average type or the normal type, while deviations are pathological (Durkheim 1972: 61–62).

To be more specific, according to Durkheim, the sociologists, based on their observations of social life, must put forward hypotheses that will aid them in organizing their empirical material, discover regularities herein, and prove these regularities. Another working tool is classification. In Durkheim's view, different societies can be classified by analyzing their constituent elements: i.e., the groups that are part of them. Durkheim termed this aspect of sociology concerned with classifying social types, social morphology (Durkheim 1972: 76–80).

If this is Durkheim's manifesto for sociology, which practical results will it lead to? How does this approach gain him insight into the role that social institutions play in the collective life of mankind? The answer can be summarized by the concept *collective consciousness.*

! **Collective Consciousness:** Durkheim's term for social institutions, such as religion and morals, that control individual behaviour, function in the individual consciousness, but exist independently of the individual.

As mentioned, we all play a part in society's moral code. We know what is socially accepted behaviour, and this knowledge controls our lives. Precisely because everyone is included in the moral code, it becomes clear that morals cannot be bound to each separate person's individual consciousness. These do not disappear when the individual dies. Morality is independent of each of us, even though we all share in it, and it is because we all share in it that it influences us. In this sense, morality is an example of Durkheim's concept of social institutions as a collective consciousness. Our language is another example. We live our lives through language, and it exists in every separate person's individual consciousness; however, at the same time, language exists independently of the individual, and both morals and language will outlive us all.

Collective consciousness thus connects people to the society they are a part of, and individuals experience themselves as social beings because they share in this consciousness. Furthermore, society as a whole becomes aware of itself and its history through the collective consciousness, the original form of which is religion (Durkheim 1972b: 239–249). According to Durkheim, religion is therefore not primarily characterized by the idea of a deity. There is no god in Buddhism for instance. What really characterizes religion is that it functions as a collective consciousness that unites a society and imparts on it a strong sense of community. Unlike the idea of a deity, the distinction between the sacred and the profane (un-sacred) is central to religion. On the basis of this distinction, it is able to establish taboos (i.e., forbid certain behaviour). Religion is a community, and one can be accepted into this community by heeding its taboos.

By emphasizing the significance of the taboo in religion, Durkheim has already connected it to morals. Morals, in their origin, constitute the observance of the rules of religion. Through this adherence, we display solidarity with the society we are a part of. Morals are therefore first of all based on rules, not actions. We obey the rules because the moral code tells us to, not because certain actions are inherently reprehensible. Herein lies the obligatory nature of morality (Durkheim 1972b: 89–107).

Durkheim's answer to the two questions formulated above is therefore that the social institutions that unite people are what characterize society. For this reason, the sciences must focus on these institutions in their attempt to understand society. According to Durkheim, researchers must adopt a positivistic approach; i.e., they must observe social facts in an objective and unbiased manner.

The next author we will consider is Karl Marx. He has a very different view of both society and social science.

Karl Marx: Science, Politics, and Ideology

Among all the authors examined in this book, none has been as influential as Karl Marx. Theorists as diverse as Lévi-Strauss, Althusser, Habermas, Sartre, Weber, and Bourdieu have all been inspired by his work.

Does this mean that Marx himself was a philosopher of science? As a matter of fact, he was not. Marx was a politician, a journalist, and a social theorist. On the basis of this, he strongly criticized the way contemporary researchers and philosophers understood the sciences and their role in society. The first and most important question of this section is, thus, what Marx considers to be the problem with philosophy and the sciences.

It is not difficult to find an answer, as it is clearly formulated by Marx in one of the world's most famous aphorisms: "The philosophers have only *interpreted* the world in various ways; the point is, to *change* it" (Marx 1994: 98). However, the clarity of this statement is misleading. What does it mean to "change the world"? As we will come to see, it means different things but, first and foremost, Marx believes that we, as people and as society, cannot avoid "changing the world". We need food on the table and a roof over our heads, and since food does not simply drop from the heavens, the first characteristic of the life of the individual and society is the necessity of "bringing home the bacon".

For the same reason, any understanding of the world must take its point of departure in work and production. This is a fundamental necessity.

Therefore, "to change the world" first of all means to work and to produce. Metaphysicians have missed this aspect for centuries while discussing how "man" differs from animals. According to Marx, this discussion could have been avoided, if they had just glanced out the window and noted that humans quite specifically differ from animals, by *producing* the material foundation of their existence (Marx 1953: 17).

The positivists criticized metaphysics as well, but, according to Marx, they had no reason to do so, as they in fact share its prejudice. As we have seen, the positivists believe that the road to true knowledge is "objective" observation. Marx claims that this is a classical metaphysical prejudice. According to him, we do not primarily understand the world through observation, but through our productive interaction with the world. Furthermore, this interaction is always concrete. This means that it is not "objective" but practical, i.e. determined by a specific place, time, and purpose. In other words, we always view the world practically; we are never a disconnected "eye" soaring above the world and observing it from above. Marx uses the concept *ideology* to describe the way our understanding of the world is tied to our practice (Marx 1953).

> **Ideology:** According to Marx, we always view the world and ourselves on the basis of our function in society. Our worldview reflects this function and does not, therefore, possess objective validity. The concept of ideology expresses the correlation between our daily practice and our worldview. At the same time, Marx also uses it to explain how the differences of power in society lead to the manipulation of human consciousness.

To properly understand the consequences of Marx's concept of ideology, one must, however, transcend the narrow epistemological horizon of understanding and instead take a look at the society in which individuals and groups produce their own lives as well as their worldviews, as the conflicts in society mean that the function of ideology is not only epistemological but also political.

Marx's Criticism of Capitalism

According to Marx, production in modern society is characterized by being based on the investment of capital, or monetary sums, which the owners do not actually need for immediate survival. The owners of this capital (the capitalists) control the production of society and therefore secure the profits it makes. This type of production requires a market society where products can immediately be sold and converted into new capital and where most production is for the market. Marx calls this combination of production and market society, *capitalism* (Marx 1970).

! **Capitalism:** The production of a modern society is characterized by its:

1) Being based on the investment of capital.
2) Being based on buying labour from people who do not possess capital.
3) Being a production aimed at a market.

These three features characterize capitalist production.

Capitalism requires another crucial precondition: labour must be a commodity that can be bought on a labour market. This precondition is the key to understanding why the great political conflicts of modern societies stem directly from the way their production is carried out. Labour can only be bought because the majority of the population (the workers) are unable to live off their own capital, as they have none. When people have no capital, they are forced to sell their labour; thus, capitalist production is conditioned by great economic inequality between different social groups. Moreover, it sustains these inequalities, as only the owners of capital receive the profits of production. The social divisions in modern society are therefore not individual coincidences. They are systematically reproduced because of the way all of society's production is organized. Different groups thus have fundamentally unequal living conditions, and it is this continuous reproduction of social division that establishes capitalism as a *class society*. At the same time, the inner social tension of society leads to a chaotic societal development, where intense economic growth is replaced at intervals by deep crisis (Marx 1970: 649).

> ! **Classes and Class Society:** A society is a class society when one or more groups monopolize society's means of production and thus the values that are created. Because of the unequal control of social production, this society constantly reproduces fundamentally unequal living conditions for the population. Marx calls these different living conditions, classes.

Capitalism is not merely a way of producing, it also constitutes the constant reproduction of social inequality. The rich become richer at the expense of the poor, because they monopolize the factories and machines—the means of production—which the entire society relies upon to thrive and develop. This is where we discover the political point of Marx's emphasis on "changing the world". If one is to do something about the social inequalities, then society must be transformed and change must begin at the very source of these inequalities: the capitalist monopoly of the production of society. In other words, Marx wants to get rid of capitalism: Becoming rich at the expense of others should no longer be possible.

According to Marx, any class society will always contain an element of what he refers to as class struggle (Marx 1970: 998–1025), i.e. political and social tensions due to the relations of exploitation between the classes. The question is, then, how so few capitalists are able to preserve their position of power in spite of the class struggle, when the workers constitute the majority. Why do the workers not revolt? The state apparatus might be there to keep the order, but this apparatus is also made up of regular wage earners like, for example, policemen or prison wardens. The answer to this question has to do with the concept we mentioned to begin with: ideology.

Science as Critique of Ideology

As stated above, we create our understanding of the world through our practical interactions with it, as well as with each other; however, what is it that dictates these interactions? It is capitalism. The entire modern society is shaped by capital and its central concern with the creation of constant economic growth to the benefit of the business owners. This is, among other things, the goal of modern wage labour—a life form created for and by capitalism. And as capitalism comes to define our practical interactions, it also comes to control the manner in which we understand the world and ourselves. This is how ideology contributes to stabilizing class society in the interest of the ruling classes. When we today consider wage labour as a natural way of life, it is because of capital's dominance (it defines what we consider to be "natural"), and at the same time it prohibits us from adopting a critical distance from capitalist society (you do not rebel against something that you consider to be natural).

Previously, religion constituted the best example of how the ideology of the upper classes manipulated the poor into accepting the present circumstances. The priests told the peasants to refrain from rebelling against the squires and instead find comfort in going to heaven *after* death. This is the reason for Marx's famous description of religion being the "opium of the people" (Marx 1994: 28). Contemporary Marxist researchers have pointed out that the educational system has the same function in modern society. For two decades, the child and adolescent is indoctrinated to respect authorities, exhibit discipline, and carry out a well-defined function in social production without questioning its fairness and ownership relations (Althusser 1976: 92).

By means of the problem of ideology, Marx is the first theorist to ever thematize the way in which economic resources can be converted or translated to other resources, first and foremost, to ideological dominance. The question is where the sciences position themselves in this discussion. The concept of ideology clearly contains a strong criticism of classical philosophy and the sciences. It is no coincidence that they have "overlooked" the significance of social production for human knowledge and society. In other words, classical science and philosophy are also ideological; they have consistently seen the world from the perspective of the ruling classes.

This is why Marx's concept of ideology is so provoking. It is not just a philosophical idea about the correlation between practice and thought. It is an attack, not only on the content of philosophy and science, but also on the traditional self-understanding of these disciplines. In reality, they have never sought nor found eternal and universally valid truths about the world and society; instead, the researchers' theories, without their being aware of it, have functioned as the most abstract expression of concrete, historical class interests.

This is also the reason why we must view Marx's concept of ideology in light of his critique of capitalism. First of all, ideology can only be understood according to its function in a specific historical class society. Secondly, Marx's criticism is aimed at this function, and thirdly, the purpose of this critique is not theoretical but political. Marx wishes to raise the workers' awareness and clear the way for a confrontation with capitalism. This is obvious when he criticizes classical economists, such as Adam Smith and David Ricardo (1772–1823). His critique is not just based on their lack of understanding of the capitalist economy but also on the political (i.e., ideological) function of this lack of understanding (Marx 1970).

Nevertheless, Marx is not a relativist. He does not reject the sciences. On the contrary, he considers his own criticism of, for instance, the classical economists as being scientific. According to Marx, the sciences must therefore be a *critique of ideology*. In other words, their task is to identify ideological prejudices in texts as well as in other cultural products.

! **Critique of Ideology:** As critique of ideology, research is concerned with analyzing, for example, a text to show which ideological prejudices are hidden therein. In order to perform this task, the sciences must apply the same criticism to themselves.

The purpose of science as critique of ideology is: firstly, to make these prejudices evident so they can be discussed and considered critically; and secondly, to strengthen the theoretical foundation of the left-wing political struggle. This is the third meaning of Marx's message to change the world: science and philosophy must be changed so they can contribute to society's development in a more democratic direction.

The critique of ideology is one of the elements of Marx's work that has most inspired the sciences in later years. Symptomal reading, Althusser's strategy of (textual) reading, is one of the many suggestions of how to perform it in practice. To this day, the critique of ideology is still being developed, for example, by the Slovenian philosopher Slavoj Žižek (born 1949).

As mentioned earlier, Marx's political significance comes from the modern European left wing (social democrats, communist parties, and trade unions) taking his work to heart and making it the theoretical foundation of their agenda; however, from a scientific point of view, his analyses of society are of particular interest. They mark a milestone in the development of the social sciences. Finally, from a philosophical perspective, Marx is interesting because he united all these different themes in his theory: science, philosophy, politics, philosophy of science, and practical work. This constitutes such a revolutionary breakthrough that the discussion of how his works are to be understood goes on to this day.

Marx's answers to our two questions are as follows: a society is many different things, but first of all it is our collective production of society. The task of the sciences is therefore primarily to create an overview of the organization of this production and the way in which it influences one's way of acting and thinking. The critique of ideology establishes this connection between production and thought.

Max Weber: A Hermeneutic Understanding of Society

What is the object of the social sciences? According to Max Weber

(1864–1920), the answer is social behaviour; i.e. actions aimed at others. Behaviour, of course, is individual, and seeing that this is the object of study of the social sciences, they can therefore not disregard the individual. The attempt to understand the social must, on the contrary, start with the individual and his actions. This view is termed *methodological individualism* (Weber 2003b: 192–207). It is, however, important not to misunderstand Weber's point. He does not consider the individual to be especially valuable or significant. In this sense "individualism" exclusively means understanding social phenomena on the basis of the motives and actions of the individual person.

! **Methodological Individualism:** The view that the point of departure of sociology is the interpretation of individual behaviour.

Seeing that Weber has established that researchers must make the study of individual behaviour their point of departure, it becomes natural to ask: How are they to study it? The concept "behaviour" may seem to imply that Weber agrees with the behaviourism of positivism, but this could not be further from the truth.

Weber is namely inspired by hermeneutics. This causes him to view positivism very critically, as the positivists do not take into account that the object of social science is the person as a cultural being. Having culture means to have an opinion of the world, to infuse it with meaning, and to have intentions. Positivistic observations are unable to capture this; they are only capable of describing *how* human beings behave, not *why* they behave as they do. According to Weber, the goal of the sciences, on the other hand, is *to understand* human behaviour.

Behaviour can mean many different things. A man hiding behind a tree may be lying in wait to attack a passer by. He may, however, also be hiding from people wanting to attack him. If we are to understand his behaviour, we must understand the *meaning* of it (Weber 2003b: 196). It is rarely made clear by the action itself, and for this reason it is necessary to relate to and identify with the motives of the actors; however, there are limits to the hermeneutic inspiration. For instance,

Weber does not share the hermeneutic aversion to causal explanations. They play an important role in scientific understanding although they cannot stand alone. Sociology must therefore integrate the aspects of causality and meaning into a collected account of the studied behaviour (Weber 2003b: 198).

So far, we have seen how Weber pinpoints what he believes is the object and method of sociology by, first of all, demarcating his position in relation to positivism. Inspired by hermeneutics, the sciences must understand human behaviour and must therefore be based on a methodological individualism. Yet how are they to progress from the individual? It is not self-explanatory. What should individual meaning be compared to? Weber's answer to this is contained in his concept of *ideal types.*

Weber's Application of Ideal Types

What do "power", "democracy", "Christianity", or "capitalism" mean? What do these concepts encompass "in the real world"? On scratching the surface just a little, one will quickly come to the conclusion that they encompass far too much to be functional. The unambiguous nature of the concepts contrasts with the complexity of reality; therefore, applying them directly and unreflectively poses a problem. This problem can, however, be solved by means of Weber's understanding that the concepts, in fact, do not refer to anything "in the real world", but must instead be compared to reality if we are to better understand the latter. In this sense, concepts function as ideal types (Weber 2003: 106).

> **Ideal Types:** Weber's tool for understanding social phenomena. The ideal type encapsulates recurring characteristic features of, for example, power, democracy, or Christianity, in the different ways these phenomena have been expressed at different times. The ideal type does not, therefore, correspond to a specific historical example of what the concept covers, but it can be used to guide the study of historical reality.

When constructing an ideal type, you begin by considering reality. For example, when working with the issue of "the political consumer", you must begin by taking a look at the different historical examples of, among other things, the consumer boycott of companies. These examples may vary greatly, but among this empirical multitude there will still be a few recurring characteristic features, even though they are not realized to the same extent in all cases. The sociologist can then create an ideal image of the behaviour of political consumers based on the summarization of these characteristic features. It does not constitute a portrayal of a single case, but rather of the common features of a number of different political conflicts in which consumer behaviour has been significant. The image is not ideal in the sense of it being exemplary—an ideal to strive after. It is ideal because it does not exist "in reality", but only "as an idea"; as the summation of those common features that enable us to use the same concept, "the political consumer", in a number of different cases.

What can we use an ideal type for? As we have said, it is neither a model to be followed nor a description of a historical reality, which can subsequently be studied in real life. Ideal types do not exist in the real world, but are thought constructions based on real world experience. We can, however, use them to put forward hypotheses (Weber 2003: 105–106). If we have an ideal typical picture of the political consumer, we can construct a hypothesis of how the concrete example of political consumer behaviour that we wish to study shares some of these ideal typical features. In brief, we can use the ideal types by comparing them to reality in our attempt to understand it. They are not the goal of scientific study, but an important tool for it.

Weber's use of ideal types reflects his understanding that the sciences do not deal with *things* but with *problems* (Weber 2003: 84), and unlike things, problems are not physical; therefore, it does not matter that ideal types are thought constructions. They must be assessed solely on their ability to make us more knowledgeable about reality.

How are these types employed in practice? First of all, different contexts in which (for example) political consumer behaviour has been found can be studied. This might include the boycott of French wines and the boycott of Shell in the mid-1990s, and it could include the American consumers' boycott of French goods up to the outbreak of the war in Iraq. After this, the characteristic features that recur in most of these contexts are summed up to construct an ideal picture of the political consumer. Finally, one can put forward hypotheses that can be tested on historical reality. This could, for example, be the hypothesis that a specific example of political consumer behaviour is characterized by being controlled by a single issue.

Weber uses the ideal types when working with a number of different issues. Among other things, this applies to the study of what the concept "legitimate authority" really encompasses (Weber 2003b: 173–188). Here, Weber distinguishes between three different main types. The execution of power can legitimize itself by reference to rational rules (for example, when a social worker refuses to help a social client with the excuse that: Those are the rules) or to personal authority (for example, when the king, in ages past, could demand obedience solely because he was king). Power can also be legitimized because of a person's charisma. This is typical of the power exerted by a religious leader.

Three forms of government correspond to the three forms of legitimate authority: bureaucratic, patriarchal, and charismatic leadership. Weber is primarily concerned with *bureaucracy* because, in his view, our modern world is characterized by an extensive bureaucratization. Let us follow him in his work with this particular ideal type.

Bureaucracy: An Example of an Ideal Type

What characterizes modern bureaucracy's ideal type? Weber counts several characteristic features. The civil servant's area of responsibility is clearly defined and delimited, and positions are filled on the basis of previously defined qualifications. Administration is organized hierarchically; it is precisely defined to whom each government official is to refer, and administration follows clear rules. In this way, civil service operates like a well-oiled machine or military organization.

> **Bureaucracy:** According to Weber, this is the predominant form of modern government, which has progressively organized society as a whole according to its own purposeful, rational way of operating. Bureaucracy is a very efficient form of organization, yet it simultaneously imprisons people in an "iron cage of rationality".

As we have already noted, bureaucracy, as an ideal type, plays an important role in Weber's work. Because of its efficiency, the bureaucratic organization has ended up permeating and changing the entire modern society and the people who are a part of it. The individual civil servant considers work both a calling and a duty. He may well be appointed by a superior, yet his loyalty is not to this person. He is loyal to the purpose and rules of the institution, and, in return, the institution ensures him a secure existence, high social standing, and lifelong employment. The bureaucrat is, however, also tied to civil service; his life is planned out as a "running track", allowing little room for individual expression. According to Weber, he is "chained" to his office (Weber 2003b: 95).

The development in the educational sector is an important example of the bureaucratization of society (Weber 2003b: 106–111). Previously, people were educated to become "cultivated", not to obtain a degree. Education was the privilege of a small upper class, whose earnings were not dependent on this education; however, with the rise of bureaucracy, a need for a standardized workforce with well-defined competencies emerged. Education increasingly became technical training and the course of education was standardized at the expense of personal cultivation. With the disappearance of the latter, the diploma itself becomes socially prestigious. Being educated is no longer a matter of being cultivated but of obtaining a diploma.

The development of the educational system illustrates well the consequences of the bureaucratization of society. On the one hand, it leads to a great increase in efficiency, while on the other hand all of social life becomes increasingly dictated by purposeful rationality, the principle of the bureaucratic mode of operation (Weber 2003b: 106–111). This limits the free development of the individual, as there is less room for actions motivated by, say, emotions or values. Weber considers this development with such gravity that he famously likens modern, bureaucratized individuals to those living life imprisoned in an "iron cage of rationality".

The educational institutions are part of this iron cage, and modern students, as well as their teachers, are a product of a bureaucratization that has spread to all areas of social life. Educational institutions in fact play a central part in this development, as they produce the actual raw material of civil service: top-ranking functionaries. Weber therefore problematizes the role of universities in society and thus points towards the questions we will consider in the next chapter, including: Should researchers reflect more critically on the impact of their activities in society and politics?

But before we get to that, let us summarize Weber's answers to our two basic questions on the basis of the above example. Society must be understood according to the social behaviour of individuals; for instance, a bureaucracy is made up of the functions and conduct of civil servants. We understand behaviour through work with ideal types, in this case, with "bureaucracy" as the ideal type. In this way, the example demonstrates both the object and method of the sciences.

What Is a Society? A Summary

As we have seen, according to Durkheim, the social sciences must study social facts: collective phenomena of consciousness, such as religion, morals, and language. These phenomena are institutions governing the life of the individual, but existing independently of all individuals. The institutions must be examined through objective and neutral observation.

In Marx's view, society must be understood according to the way in which we create and maintain it through productive work. The distinction between the individual and the collective is less important because production can only be understood as a collective process. The historical conditions under which production takes place are, however, interesting to consider. These conditions are expressed at all levels of social life. The critique of ideology is Marx's method of showing how the roles different social groups play in production also find cultural and political expressions.

Weber differs from both Marx and Durkheim, as his point of departure is methodological individualism. Through work with ideal types, he attempts to understand individual behaviour and pinpoint what characterizes the modernization of society. In his view, the key to understanding modernization is the bureaucratization of society, which spreads to all areas of life.

These three theorists each explain social development according to different constituent elements of our collective existence. Durkheim views mankind's *conscious* interaction, through for example morals and religion, as the defining element of social life and our self-understanding. According to Marx, the sciences must be based on the analysis of social production. Weber finds himself between the study of ideas (Durkheim) and production (Marx). He is primarily interested in the forms of organization that constitute the framework of the individual's life. Both economics and ideas play a part in this, but institutions can never be reduced to either ideas or production.

Sociological Research in Practice

All social sciences must be based on an idea of what a society is and what characterizes one's social interactions. In other words, they must all make sociological assumptions. Because of this, sociology is applied across the entire knowledge level of social science.

Example: Sociology and Market Economy

The fact that sociological insight is the condition for understanding a modern, developed market economy may not be directly apparent; however, in an article from 2007, the German sociologist Jens Beckert explains why this is the case (Beckert 2007). The exchanging of goods is not, in itself, enough to ensure a stable economic system. Among other things, this also requires that buyer and seller trust one another, and trust cannot be explained by economics. It has social and cultural roots, and furthermore, it necessitates the existence of governmental institutions capable of punishing those who abuse the trust of others in the market. Trust must therefore be explained by social structures, governmental institutions, and cultural conventions; in short, it must be explained sociologically.

The market economy is thus not a self-reliant system. It requires a multitude of social relations. These must be studied when attempting to understand the way in which the economy functions. From this perspective, the task of the scientist is to account for how the social dynamics of society enable the economic system, by, for example, creating trust between the different actors in the market. Questions of this type have kept economic sociologists engaged since the 1970s.

Example: Sociology and Marketing

Sociological deliberation is also relevant on the practical level of knowledge. This is completely obvious when it comes to predicting and influencing consumer behaviour. For example, when planning an advertising campaign, the age, income, cultural background, et cetera of the target group must be taken into consideration. This information discloses details about the tone and social conventions of the group, and these must be respected in an advertising campaign, if the campaign is to be well received. Before the campaign, a sociological charting of the recipients must therefore be carried out. This is a precondition for successful communication, and therefore marketing requires sociological insight.

Example: The Austrian School of Macroeconomics

It is not surprising that two of the three classical sociological theorists we have considered in this chapter have had especially direct influence on the economic sciences. Marx's analysis has formed the foundation for the work of numerous Marxist economists. Weber's ideal types have inspired the Austrian school of macroeconomics. In particular, Alfred Schutz (1899–1959) argued in favour of using ideal types as a methodological tool (Koppl and Whitman 2004). According to him, their strength lies in the fact that they enable us to understand how actual historical actors think and act. They thereby constitute an important supplement to the rational choice models of neo-classical economics. In reality, human beings do not act as rationally and as optimally as is presumed by these models. Even when they apparently do follow the models, it is not always because of economic interests. For example, the commitment of professional football players to the game cannot be explained solely by the fact that they receive a bonus when winning. Commitment is caused by several other factors, not least the desire to not let their teammates down. Their commitment must therefore be understood on the basis of the norms of the group they are a part of; in other words, it must be understood sociologically. This cannot be done according to the rational choice perspective; however, an ideal type that takes economic, psychological, as well as social factors of motivation into account can be constructed.

Example: How *You* Can Work Sociologically

How can our group of students add a sociological aspect to their study of corporate communication? Obviously their problem and method will vary greatly according to which sociologist they are inspired by. In this chapter, we have looked at three classical approaches, but these are not the only ones. For example, the chapter about social constructivism discussed how Bourdieu, inspired by both Marx and Weber, subjected the question of the nature of scientific opinion polls to critical scrutiny. However, let us briefly consider the recommendations each of this chapter's three theorists would offer our students.

Durkheim would view corporate communication as a typical social fact. It does not depend on each individual employee but it still determines the individual's ways of expressing himself. Communication is carried out in one way in a travelling circus and in another at a large bank. The individual learns to adapt his individual expression to the organization. In this sense, corporate communication and the moral code of society are similar. To study corporate communication the students must observe it, while remaining as value neutral as possible. In this way they can create an overview of the characteristics of the company's "normal" communication, and it is this normality that must be their focus. For example, internal communication will typically differ greatly from external communication. Sometimes this distinction will not appear as clearly in individual cases, but the normal and regular is still what must be studied. Once the students have mapped out the communication of the company they can begin looking for causal relations in their collected material: Why does the company communicate in this particular way? The uncovering of these causal relations is the actual goal of the studies.

According to Marx, on the other hand, it will be interesting for the students to look into how society's ruling ideology is expressed in the company's communication, for instance in the way in which the organization presents itself to the public. It may, for instance, paint a picture of itself as a unity or maybe even as a community where everybody works towards a common goal and have common interests. Maybe this is how the employees themselves view the company, yet it is still an ideological narrative as it is based on the repression of the real conflicts of interest between owners and employees that characterize any company in a capitalist economy. Another example could be the internal communication between the employees, presenting work as something they do for fun, for the challenge, and to develop their own personal skills. While this may not be untrue, it is also an ideological view, as it overlooks the fact that the fundamental purpose of the work is to create a profit for the owners of the company. For Marx, the real purpose of examining the organization's communication would not simply be to unearth, but also to criticize ideological prejudice. Without this criticism, the employees will be unable to critically assess how the ideology is forming their way of thinking and talking—and that of the management as well.

Finally, Weber would recommend that our students begin by looking at different examples of corporate communication, not just examples from the specific company. In this way they will be able to gain an overview of what their object of study truly is. Once they have discovered the common features connecting the different examples, they will be able to construct an ideal typical concept of corporate communication. They can then use this ideal type to formulate hypotheses about the specific company's communication. These hypotheses can subsequently be compared to the actual communication observed in the company. By comparing the ideal type to the empirical material the characteristics of communication in this particular workplace will become clear.

Questions

1. Explain Durkheim's concept of social facts.
2. Explain what Durkheim's concept "collective consciousness" is referring to.
3. What characterizes capitalism according to Marx?
4. Explain Marx's concepts of class society and class struggle.
5. How are we to understand Marx's concepts of ideology and critique of ideology?
6. In what sense is Weber inspired by hermeneutics, and how is his methodological individualism to be understood?
7. Explain Weber's use of ideal types.
8. What characterizes bureaucracy as the most widespread modern form of government, according to Weber?
9. What assumptions are made about society and social life in your own field of study?
10. In your opinion, what are the strengths and weaknesses of the approaches of Durkheim, Marx, and Weber respectively?

Science, Politics, and Society

In this chapter, we will take a closer look at some of the most important views on the role the sciences play and ought to play in society; however, we need to start somewhere else, for the sciences do not merely drop from the sky to be received by an astounded public. They are actively produced, and this production mainly takes place at the universities and other institutions of higher education. We must therefore first take a look at the university to find out what it really is.

The University: Principles and History

In chapter 1, we noted how universities play a central part in the knowledge dynamics of modern society. The knowledge workers of the future are educated here. But what exactly is a university? For instance, what is the difference between a university and a high school?

The university institution has undergone great changes throughout the ages and is still under development; however, it is possible to point to principles that have remained relatively constant during its many organizational changes. The Danish philosopher, Hans Fink (born 1944), mentions five such principles (Fink, Kjærgaard, and Kristensen 2003: 9–29). A university is fundamentally characterized by the close connection between research and education; by the freedom of researchers to carry out research and teach as they find best; by the institution's self-governance; and by science being understood as a united whole. Let us take a closer look at these principles.

> **The Five Basic Principles of the University:**
> 1. Universities offer research-based teaching.
> 2. Researchers have the freedom to do research.
> 3. Researchers have the freedom to teach.
> 4. A university is a self-governing entity.
> 5. Universities, in principle, encompass all sciences.

The direct connection between research and education is often seen as the one thing that sets universities apart from other institutions of education. In practice, this connection is secured by active scientists being in charge of teaching. This means that students are provided with the newest knowledge within their fields of study, while researchers are given the opportunity to discuss their findings and results with their students. Furthermore, research-based teaching is conducive to the students' own independent studies.

The principle of freedom of research means that neither government nor church, nor other authorities, are to determine what must be researched, which methodology is to be applied, or how researchers are to publicize their studies. On the other hand, the scientific staff at the university are obligated to conduct research as well as publish the results of their studies. This principle is based on the experience that controlled research is poor research and that the best results for both the sciences and society are achieved if the government, for example, does not interfere with the work of researchers.

Freedom of teaching means that the individual researcher is at liberty to organize his teaching according to his own judgment. For instance, the Ministry of Education has not issued a decree that only one particular textbook on philosophy of science is to be used by lecturers in this particular field of study. For researchers, this freedom is a precondition for the ability to unite research and teaching, and it makes it easier to target their teaching to different groups of students.

The principle of self-governance originates in the Middle Ages, and has followed universities throughout their history. The underlying thought is that protecting the above-mentioned freedoms of research and teaching requires that neither government nor church be in direct control of the individual university.

Finally, the point of the sciences being perceived as a united whole is that a university in principle must encompass all known sciences. The classical university's division into faculties is an expression of this way of thinking. This principle must not, however, be confused with positivism's idea of a unitary science. The different sciences can vary greatly, and the same model should not be used for them all, but the university, as an institution, is what unites them.

From where do these principles originate? Some can be traced back to the Middle Ages, but this does not apply to, for instance, the principle of freedom of teaching. The institution we today recognize as the university has undergone a long development starting with the founding of the first universities in Paris, Bologna, and Oxford in the twelfth century. According to the Danish intellectual historians, Peter C. Kjærgaard and Jens Erik Kristensen (Fink, Kjærgaard, and Kristensen 2003: 35-90), the universities of the Middle Ages were not institutions of research, but centres for the preservation of knowledge handed down from antiquity and the church. Naturally, this led to a growing distance between a developing society and a retrospective university.

The seeds of the modern university were sown during the *Enlightenment,* in the second half of the eighteenth century (Fink, Kjærgaard, and Kristensen 2003: 80–90). The leading philosophers of the age believed society must be reformed and improved through critical reasoning and the enlightenment of the population, who, for the most part, were still poorly educated. For this reason, some of the philosophers of the Enlightenment, for example Voltaire, forcefully attacked the Catholic Church for being based on dogma and tradition rather than reason. This critique also affected the universities. For instance, it is reflected in the Danish Enlightenment playwright Ludvig Holberg's (1684–1754) satire about Erasmus Montanus, who returns to his village after having studied at university. He has acquired substantial amounts of irrelevant knowledge as well as a talent for useless pedantry, which he uses to "prove" that his own mother is a stone. In Holberg's view, the university student is a buffoon.

> **The Enlightenment:** The period in the eighteenth century in which the dominant view of philosophers and intellectuals is that society is to be improved through the enlightenment of the people (e.g., by education) and that society should be organized rationally. Enlightenment thus constitutes a violent attack on society's institutions, for instance, the church, because their authority was based on tradition and not rationality.

The German scientist and civil servant, Karl Wilhelm von Humboldt (1767–1835), reinvented the university in its modern form according to the principles outlined above. In 1810, he was behind the founding of a new university in Berlin, the model of which came to inspire the reformation of universities throughout the world. With Humboldt's reform, research became part of the university's core activities, and the principles of research-based teaching and the freedom of teaching and research were formulated (Fink, Kjærgaard, and Kristensen 2003: 91–102). Furthermore, the preparatory studies that previously constituted the first year of a university education were moved to preparatory schools, now known as upper secondary or high school. Moreover, Humboldt believed that studying at a university should not merely establish a path to education, but also to cultivation. It was intended to shape people with a cultural and intellectual perspective. The reason for this was the view that graduating "whole human beings", rather than specialized geeks, was more useful for society.

> **Humboldt's University:** The archetype of the modern universities inspired by the university Humboldt founded in Berlin in 1810. Here, teaching and research merge and the principles of freedom of teaching and research are formulated. At the same time, education is considered a project of cultivation.

To a great extent, Humboldt's vision for the modern university was determined by what he considered to be the need of society; thus, his reform is typical for the development of universities. Since their foundation, they have played a significant role in society, and for that same reason, an unstable relationship has existed between them and the various authorities of society. The universities have sought to enforce their own autonomy and the autonomy of science, while church, emperors, monarchs, and economic stakeholders have attempted to control research and teaching. This was the case in the Middle Ages and it is the case today.

If science, as an institution, is tied to the rest of society in a multifarious manner, rarely free of conflict, where does this leave the individual researcher? Is he solely meant to seek the truth and allow others to determine how this "truth" can be used in practice? Or should he instead be critical of the role his research plays in society? In the twentieth century, this has been greatly disputed. In the following section, the two most typical answers to this question will be described briefly, based on the views of some of the most important participants in the discussion.

The Scientist, His Research, and Society

The researcher is not only a scientist, but also a fellow citizen. This means that, on the one hand, he is hired to uncover the truth in an area of importance to society, while, on the other hand, as a citizen, he is required to share the responsibility for society's development. Usually these two roles are compatible, but at times they clash; for example, if the scientist's work is used for political purposes that are in conflict with his views as a citizen. In this case ought he be loyal to his science or to his role as a citizen?

The view of the scientist's role in society is naturally connected to the view of society in general. In modern European democracies, political life is structured according to the contrast between the conservative and liberal right wing and the socialist and communist left wing. This contrast summarizes a large number of disagreements and different sources of inspiration. The classic theorists of the right wing are, among others, Edmund Burke (1729–1797) and John Locke, while the classic theorist of the left wing is Marx. These different sources of inspiration signify how the two political wings view society in fundamentally different ways.

Taking inspiration from Weber, we can point out different ideal views of society, science, and researchers according to the political worldview of both left and right wing. Seeing that we are dealing with ideal types, they are not necessarily in concordance with the views actually put forward by politicians; however, they summarize a number of general features of the two main political directions.

According to classical conservatism, people are united as a nation bound together by a common culture and tradition. This community is stronger and more fundamental than the inner conflicts of society. From the classical liberal point of view, all people are born as equal and free individuals and, by means of the parliamentarian democracy, all people influence society's development equally. The actual social inequalities found in society are caused by individual differences; they are not structural. Common to the two traditions of classical right-wing politics is the view that society is not fundamentally characterized by conflicts of interest and social inequality.

From this point of view, the scientist does not control the results of his own work. The conservative would claim that these are the property of the nation and not the researcher as an individual. The liberal would claim that democratically elected representatives of the population are to decide how to use the results of research. Science itself must be objective; therefore, the scientist oversteps his authority by politicizing it. He is only hired to uncover the facts in his field of research. Naturally, being critical of the sciences is necessary, yet this task applies to everyone, not just the scientist.

According to the view of the classical left wing, on the other hand, society is not characterized by harmony, but by continuous conflict between economic interest groups (classes). The fundamental structural inequality of these groups is maintained through society's production. Because of this, some people influence the development of society more than others. Financially strong interest groups will, for instance, through lobbying distort the democratic process.

According to this perspective, research is unequally divided like all other resources in modern society. There are not unlimited means for supporting the sciences and not all groups benefit equally from the research. The sciences are unable to be politically neutral as they are part of society, and thereby part of society's political conflicts of interest. Unless scientists take a stand regarding these conflicts, they are, therefore, really just upholding the current power distribution in society. From a left-wing perspective, being critical of the sciences is therefore necessary. Who should, for instance, benefit from society's investment in the sciences: Third World countries, large financially strong corporations, or the military? No one is more capable of informing the public on this issue than the scientist himself. It is, therefore, the scientists' duty to be critical of their own research.

The question of whether society is fundamentally harmonious or fundamentally marked by conflicting interests is crucial to this ideological dispute. If society is harmonious, the sciences must be neutral in order to benefit everyone equally. However, if society is characterized by conflict, neutrality is impossible and the sciences will never be equally beneficial to everyone. In this situation, the scientists themselves must critically determine whom their work is to benefit.

As stated above, it is certainly possible to find examples of people from either wing who deviate from this highly schematic account. This is partly because ideal types do not constitute a depiction of society, and partly because the distinction between left and right is not as pronounced today as it once was. We have now seen how each of the two wings traditionally viewed the question of the researcher's position between his dual roles as scientist and citizen. This shows how the question of science is also a political question.

This discussion is naturally reflected in philosophy of science. In the following we will take a closer look at a number of theorists who each view the question of the scientist's role in society differently.

"Science Must Be Neutral": A Critique of the "Arbiters of Taste"

It is very rare that a foundational question of philosophy of science becomes the object of fierce political debate and polemic, but this proved to be the case when Anders Fogh Rasmussen, Denmark's prime minister at the time, made the following statement in his New Year's speech in 2002:

> "Recent years have seen the budding and growth of a true wilderness of state councils and committees and institutions. Many of these have developed into state-authorized arbiters of taste determining what is good and right in different areas. There is a trend towards a tyranny of experts, which is at risk of stifling free public debate. The population should not put up with reprimands by these so-called experts who claim to know best. Experts may be capable enough of presenting factual knowledge, but when it comes to making personal decisions, we are all experts. This government intends to get rid of superfluous councils and committees and institutions. It will be a very comprehensive clean up. We will sort out this middle layer, which drains resources and distracts attention from what is important."

The prime minister may not have been aware of it, but in this speech he not only expresses the classical right-wing view, as identified above, but also a specific understanding of science that is deeply rooted in history. Scientists, or the "experts", must communicate "factual knowledge" but are not to determine "what is good and right in different areas". In other words, Rasmussen clearly distinguishes between commenting on the world as it *is,* and on how it *ought* to be. This distinction was first put forward by the Scottish empiricist, David Hume (1711–1776). He was an Enlightenment philosopher and therefore thoroughly annoyed by the contemporary authorities. They argued that the existing order of society was right and good, because it was old tradition or in accordance with "the order of nature". Hume believed that it is impossible to conclude how something *ought* to be on the basis of how something *is* (Hume 1985). For instance, hunger has always been an issue in the world but this is not a reason for refraining from trying to solve the problem. People have always cheated on their taxes, but this does not make it less unacceptable. Hume's views on this point have since been developed by the English philosopher G.E. Moore (1873–1958), who called the misunderstood conclusion from "is" to "ought", *the naturalistic fallacy* (Moore 2005: 11).

> ! **The Naturalistic Fallacy:** According to, among others, Hume and Moore, it is a fallacy to conclude what the world ought to be like on the basis of how it is in reality.

The problem with the naturalistic fallacy is that it mixes two different perspectives on the world: an ethical discussion of what the world ought to be on the one side and a discussion of facts on the other. This is where Hume and Moore's arguments become relevant for the philosophy of science. According to Hume and the rest of the empiricists, science is about observable facts, but while it is its task to uncover what the world is like, it does not give scientists the right to pronounce value judgments; i.e., to comment on how things ought to be.

As we saw in chapter 2, the positivists, the nineteenth-century heirs of empiricism, also discussed the question of the role of the sciences in society. Comte believed that the sciences should reshape the social order to be rid of political conflicts; however, he did not believe the sciences should make value judgments. Instead, he imagined that the sciences in themselves constituted "pure" value-neutral rationality. In other words, all the conflicting value judgments in society resulted in political conflicts, and the solution was to organize social life on the basis of value-neutral science.

If science is to be useful in political decision-making, it is of decisive importance that it is not itself political. This is the view that we also find among the logical positivists. As we have seen, they believe that statements about values are not only unscientific, but meaningless. The sciences are only meaningful as neutral and objective observations of reality. For this reason they must not only abstain from dealing with questions of value, they must also be free of values themselves. Science has, therefore, no hidden core values and, as a result, it is up to others to determine how to apply its results.

This positivist understanding of the role of science in society has gained new relevance over the past few decades, with the idea of evidence-based policymaking. It has spread from the USA and Great Britain to many other countries, including Denmark, where it has influenced policies in fields like healthcare, public welfare, and education (Hansen and Rieper 2010). The fundamental idea behind this development is that politics should not be based on political ideologies and values, but on scientific studies of what actually works. Before passing new legislation, one should therefore present clear evidence that it will have the desired effect.

! **Evidence-based Policymaking:** This movement from the USA and Great Britain argues that politics is to be formulated based on scientific enquiry. There must be empirical evidence that a given law will work before it is passed.

That we are dealing here with a positivist view is clear from the fact that evidence-based policymaking is based on the explicit contrast of science and values ("ideology"), and therefore also on an implicit idea about the value neutrality of science; however, the idea of evidence-based policymaking is also highly disputed. For instance, researchers often disagree about what policies may be backed by evidence and even about what "evidence" really is. Furthermore, some studies (Vohnsen 2012) have shown how science can be abused and manipulated to legitimize ideological lawmaking. In these cases, evidence-based policymaking becomes "policy-based evidence making", which is damaging to democratic debate and to the transparency of the political system.

Among the philosophers of science who agree with the former prime minister, we find not only positivists, but also one of the authors from the previous chapter, Max Weber. Neither he nor the positivists are politically right wing, yet, regarding this issue, their views correspond to the classical right-wing idea of society.

Moreover, Weber does not entirely agree with the positivists. He does not claim that researchers should refrain from making value judgments in all contexts; on the contrary, these are impossible to avoid. His point is that the researcher must always *attempt* to avoid these judgments. The question is: Why?

In Weber's age, few people had as much authority as a university professor. Students considered his word truth and law; however, not everyone handled this prestige well. Many believed that since they were such great authorities within their field, they must also be accomplished in other fields, such as politics. According to Weber, his colleagues abused the freedom of teaching when putting forward moral and political precepts during their lectures. Worst of all, they wrapped up their personal beliefs in their teaching, making these appear as scientific truth. To use a modern expression this can be termed "indoctrination" (Weber 2003: 139).

This forms the basis for Weber's insistence that researchers must refrain from making value judgment whenever possible. When it cannot be avoided, they must at least indicate clearly when they move beyond strictly factual dissemination to presenting a personal assessment. In this way the students are able to distinguish between knowledge and opinion, and can be critical of any value judgments.

Weber thus believes there is a crucial difference between uncovering truths about the world and judging the world ethically or politically. Lecturers must stick to strictly factual teaching, the aim of which is to provide students with the necessary competencies for their future work (Weber 2003: 135). The sciences are allowed to be concerned with questions of a normative nature as long as they do not approach these questions normatively. For instance, if a sociologist studies the moral code of a specific group, he must describe and explain it, but not assess its validity.

In spite of his criticism of positivism, Weber agrees with the positivists' sharp distinction between descriptive and normative perspectives, and their emphasis that the sciences must solely observe and communicate facts. His argumentation is directly and intuitively comprehensible to everyone. It makes sense that students must be presented with scientific facts and not the professor's idiosyncrasies, but is the matter really that simple, or are we deceived by the intuitive reasonableness of Weber's argument?

"Scientists Must Take a Stand": The Necessary Criticism of Society

On August 6th, 1945, the premises for understanding the role of science in society changed forever. Previously, it was considered obvious that research led to progress and wealth, but the nuclear bombing of Hiroshima suddenly made it clear that science could have the diametrically opposite result. Its most extreme consequences could indeed lead to the destruction of mankind. At the same time it became clear to many that science was at the centre of the political conflicts of modern society and could no longer remain neutral.

With the invention of the atomic bomb, human reason and intelligence seemed to have turned against mankind. Even before Hiroshima, the German philosophers Theodor Adorno (1903–1969) and Max Horkheimer (1895–1973) reflected on this development to try and understand how it could have gone so wrong. They are the most important representatives of the philosophical school of thought called *critical theory.* Much simplified, this approach is inspired by Marx and Freud, but it is neither Marxist nor Freudian; instead, it uses these two authors as sources of inspiration for a relevant criticism of society.

> ! **Critical Theory:** A philosophical school of thought critical of society and civilization founded by Adorno and Horkheimer in Frankfurt in the 1920s. For this reason it is also known as the Frankfurt School. The school's primary sources of inspiration are Marx and Freud.

Adorno and Horkheimer's analyses result in the work *Dialectic of Enlightenment* (Adorno and Horkheimer 1995). They focus on the optimistic faith in reason and rationality. This faith is the core of modern science. By reducing the world to what can be measured and weighed (i.e., what can be comprehended by means of our rationality) modern science has achieved near complete control of nature; however, man is more than his rationality, and nature is much more than that which can be measured and weighed. As a result, modern society's one-sided scientific, rational approach to the world leads not only to the control of nature, but also to people's *alienation* from nature and themselves.

> **!** **Alienation:** A concept the Frankfurt School adopts from Marx. According to this theory, society can be organized in a way that runs counter to human nature; for example, by everything having to be organized in a rational manner. When this happens, man experiences the world as a foreign power, in which he has no natural place or home, and since he sees a reflection of his own being in the world, man no longer understands himself.

Science and rationality are not merely forms of neutral reasoning as the positivists believed. They are a means for controlling, manipulating, and exercising power over nature in general. This was a useful skill when mankind were the weakest animals roaming the savannah; however, today our survival is no longer threatened and so the rational control of nature begins working against its original intent. It finds expression in the control of mankind. According to Adorno and Horkheimer, this explains the atomic bomb and the Nazis' mass-extermination camps. Here, high technology and irrationality form a synthesis because the scientific control of nature has become the control of mankind. It has become irrational; thus control, the raw exercise of power, is all that is left of the Enlightenment dream to create a better society through the rational control of nature (Adorno and Horkheimer 1995: 99).

In the previous chapter we saw how Weber turned our attention to the ambiguity of purposeful rationality with his concept, "the iron cage of rationality". Adorno and Horkheimer continue this theme, as does a third critical theorist, Jürgen Habermas (born 1929). According to him, not only do extremes, such as Nazism and the atomic bomb, reflect scientific rationality's influence on social life, but democratic politics do so as well. Just as science's control of nature is technical, politics too are reduced to discussions of technical solutions for technically defined issues. The dominant classes define the overall political goals beforehand and there is therefore no room left for ideological discussions of values and objectives. This type of political culture alienates people from democracy (Habermas 2005: 39–83).

According to Habermas, this development proves that the positivists were wrong; for when a society becomes increasingly technical by means of science, a large number of political discussions are excluded. Clearly this is in the interest of some groups but not all. For instance, it is immensely disadvantageous to groups wishing to discuss whether the technically defined goals of society are the right goals. In this way, the sciences play a very direct political role in the conflict between those who want to change the present order of society and those who wish to preserve it. Therefore, Habermas would also be of the opinion that the idea of evidence-based policymaking misunderstands both science and politics. Scientific research is never value neutral, and politics is never a matter of simply finding technical solutions, but about values, ideologies, conflicts of interest, and power struggles.

According to Habermas, the positivists' belief in "objective and neutral sciences" is an illusion. The reason we begin studying something is always that we have a particular interest in it, not because we find "observing" amusing. The point of departure of scientific knowledge is, therefore, exactly that which Hume and the positivists believed it ought to steer clear of; namely, norms, values, and interests (for example, economic). In other words, science is never neutral. Habermas specifically states that the driving forces of scientific work are different *cognitive interests* (Habermas 2005: 119–136). The natural sciences are characterized by a technical cognitive interest. Their purpose is to create knowledge that can be applied in, for example, the business world. On the other hand, what Habermas terms practical cognitive interests drive the hermeneutic-historical (human) sciences. Their objective is to create a common horizon of understanding in society. Finally, the "sciences of action", such as sociology, economics, and political science do not only uncover social life but also enable us to reflect critically on the organization of society. This is the first condition of being able to change society in a positive direction, and these sciences are therefore borne by what Habermas terms an emancipatory (liberating) cognitive interest.

> **Cognitive Interests:** According to Habermas, the sciences are never objective and neutral but driven by different cognitive interests. He distinguishes between technical, practical, and emancipatory cognitive interests.

Seeing that the sciences are never objective and neutral but always directed by different interests, scientists, as citizens, ought to consider the purpose their research actually serves. The contrast between "arbiters of taste" and "the people" is false, not just because the scientists themselves are also "the people", but especially because their discussion enriches rather than excludes democratic debate. This completely free and emancipating democratic discussion, unrestrained by technical rationality, is Habermas's goal.

The French philosopher, Jean-Paul Sartre (1905–1980), is even more critical of the relationship between scientists, society, and the sciences. He places scientists in the same category as judges, teachers, and functionaries; the category he calls "the technicians of practical knowledge" (Sartre 1979: 26–30). Through their work in government and companies, they contribute to the preservation of the ruling order in the class society, thereby contributing to the oppression of the underprivileged social groups. As persons they do not wish to fill this role, yet their job function forces them to. This conflict between, on the one hand, contributing to the maintenance of an unjust social order, while on the other hand being able to see through this order and one's own function in it because of one's education is what Sartre terms "the unhappy consciousness".

According to Sartre, the scientist must accept the consequences of his understanding of society. He must transcend the role of the technician of practical knowledge and instead criticize social injustice. According to Sartre's terminology, the scientist must become an *intellec-*

tual. The intellectual is the knowledge worker who breaks with his role in society, criticizes the ruling ideology, and joins the fight of the underprivileged classes for a more just society (Sartre 1979: 26–45).

> ! **The Intellectuals:** The classic collective name for knowledge workers and other groups that use their intellect and not their hands for work; for example, poets, artists, authors, and philosophers. Sartre and Jørgensen depict the societal role and responsibilities of the intellectuals differently.

The question of the intellectuals is therefore concerned with the role that, for instance, scientists play when they pose critical questions about society and their own function in it. Sartre's opinion on this matter is not the only one, and the Danish intellectual historian Dorthe Jørgensen (born 1959) presents a different view. According to her terminology, "the intellectuals" are not a specific group of professions, but rather people who seek the truth about the world, society, and themselves. Intellectuals see meaning and coherence in the world. For this reason they possess not only knowledge but also wisdom, and they are capable of putting our life experience into a greater perspective, creating what Jørgensen terms a metaphysics of experience (Jørgensen 2002: 80).

Society needs intellectuals, not to revolt (as Sartre believed), but because they reflect on the myths of society and criticize those that are harmful (e.g., the myths of "them" and "us", "the people" versus "arbiters of taste", "westerners" versus "Muslims"). The intellectuals' approach is political as they always raise questions that go beyond the concrete, continually insisting that things could be different. Because of this, they continue to be a thorn in the side of bureaucrats who wish to focus on the concrete. According to Jørgensen, Anders Fogh Rasmussen's New Year's speech really expresses a conflict between intellectuals and narrow-minded bureaucrats, not a conflict between "arbiters of taste" and "the people" (Jørgensen 2002: 109–114).

Left-wing views on the sciences range from relativism and social constructivism to an understanding of Marxism as a social science. A crucial common feature is, however, that left-wing theorists all refute the possibility of making a sharp distinction between facts and values, and between a theory and its application; thus, they also deny that scientific knowledge can be objective and neutral. Although it is unlikely that Marx would agree completely with any of the theorists explored in this chapter, they all share the view he advocates; namely, that it is crucial for the sciences that researchers maintain a critical reflection on the ideological and political roles and prejudices of both themselves and others.

Science, Politics, and Society: A Summary

In this chapter, we first looked at the sciences as an institution. We examined the principles that characterize universities, as well as the connection of these principles to Humboldt's nineteenth-century university reform. This is an interesting topic because the sciences are communicated by scientists to society through the university; however, there is also a subjective aspect of this communication. Should the scientist be critical of the role of the sciences in society, or is the application of research the responsibility of politicians? Historically, the answers to this question have followed the classic political division between the right wing and left wing.

Weber and the positivists both support the right-wing view that researchers must refrain from politicizing and exclusively communicate "factual knowledge". The logical positivists continue the strict Humean distinction between fact and assessment, and emphasize that the sole task of the sciences is to uncover facts. Weber insists that students taught by the researcher have a right to be presented with factual knowledge and not the professor's personal assessment of this or that.

Traditionally the left wing has paid more attention to the question of the role of the researcher in society. In this context, we have considered critical theory and the discussions of the role of the intellectuals. We noted that, although the theorists do not agree in all respects, they all refute the idea that the sciences are politically and socially neutral. Furthermore, they believe that the scientists must be critical of the social consequences of their research.

No view is more "correct" than the other. Both sides present reasonable arguments. Whether you agree with the positivists or Habermas depends on your political worldview rather than the strength of the arguments. If you believe society fundamentally constitutes a community with common interests, then the sciences must remain politically neutral in order to benefit everyone; however, if you believe society is fundamentally marked by social inequality and conflicts of interest, the sciences cannot remain neutral, and scientists must be critical of who benefits from their work, as it will never be equally beneficial to everyone.

The next chapter will continue to deal with the responsibilities of science, though in relation to individuals and groups rather than society as a whole, as we will be considering the question of the sciences and ethics. But before we get to that, we will once again embark on the journey from philosophy of science to the scientific, as well as to the practical levels of knowledge.

Science and Politics in Practice

There are numerous examples of researchers interfering with politics, and there are even more examples of them refraining from doing so. Although no unequivocal conclusions can be drawn from these cases, they are still highly educational.

Example: The Sciences in 1930s Germany

During the 1930s, German researchers ought to have taken a stand regarding the political use of their work (Szöllösi-Janze 2001). Hitler's regime aimed at substantiating its racial theories, and for this reason research in this area promised rewards: money, power, as well as prestige. Physicians, anthropologists, historians, and several other academic groups were involved in the attempt to prove the existence and superiority of the Aryan race. Researchers were, for instance, given free rein to experiment on prisoners in the concentration camps. In this case, scientists allowed both themselves and their sciences to be corrupted because they refrained from being critical of the political system and its abuse of the sciences.

Example: The Lysenko Affair in the Soviet Union

Supporters of the ideals of objective and value-neutral sciences can, on the other hand, refer back to the Lysenko affair from 1928 (Joravsky 1986). At that time, the young biologist Trofim Lysenko's (1898–1976) career skyrocketed in the Soviet Union, but not because he was a talented researcher. In fact, he was not. On the contrary, he was proved to have falsified his scientific results. He claimed that these results supported Stalin's official political doctrines, and this turned out to be enough to make him the darling of the Soviet leaders. He was appointed leader of the country's agricultural research and any critics were threatened to be silenced or imprisoned. Lysenko's fraud was first discovered after several decades, and by then the biological sciences in the Soviet Union had suffered irreparable damage caused by his political purges.

The Lysenko affair exemplifies the extent of damage that can be caused when a researcher begins to play the politician and actively interfere in political discussions. While the sciences in Germany were destroyed by their imagined political "neutrality", the biological sciences in the Soviet Union were corrupted by Lysenko's politicization of them.

Example: Niels Bohr's Letter to The United Nations

One of the best-known examples of a scientist being critical of the political consequences of his work is the world-famous Danish nuclear physicist and Nobel Prize winner, Niels Bohr (1885–1962). During World War II, Bohr fled to the US, where he contributed to work on the development of the American atomic bomb as part of the war against Nazi Germany; however, with time he became increasingly concerned about the bomb's long-term consequences. He feared that a nuclear arms race between the US and the Soviet Union could potentially put the survival of mankind at risk. To prevent a development of this kind, Bohr wanted it to be possible for all countries to use nuclear technology for peaceful purposes, while subjecting nuclear materials to international control. After several years of presenting his arguments in vain to the political leaders of the US and Great Britain, he chose to intervene directly and politically by means of an open letter aimed at the UN general assembly in 1950 (Bohr 1950). Although Bohr's views did not gain immediate support, they eventually inspired the establishment of the UN's International Atomic Energy Agency. This organization monitors the spreading of atomic material, and in 2005 it was awarded the Nobel Peace Prize for its work.

Should Bohr have acted in this way? Churchill was greatly irritated by what he considered a scientist's misplaced interference in political issues. Bohr had, for his part, decided that his conscience as a citizen obligated him to intervene in political affairs in his capacity as a scientist.

Example: How *You* Can Work with the Question of Science and Politics

The way our students will approach the question of science and politics will depend on whether they adopt a classical right- or left-wing point of view. If they choose to follow the approach of the positivists and Weber, it is crucial that their own assessment of the company does not influence their study. Communication may be characterized by conflicts between management and employees, but the students are responsible for presenting these conflicts without judging them. They must be as objective and neutral as possible. On the other hand, if the students choose to adhere to a more left-wing understanding of science, they will consider the idea of a neutral and objective account as illusory. Furthermore, they will believe that attempting to stay neutral regarding a conflict between management and employees will strengthen the existing power relation between the two parties. If the students discover that management's communication manipulates its employees, they will note this in their report. Furthermore, they will not refrain from criticizing management but, on the contrary, choose to side with the employees.

Questions

1. Explain the five basic principles that characterize the modern university.
2. What does "naturalistic fallacy" mean?
3. Why must the sciences, according to the positivists, remain politically neutral?
4. What is Weber's argument for claiming that scientists must keep research and politics separate?
5. How do Adorno and Horkheimer explain the emergence of, for example, the atomic bomb?
6. Explain Habermas's view of the relation between cognition and interest.
7. Why did Sartre believe the intellectuals ought to revolt?
8. According to Jørgensen, what role do intellectuals play in society?
9. Which examples of clashes between the sciences and politics do you remember hearing about, for example, in the daily papers?
10. In your opinion, what are the strengths and weaknesses of the different views on the question regarding the critical stance of scientists presented in this chapter?

Science and Ethics

We will begin with two examples. The first concerns a large Danish company. In the summer of 2008, the UN's Food and Agricultural Organization (FAO) levelled strong criticism at the chemical manufacturer Cheminova. The reason for this criticism was the company's production of a pesticide based on the substance methyl parathion. It is one of the most poisonous substances in the world, and handling it therefore requires extensive precautionary measures; however, FAO's critique did not pertain to production itself, but rather to the fact that Cheminova exported the poison to Brazil. According to FAO, the problem was partly that Brazil's tropical climate made it too warm for the safety equipment to be used, and partly that the Brazilian agricultural workers were not sufficiently trained to use the equipment correctly and therefore risked becoming severely ill. For this reason, FAO deemed Cheminova's export *unethical*. The company defended itself by claiming that pesticides were necessary for Brazilian agriculture, and producing them without methyl parathion was too expensive to make this a genuine alternative. Export was necessary to feed the Brazilian population and to secure the agricultural export of, among other things, cotton. Nevertheless, this explanation did not satisfy the critics in the debate that followed FAO's criticism. For instance, it was pointed out that the use of methyl parathion had been banned in the EU for several years and, for this reason, it was wrong to export it.

The second example is from the world of fiction. In Steven Spielberg's film *The Terminal* from 2004, Tom Hanks plays the role of Viktor Navorski, a passenger from the former Soviet Union who, because of bureaucracy, is stranded in JFK airport. He is unable to fly home or leave the airport. One day a Russian-speaking man goes berserk when airport staff attempt to confiscate the medicine he is carrying. He does not have the required export license, but no one is able to explain this to him, as the airport officials cannot find an interpreter. The situation is so desperate that the airport manager promises to help Viktor if he acts as interpreter, and Viktor accepts. However, it turns out that the Russian speaking man is hysterical because the medicine is for his dying father. He cannot buy it in his own country so he travelled to America to collect it. What should Viktor do in this situation? If he interprets correctly, the man's medicine will be confiscated and his father will die. Viktor can also choose to say the medicine is for an animal as this makes export legal; however, he will then be lying to the authorities, abusing his position as interpreter, and will incur the airport manager's anger and thus not be allowed to leave the airport.

What Is Ethics?

What the two examples have in common is that both deal with moral dilemmas and therefore require ethical deliberation. But what exactly is a moral dilemma, and what does "ethical deliberation" entail? We will seek to answer these questions in this chapter and, at the same time, make visible their particular relevance for the sciences.

The concept of morals identifies the unwritten rules that regulate our coexistence with other people. Normally we are hardly aware of these rules. Most of us need barely remind ourselves that lying or stealing is wrong, as these moral precepts seem self-evident. We usually first become aware of ethics when the rules are broken, or are in conflict with one another. The problems of both Cheminova and Viktor Navorski exemplify how different values can require people and companies to act in conflicting ways. This is why these problems are typical of ethical dilemmas. In other words, ethics steps in when our inherent moral system is no longer applicable, and we are required to stop and consider how to act. Put differently, ethics is the discussion of and reflection on what is morally correct. It is concerned with the way we interact with each other, and which values we choose to let our social coexistence be governed by.

The examples of Cheminova and Viktor Navorski demonstrate how we encounter ethical dilemmas in all areas of life. This applies to microeconomics and corporate management (were Cheminova's actions ethical?), and also to working with language, interpretation, and communication (as in Viktor's case). Sometimes these dilemmas seem easy to solve. Most people, for instance, would make the same decision as Viktor. He tells the airport manager that the man's medicine is for his family's goat, thus allowing him to travel home with it. This does not, however, make the dilemma any less real. Furthermore, it is possible to imagine other, less dramatic, yet difficult problems. If translating or interpreting for a person who, because of ignorance, ends up insulting the recipient of the communication, should my translation be loyal to the message, leaving the person to suffer the consequences, or should I "make up" a translation; i.e., lie to save him? Sometimes finding any kind of satisfactory solution at all seems difficult. What should we do if we are unable to ensure both effective agricultural methods and safe working conditions in Brazil? There are no easy solutions to the Cheminova dilemma.

Ethical problems are, however, found not only on the practical level of knowledge, but also in the sciences. Here they appear in various different ways. First of all, scientific and technological breakthroughs can change our established conventions of morality and create conflicts between rights and values not previously at odds with each other. This applies, among other things, to instances where the sciences manipulate the human body. For instance, the development of abortion technologies has resulted in ethical tension between the mother's right over her own body and the unborn child's right to live; an area of tension which did not exist to the same degree earlier, but has appeared because of science. Secondly, the actual way in which scientific studies are conducted can prove ethically problematic, not least when experiments are carried out on human beings. For this reason, all applications to the governmental research committees in Denmark must today include a description of the project's ethical aspects. Therefore, if you wish to understand the sciences, you also need to know something about ethics.

We are, fortunately, not forced to start from scratch when attempting to deal with ethical issues. At the philosophical level of knowledge, theorists have for centuries sought to provide rules and guidelines that would enable coexistence without ethical dilemmas. It has not yet proven possible to reach an agreement on such a moral code, and it is highly unlikely that anyone will succeed in putting forward a system of ethics that takes all isolated cases into account, as well as being free of internal contradiction or paradoxes. The practical coexistence of mankind is a tricky matter, especially in theory; however, there are a number of traditions in moral philosophy that have proven sufficiently applicable and useful to still be used as tools for attempting to solve ethical dilemmas today. In this chapter, we will begin by examining the three most important moral philosophies, and following this, we will explore how these can be applied in science.

Utilitarianism

Utilitarianism can be traced back to the British philosophers Jeremy Bentham (1748–1832) and John Stuart Mill (1806–1873). Even though it has existed for less than 200 years, it has become one of the predominant schools of thought in normative ethics. It may even seem puzzling that no one thought of it earlier, as its fundamental assumptions at first glance appear intuitively obvious.

What do all human beings essentially strive for? The short answer is: happiness. We each have different ideas of happiness. For some it is relaxing on a beach in Fiji, for others it is being appointed professor at a university, and for others it is something else entirely; however, we all strive for what we personally believe to be happiness. According to the utilitarians, the ethical value of an action should therefore be measured on the basis of whether it produces happiness, or at least utility, for the people involved. An action that results in utility and happiness is good, while an action that leads to unhappiness is bad. The utilitarians do not believe we should be in a constant state of ecstasy. Happiness should rather be understood as living an active life with few sorrows and pains and many lasting pleasures (Mill 1995: 25).

> ! **Utilitarianism:** The ethical theory that holds that the action that is morally right is the one that results in the greatest possible utility (or greatest possible happiness) for the greatest number of people.

This may seem obvious, and yet it is not; for this view entails that the moral agent's *intentions* have no significance at all for our judgment of an action. Let us imagine a forked road: one direction leads directly to a precipice while the other leads to the nearest town. An extremely callous road worker is situated at the fork in the road, hired to warn drivers from taking the dangerous road; however, because he is evil, he instead intends to lure as many travellers as possible to their deaths. But he is not only cruel, he is also slightly confused, so when a car finally approaches he sends it in direction of the town—much to his annoyance. According to the utilitarians, the road worker acts morally right. His intentions make no difference. On the other hand, it would be morally wrong if a person were to jump in a river to save a man from drowning only to discover that the person he has saved is Hitler (Smart and William 1973: 49). This way of viewing ethics is termed *consequentialism* because actions are solely assessed on the basis of their outcome.

> ! **Consequentialism:** The view that the moral quality of an action is determined solely on the basis of its outcome. This view is primarily represented by utilitarianism.

Based on the premise that we all seek individual happiness, the utilitarians draw the conclusion that the action that maximizes happiness for the most people is a good one. Social ethics is therefore derived from one's individuality. In other words, the goal of utilitarianism is not the happiness of the individual, but the total amount of happiness in the entire population. Mill emphasizes that, according to this principle, we must focus on education as well as the fight against poverty and disease, as these are the most effective ways of increasing the population's collective happiness (Mill 1995: 27–41). Derived from this, some thinkers have suggested the principle of negative utilitarianism, in which the main focus is to minimize pain rather than maximize happiness (Smart and Williams 1973: 28–30).

But who is to say that education makes people happy? Since the utilitarians justify their position by claiming that we all strive for happiness, are they then not bound to what people, in actual fact, consider happiness? And will this then lead to "an ethics of the lowest common denominator"? Should we close down the art museums that only please a minority, and instead prioritize reality TV, and other types of "cultural junk food", which apparently bring happiness to many people? The utilitarians disagree among themselves on this matter. Bentham and the so-called hedonistic[1] utilitarians believe that one form of happiness is no better than another (Smart and Williams 1973: 12–27). If the people want reality TV, reality TV is what they should be given. Other utilitarians would claim that some forms of happiness are more valuable than others. For instance, visiting an art museum, reading a good book, or spending time with your children is considered of more value than watching reality TV. As Mill puts it: "It is better to be a human being dissatisfied than a pig satisfied; better to be Socrates dissatisfied than a fool satisfied" (Mill 1998: 140). He argues that people who can appreciate all the above-mentioned forms of pleasure—good books, children, art museums, and reality TV—will always prefer the first three to cultural junk food. The problem with this argument is, however, that it will never be more than a postulate.

Of course, there will be people whose idea of happiness does not fit within the boundaries of society. Keeping a serial killer happy may prove challenging if the rest of the population is to coexist alongside him. People who consider money or power to be happiness may also

1 Hedonism is the ethical view that pleasure is the highest good.

cause harm to many others. According to Mill, the individual's concept of happiness can only be accepted insofar as it is not harmful to others. For instance, it is acceptable for a person who loves money to open a shop, but he cannot commit an armed robbery (Mill 1995: 53–61). The law must regulate different individuals' pursuit of happiness. In general, utilitarianism finds its primary strength in the political system, which in turn has embraced it. According to utilitarians, the fundamental issue of parliamentarian politics is the fact that the state has limited means, while the people have nearly endless needs; therefore, the important thing is to prioritize society's resources to ensure they yield the greatest possible happiness. In the words of the utilitarian, the challenge the politicians face is to make the greatest possible number of people as happy as possible with the funds available.

How would the utilitarian view our two ethical dilemmas? He would consider the consequences of the various actions available, and in the first case there would be no doubt. If Viktor tells the truth, the Russian man's father dies and if he lies, the father survives; therefore, lying obviously leads to the greatest benefit and happiness. Of course he breaks the rule "you must not lie" and he betrays the trust of the airport manager, yet these consequences are of less importance than saving the father. Most of us are able to follow this chain of reasoning; however, when considering the Cheminova case it becomes more complex, because what is more important: the health of the agricultural workers or maintaining Brazil's agricultural production? Which of these produces most utility? Many would protest against attempting to fit the protection of life and rights of the individual into this utility calculus, but this is how the utilitarians would view the issue. They would likely conclude that the export of methyl parathion produces more happiness than the banning of it.

This already suggests that utilitarianism is not always without problems. Furthermore, it leads to some difficult dilemmas. For instance, should politicians aim to increase the collective amount of happiness in society, or should they instead increase the average happiness? To achieve the first goal, they could, for example, choose to exempt the richest people in society from paying taxes. This would most likely make them much happier, and the remaining population would hardly feel the difference; thus, the total happiness in society increases. This does not, however, ring true in most people's idea of justice and, moreover, the majority of the population would not be happier. In the second scenario, the happiness of the entire population could be increased slightly but no one would be really happy. This is not necessarily a good scenario either. The prioritization of the different needs in society poses another problem. If a hospital manager is forced to choose between operating on either fifty patients in need of a hip replacement or one heart patient, the utilitarian can only answer that he must choose the action that leads to the greatest possible happiness, but how can saving the life of one heart patient be compared to removing the disabling pain experienced by fifty hip patients? How can the usefulness of the Royal Theatre be compared to the usefulness of the Maritime Authorities? In these cases, the utilitarian can only respond that decisions must be made based on an assessment of the particular case. He may be right, but his answer also implies that utilitarianism cannot be used as a guiding principle in the decision-making process.

As already indicated by the Cheminova example above, being consistently utilitarian implies being prepared to accept decisions that few people would consider to be morally acceptable. The utilitarian J.J.C. Smart (1920–2012) discusses a hypothetical example: The sheriff of a small town has arrested a crime suspect but interrogation shows that the man is innocent. In the meantime, an angry mob has gathered outside the prison. They demand revenge and are convinced that the man is guilty. The sheriff is left with a dreadful choice. If he sets the innocent man free, the angry crowd will run riot and many people will be killed; however, if he chooses to hang the innocent man, the crowd will be satisfied and additional deaths will be avoided. According to a utilitarian thinker, the latter scenario must be favoured. He would not be happy about it, but it would be the lesser of the two evils (Smart and Williams 1973: 69–71).

Obviously many will object to this conclusion, protesting that the dignity of man, the inviolability of human life, and the fundamental rights of the individual cannot be compromised. This must apply to both Brazilian agriculture and the sheriff's law enforcement. These critics would emphasize that the two examples precisely demonstrate the fundamental problem of utilitarianism: the one-sided focus on utility makes the theory blind to these fundamental and inviolable rights. Some of these critics will undoubtedly be inspired by Kant.

Kant's Ethics of Disposition and Duty

As already mentioned, the utilitarians' point of departure is the concrete and tangible reality that is visible to us all (namely, that we all strive for happiness); however, is the correlation between what "everyone can see" and what is morally right as self-evident as they believe it to be? The fact that utilitarianism leads to the violation of the rights of the individual seems to refute this. Kant makes an additional objection: The motive underlying a person's actions cannot be deduced from these actions themselves. In most people's opinion (and definitely in his own) the callous road worker acts more foolishly than morally right. How about the fast food chain that donates money to a family house attached to a hospital? This appears to be a moral action; however, if the intention is in fact to improve PR and induce goodwill in the population, as well as distract attention from the poor working conditions for the chain's employees or the poor quality of its food, we would be tempted to call the chain's actions cynical rather than moral.

This can also be expressed in a different way: the only thing we can know with certainty that is good, is goodwill, and "will" cannot be observed in reality. It remains hidden in the human mind. We must therefore ignore the ambiguous and deceitful empirical reality and instead consider what our reason tells us to do. Whereas the utilitarians focus on the good or bad *consequences* of an action, Kant therefore considers the *intentions* underlying the action. This is why his moral philosophy is known as *ethics of disposition.* In his *Groundwork of the Metaphysics of Morals,* Kant seeks to study which ethics can be derived from reason. This also requires him to find out what characterizes the good will (Kant 1993: 21).

Ethics of Disposition: The ethical theory that holds that the moral qualities of an action are determined by the motives of the moral agent.

There is an additional reason why morality cannot be derived from empirical reality. It is a series of isolated cases with no clear-cut common features, and special circumstances will always have a part to play. For instance, we know we should not steal, but we cannot derive this general rule from reality. On the one hand we condemn a burglar, yet on the other hand we do not consider it a crime when a poor mother steals bread to feed her starving child. This example does not invalidate the universal rule, as it is generally acknowledged that stealing is wrong, but it proves that these universal moral laws must be based on our reason and not on empirical reality (Kant 1993: 37–39). Kant's task is therefore to find a universal moral law based on human reason—an ethic no rational being can dispute, and that defines the good will.

When I perform an action, I am not merely acting. Indirectly, I am claiming that my action is right in the particular situation. We do not usually consider this, yet it can easily be shown to be true. If someone else acts precisely as I did in the same situation and I criticize this other person, everyone would immediately accuse me of being self-contradictory: "How can you possibly criticize him, when you have done the exact same thing?" Everyone would instantly be aware of the fact that reproaching others for behaving as oneself conflicts with reason. In other words, the understanding that the principle of our action transcends the isolated action itself is inherent to our reasoning. Kant uses this understanding when putting forward his famous moral law, the *categorical imperative*: "Act only according to that maxim whereby you can at the same time will that it should become a universal law" (Kant 2012: 34). In other words, we must always act in such a way that we would be able to accept, as rational beings, that everybody else acted according to the same principle. That is to say, we must act as if we were legislators or role models for the entire world.

! **The Categorical Imperative:** Kant's moral law. The point of this law is that we must always act in such a way that we would be able to accept, as rational beings, that everybody else acted in the same manner.

Let us consider a concrete example. I could really use ten million dollars and I know this amount can be found in the bank. My first impulse is therefore to rob the bank; however, according to Kant, I ought to stop to ask myself whether it would be a good idea that everyone did the same thing that I was considering doing. In this case, the consequences would be immeasurable. My action would not merely result in the collapse of the monetary system, but also in the complete breakdown of social order, which in turn would lead to anarchy and human misery. Reasoning leads me, therefore, to understand that the considered action is morally wrong.

In fact, this example goes even further; for it is one thing that I have no desire for society to disintegrate, but it is quite another that my own property would also be lost if my action made armed robbery a universal law. It would only be a matter of time before I would be robbed myself. As a reasonable being, I cannot therefore want something that would turn out to be self-harming. Consequently, I would not want to hurt other people either, for if my action were to become a universal law, it would result in others hurting me in turn. We can therefore directly derive an additional rule from Kant's philosophy, which is a rephrasing of the categorical imperative: "Act in such a way that you treat humanity, whether in your own person or in the person of any other, never merely as a means to an end, but always at the same time as an end." (Kant 2012: 41). In other words, we must always treat other people with respect and not merely as objects, or as a tool to satisfy our own needs. Kant calls this rule *the practical imperative,* and together with the categorical imperative it constitutes his moral law; however, what does it mean in practice?

The Practical Imperative: Understanding the categorical imperative means never using other human beings purely as a means to achieving your own goals, but always respecting them as an end in themselves; i.e., treating them as persons with the same rights and dignity as yourself.

If I rob a bank, I use the employees as well as the owners of the bank purely as a means to obtain ten million dollars. At the same time, I make it permissible for others to treat me in the same way. When the police arrest me, they are consequently permitted to treat me as a means to restoring law and order without considering how the arrest will affect me. If I instead sign a business deal with the bank, I am still using it to pursue my own interests, but I am no longer treating the bank solely as a means to satisfy my own selfish needs, as both parties must agree to the deal in order for it to go through. Kant does not claim that we can never treat each other as a means. For the bank, I am a means to increasing profits, just as the bank for me is a means of obtaining ten million dollars. The point is that we must *never* treat each other *solely* as a means, but that we must *also always* treat each other as an end. This is the difference between the business deal and the bank robbery.

When we give it some thought, we know how we ought to behave. The answer lies in our reason. If reason alone reigned, ethics would become redundant. Kant expresses it in this way: if we always acted according to the categorical and practical imperatives we would live in a "kingdom of ends"; that is, a society in which everyone treats each other not merely as a means but also as an end (Kant 1993: 68–69). In practice, however, our will often conflicts with our reason. There are many people who rob banks or who, in other ways, treat others as a means to satisfy their own desires. If we are to be perfectly honest, this description fits all of us. This is why the moral law is not merely a description of the actual present circumstances, but an *imperative*; a command we must strive to comply with, even though we will probably never live in a "kingdom of ends" in reality. For this reason, Kant's moral law is also termed duty ethics or deontology.

The action that is morally right is identified on the basis of the moral agent's intentions. What does it mean to have good intentions? It means that your actions are motivated by respect for the moral law (the two imperatives). This is the core of Kant's ethics. On this basis, how would he assess our concrete ethical dilemmas?

In Kant's view, lying is the very essence of an immoral action. It can never be justified. And for this reason, he would not accept Viktor's action, even if the consequences of telling the truth in this case would be dire. Nor would he hesitate to pass judgment in the Cheminova case: We can never make it a universal law to disregard human lives to make a profit. This is also the reason why Kant would condemn the manner in which utilitarians weigh up economic interests and human lives against each other. In this case, therefore, the practical imperative dictates that Cheminova's export of methyl parathion is unethical.

However, Kant's conclusion in the case of Viktor Navorski also indicates that his theory too may contain serious problems. For example, the majority of people would be of the opinion that no moral law possesses absolute validity. Although most of us agree that, as a general rule, lying is wrong, most of us would reconsider if the Gestapo knocked on our door asking questions about the Jewish refugees hidden in our attic. In this case, the majority would consider lying to be moral even though they would not want lying to become a universal law.

Nevertheless, Kant's ethics is clearly stronger than utilitarianism in one respect. Kant would never compromise the rights of the individual; he would never allow the sheriff to execute the innocent man.

Virtue Ethics

Virtue ethics is the oldest system of ethics in western culture. It originates from the Greek philosophers of antiquity, Aristotle being the primary classical representative of this moral philosophy.

For Aristotle, the aim of ethics is to understand what the good life is. This may sound a little like utilitarianism, but this is definitely not the case. Firstly, the utilitarian's goal is not the individual but rather the total amount of happiness in society as a whole. Although Aristotle believes there is a close correlation between the happiness of the person and of society, he never disregards the individual. On the contrary, good human beings are the condition for a good society. Secondly, his concept of the good cannot be contained in the utilitarian idea of utility. Thirdly, for Aristotle, the good life is tied to a concept that is completely foreign to the utilitarian way of thinking: the concept of *virtue*.

> **Virtue Ethics:** The ethical theory that views ethics as being a question of a person's character traits (virtues); i.e., the actions and dispositions of a person viewed over a longer period of time, in principle throughout an entire life.

Today the concept of virtue has a slightly outdated ring to it, but undeservedly so. In Aristotle's view, virtues are simply the traits a person must possess in order to live a good life, which, per definition, is a life in society. In other words, these virtues are the features required to live a good life in the company of other people. This means that there is no difference between "feeling good" and "doing good". For Aristotle, we are not forced to choose between doing good for oneself (egoism) and doing good to others (altruism) as we have become accustomed to believing today. The well-being of the virtuous person cannot be separated from the welfare of society and contrasting the two is, therefore, a great misunderstanding. Another modern contrast is the one between intentions (Kant) and consequences (utilitarianism). According to Aristotle's perspective, this too is nonsensical, as virtues lead to good actions and in turn, these actions lead to a virtuous life.

Aristotle presents a vast number of virtues, among others: courage, moderation, and generosity. But is courage a virtue in all situations? Would not the courageous person get involved in problems that could have been avoided in the first place? In other words, how do we identify what defines the individual virtues? Aristotle's answer has later become known as the "golden mean". Virtue is the middle ground between two extremes (Aristotle 1976: 100). When it comes to courage, the golden mean is the middle ground between recklessness and cowardice. When it comes to generosity the golden mean is the middle ground between miserliness and extravagance. This also implies that not all virtues are equally important. For instance, it is because of the virtue Aristotle calls *phronesis* (intelligence) that we are able to navigate according to the golden mean (Aristotle 1976: 209).

However, it is not for the sake of virtue we should strive to find the middle ground. If we stuff ourselves with food we will become ill, and if we do not eat enough food we will also get sick. Living in the middle ground, between extremes, is simply what is best for us. It is living according to human nature and this is how we function best. Living a life in moderation therefore leads to happiness.

According to Aristotle, the greatest happiness is living a life of *sophia* (wisdom), which is to say, a life with time for philosophical reflection (Aristotle 1976: 221–222). Why wisdom you might ask? This is what enables us to comprehend that a moral life is equal to the good life. In other words, through wisdom, we find happiness in a life that is best for us, not in one extreme or the other, such as gluttony and wastefulness.

Since we are social beings according to Aristotle, wisdom in itself is not enough to define the good life. The good life is not just life in moderation, but also a life among good friends in a well-governed society. In Aristotle's view, there is therefore continuity between the ethical (How should I live my life?), the social (What is friendship?) and the political (How is a good society organized?).

However, we no longer live in the small Greek city-states that constituted Aristotle's frame of understanding, and not all of his ideas can be transferred to modern society. Naturally, this raises the question: which elements of Aristotle's ethics are still of use in modern ethics?

Among others, the Danish philosopher Anne-Marie Søndergaard Christensen (born 1972) provides an answer to this question. As we have seen, both the utilitarians and Kant focus on the individual action, more specifically on the *consequences* and the *intentions* of this action, respectively. The modern virtue ethicists, however, continue Aristotle's perspective by understanding ethics as a question of *character*; that is, the sum of the actions and dispositions that characterize a person over the course of time, in principle throughout an entire lifetime (Christensen 2008: 69). Among the virtue ethicists, differing interpretations of this point of departure can be found. Some merely call attention to the question of character while others believe that a person's actions should be judged more or less exclusively according to whether the person is virtuous. The virtue ethicists also disagree on what exactly we are to understand by virtue. Some believe virtues are abilities that can be employed for good or bad purposes, while others consider it meaningless to think that virtues can be used for something bad. Most of them agree, however, that viewing virtues as mere dispositions is not enough. A virtue can only be considered such if it leads to actions (for instance, it makes no sense calling a person courageous if he has never had an opportunity to show courage).

Christensen also mentions other crucial common features of the philosophers who continue Aristotle's views of ethics. One of them is the rejection of what Kant and the utilitarians have in common: the focus on *rules* (Christensen 2008: 68). In practice, morality is neither about obeying the categorical imperative nor about abiding by the rule of maximization of utility. To understand when, why, and how we act ethically, we must instead understand human psychology. For that reason, modern virtue ethics is also based on moral psychology.

As it is, the virtue ethicists would consider the character traits expressed by the actions of Viktor and Cheminova as crucial. Is Viktor lying because he is a notorious liar, or because he is motivated by the virtue we call compassion? Is Cheminova's export coloured by the prospect of profits or by the necessity of pesticides for Brazilian agriculture? In both cases, we must consider the character underlying the action. How do Viktor and Cheminova *usually* behave? As Viktor is a fictional character, it may be hard to determine whether he "usually" lies; however, this is not the impression we get. On the other hand, the virtue ethicist would regard Cheminova's corporate history with more scepticism. The company has been involved in many similar cases, which heightens the suspicion that the company's actions on the market are governed by a desire for profits rather than by concern for Brazilian agricultural production. According to the virtue ethicist, the Brazil case is thus symptomatic of a flawed character.

The three moral philosophies examined in this chapter do not, perhaps, present us with an exhaustive view of ethics, but they do provide a fairly good impression of two characteristic features of the many different approaches to moral philosophy. First of all, it seems obvious that all the different theories have a point. Most of us can agree that morals are about character, about making people happy, about respecting the integrity of others, and, moreover, doing one's duty, but it proves difficult to unite all these different perspectives into one unified theory. Furthermore, it is characteristic that in practice these different ethical schools of thought are not necessarily in conflict with each other. Neither the utilitarian, nor the virtue ethicist would criticize Viktor's decision, yet they disagree about *why* he should make this decision.

Nevertheless, one should not be blind to the fact that different ethical approaches can have consequences for the assessment of real situations. In the autumn of 2009, it was discovered that a number of scientists had manipulated their results to create a more unambiguous picture of global climate change.[2] A Kantian would consider this completely irreconcilable with our duty to tell the truth. A utilitarian would argue, however, that the important thing is to focus attention on global warming and that the end justifies the means. We are thus dealing with direct disagreement, and this example also leads us to the question of the role of ethics in the sciences.

Research and Ethics

Scientific work is not just an abstract search for truth. It is, first of all, a social system of researchers working together. Just as in all other social contexts, the sciences are also regulated by moral norms and values that most researchers hardly think about on a daily basis, but that almost all of them adhere to. These values are, primarily: credibility, honesty, and trust, and these are all expressed in a number of norms defining good scientific practice. Among the most important are the following:

---

2 See for instance, http://nytimes.com/2009/11/21/science/earth/21climate.html?-r=1&hp

- Credit must not be taken for another's work.
- Research results must be conveyed honestly.
- The views of others must be reproduced faithfully.

The climate researchers committed an offense against the second norm by putting forth an enhanced depiction of their work. You would violate the first norm by presenting the results of others as your own, for instance, by plagiarizing their texts or by quoting without reference. The last norm is the most difficult to abide by and its violation is the hardest to trace. Many great theorists have gathered momentum in their own work by presenting more or less caricatured versions of others' theories. Nonetheless, in scientific circles it is expected that the views of others be reproduced faithfully.

The American sociologist Robert Merton examined the historical foundation of the norms of the scientific community, and in this connection, he identified four basic principles that have characterized the ethos of the modern sciences since their emergence in the eighteenth century (Rendtorff 2003: 16–18). According to Merton, the sciences are *communalist* in the sense that their results do not belong to a single person or group, but are common property. They are *universalist* insofar as scientists must be impartial and uninfluenced by external political, economic, and ideological pressures. In continuation of this norm lies the idea of the sciences as a *disinterested* search for truth. Researchers do not allow their work to be governed by personal interests. Finally, scientific work is a form of *organized skepticism* in which all theories are subjected to thorough and critical testing before they are accepted.

These norms apply to all sciences. They are a characteristic of scientific work as such. For this reason, students are, from their very first semester, "raised" to abide by them, especially in connection with exams. For committing what is basically the same offense, a professor can be accused of "scientific misconduct" whereas students will be punished for "cheating" on exams. Because of the rootedness of these norms, it is considered a serious offense when a scientist is caught violating them. In some countries, when suspicion arises that the rules for good scientific conduct have been broken, a special committee for scientific dishonesty functions as a supervisory body in the different branches of the sciences.

Of course, more specific accounts of the ethical rules researchers must follow have been compiled. The Danish Council for Independent Research for the Social Sciences (FSE) provides an example of this kind of research ethical code. In the council's guide, five fundamental ethical considerations are emphasized. Firstly, researchers must consider whether their projects are in accordance with the norms for scientific quality. Secondly, they must show consideration for the people and groups being studied to avoid undue invasion of privacy. They must ensure that their collected material does not fall into the wrong hands, and that they only include persons who have agreed to participate in the studies. Fifthly and finally, the results of the study must be made publically accessible in accordance with the scientific principles mentioned above.

The rules of the FSE demonstrate how special considerations are necessary for the study of human beings. For example, when conducting an interview, the interviewer observes and analyzes another human being. The interviewee is not an object in the same sense as an atom or molecule; rather, he is a person who is entitled to respect. The researcher must maintain the proper balance between the necessary objectification of the other and respecting him as a person.

FSE's rules therefore also demonstrate that the ethical problems in the sciences are not merely of an internal nature. They are also found in the interplay between the sciences and society. Generally speaking, this relationship has always been based on an ethical ideal. It has always been assumed that the purpose of the sciences is to improve human life; however, it has also always been the case that much scientific work does not live up to this ideal. This is true, for instance, of the development of the atomic bomb as mentioned in the previous chapter. Moreover, it is not always easy to decide when the sciences improve human life and when they instead constitute an ethical problem. This is especially the case when scientific work manipulates people socially and biologically, as this raises questions as to both the methods and results of the scientific enquiries. We previously mentioned abortion technology, and generally the most obvious examples are often to be found within the discipline of medical science.

For example, today, women of any age can become pregnant with the help of artificial insemination. In 2008 a seventy-two-year-old Indian woman gave birth to twins, and in Denmark a sixty-one-year-old woman became a mother in 2007.[3] Is this ethically justifiable? Our three ethical theories can aid us in this type of dilemma pertaining to the relation between research and society. The Kantian would claim that these women are not taking the interests of the child into consideration. The utilitarians would compare the benefits and the disadvantages of the treatment. On one hand, it appears that we are not having enough children, so it would be useful to give everyone the opportunity to increase the birth rate. On the other hand, the fact that these children will become orphans at a young age would not produce happiness, so this naturally speaks in favour of banning the treatment. Finally, the virtue ethicist would refer to the Aristotelian idea that the good life is a life in accordance with human nature. From this point of view, it is not advisable to change nature by allowing seventy-year-olds to have children.

The example demonstrates how environmental and bioethical issues take up increasingly more space in discussions of the sciences in recent years (Rendtorff 2003: 77–81). In connection with, for instance, genetic engineering researchers are often accused of "playing God" and it is a game that creates large, complex problems. They do not merely have to do with the comparison of conflicting issues (on one hand genetic engineering can aid in fighting starvation and illnesses, yet on the other hand, it constitutes such a drastic interference in nature that the long-term consequences can prove hard to determine) but also with the question of the role of the sciences in society (for instance, whether it should be possible to patent human genes).

Gene technology is naturally a brand new issue, but medical researchers have always had to take moral questions into account. For instance, it is necessary to put forward a moral code dealing with the use

---

3 See http://politiken.dk/indland/article253672.ece

of test animals, and of course this is even more necessary when dealing with test persons!

The environmental and bioethical problem-complex demonstrates how the *results* of the sciences challenge our moral code, yet in the social sciences there are many examples of how the *methods,* rather than the conclusions of a study, prove problematic.

One of the most extreme examples is the American social psychologist Stanley Milgram's (1933–1984) famous experiment from 1961 (Milgram 2009). In a study presented as an experiment about memory, people were asked to pose a number of questions to a test person in another room. If the test person failed to answer correctly, they were to administer an electric shock to him through a device he was attached to. In reality, however, the experiment was not about memory and there were no electric shocks involved. The test person was just an actor, pretending to be shocked. The *actual* test persons were the people who were asked to shock the actor.

The purpose of the experiment was to explore how far people were willing to go when influenced by a strong authority; in this case, the researcher, who came across as very authoritative. This experiment was conducted only sixteen years after the Second World War, and many people were under the impression that the Nazis must have been exceptionally evil. Through his experiment, Milgram wished to show that this was not the case. Just like the Nazis in the concentration camps, ordinary people would commit the same acts of cruelty if ordered to by a strong authority. The experiment was a success. Many of the participants obeyed the orders to shock the fake test person to such a degree that there was no doubt the electrocution would have been lethal. When the manipulated test persons subsequently realized what they had agreed to do, many of them suffered severe mental problems as a result.

As mentioned earlier, this example shows how the methods of scientific studies can prove more problematic than their results. More specifically, Milgram's experiment is irreconcilable with the second of the five criteria for ethical research put forward by the FSE, which states that participants in an experiment must not be violated. Today, it is commonly recognized that this experiment does not live up to the standards of sound research ethics, even though the experiment yielded significant results.

The experiment also demonstrates how studies in the social sciences can involve manipulation of the persons who are a part of the studies, for instance, by giving them false information. Therefore, a fundamental ethical rule in connection with such studies is that all participants must subsequently be debriefed. In other words, they must be informed of their having taken part in an experiment, and whether or not they were presented with untrue information.

Research Ethics: A Summary

Ethics is concerned with the way we interact with one another as human beings. It is about our morality, and research is fundamentally based on moral values such as honesty, credibility, and trust. For this reason, the primary obligations of scientists are to abide by both the basic scientific principles, outlined by Robert Merton, and the fundamental norms of good scientific conduct. These obligations are generally valid; however, there are also ethical issues more specifically affiliated to particular branches of science. For example, medical sciences manipulate people biologically, while the social sciences at times manipulate humans as persons, and this manipulation leads to other moral issues.

When encountering these different issues in their work, scientists can be assisted by utilitarianism, Kant's deontological ethics, and virtue ethics. These three theories respectively focus on the utility of an action, one's duty to comply with the moral law, and the character of the moral agent.

As we have seen, each of the three moral philosophies are concerned with important aspects of our social life. Often the actual actions suggested by these three views will not differ much. The difference consists in what they view as the reasons for these suggested actions. The researchers can make use of their divergent approaches to better illuminate different elements of their practical ethical issues and they can apply them to illuminate the same issue from different perspectives.

Ethics in Practice

Example: Business Ethics and CSR in Economics and Management Theory

Under the titles of business ethics and corporate social responsibility ethical considerations have, during the past fifty years, come to play an increasingly important role in economics and management theory. Whereas earlier, running a company was exclusively about profits, it is now recognized that profits are not the only parameter for the success of a company. It is necessary to take the social and environmental responsibility of a company into account, and this has led to the concept "the triple bottom line". The idea is that a firm must do well within all three parameters to ensure stable development. For example, if the company chooses to disregard its social responsibility, it may fall foul of the surrounding society, which would cause great damage to the company. Researchers in business ethics have extensively used the three ethical schools of thought examined in this chapter. Obviously they are applied in a different manner than in research ethics, yet the theoretical foundation is the same. Furthermore, research and business ethical issues will often intermingle. This applies, for example, to the Cheminova case. This particular case encapsulates a research ethical question of whether or not the company ought to have developed the poisonous pesticide. At the same time, it also poses a business ethical question of whether the company lives up to its social and environmental responsibility when it exports pesticides to Brazil. Moreover, Cheminova's bad press illustrates how a company can suffer great damage if it fails to take its ethical obligations seriously.

Example: The Stanford Prison Experiment

The most famous examples of ethically problematic research in the social sciences are found in the discipline of behavioural psychology. We have already considered the Milgram experiment, but the 1971 Stanford prison experiment, conducted by the American psychologist

Philip Zimbardo (born 1933), is almost just as famous, or notorious. It was conducted in an artificial prison designed for the purpose. Healthy and normal test persons were then divided into two groups who were to act as prison guards and inmates respectively. Zimbardo wished to observe the behaviour of the two groups, but after only a few days, the experiment had to be discontinued as it had spiralled out of control. The "prison guards" had developed sadistic character traits, while the "prisoners" showed signs of severe psychological trauma, and Zimbardo himself had proved unable to remain neutral in his observations of what took place. The experiment showed how quickly humans identify with socially defined roles, but like the Milgram experiment, because the test persons were subjected to such severe psychological stress, this experiment has been deemed unacceptable according to contemporary standards of research ethics. In fact, the experiment was so controversial, that several years passed before its findings were even published, in spite of no one having challenged their significance. They have in later years been used to clarify what went wrong in the Abu Ghraib prison scandal in Iraq in 2004, where Iraqi prisoners were humiliated and abused by American military personnel, a correlation that Zimbardo himself pointed out (Zimbardo 2008).

Example: The Penkowa case

In Denmark, the most prominent case of bad research ethics in many years took place at the University of Copenhagen in 2010.[4] The well-known brain researcher Milena Penkowa was convicted of embezzlement, forgery, and making false accusations at the Copenhagen city court. That same year she stepped down as professor. More cases in court and at the Danish Committee on Research Misconduct followed. The last ones were only decided in 2016, and in 2017 the University retracted her doctorate.

The Penkowa case was not only protracted and complicated, it also involved more than research ethics, including economic crime. But it

4 The university itself summarizes the case here: http://nyheder.ku.dk/penkowa/.

began with the fact that Penkowa counterfeited documentation for the experiments on animals upon which her doctoral thesis from 2001 was based. The high court has since found that a great many of these experiments never actually took place.

As the case demonstrates, this is a serious violation of the research ethical guidelines. To use the wording from the rules cited above, it exemplifies what it means for the work of a scientist to not be in compliance with the norms of scientific quality. This is because Penkowa's work goes against the second of the three general norms identified in this chapter: She has not been honest about her results. And if you are not honest about the results of your research, you make critical debate about these results impossible (in other words, you make impossible what Merton called organized skepticism), which constitutes the very essence of any science.

Example: How *You* Can Work with Research Ethics

In the above, we have seen how different theories can be used in work with ethical issues in research. For one last time, let us ask our students to consider how they would integrate research ethics into their study. No matter how they approach it, ethical considerations will be relevant. First of all, it is crucial that they comply with the fundamental norms of scientific work and the rules set forward by the FSE and similar institutions. Subsequently, they must consider the specific ethical issues they might encounter in their study of corporate communication. They will, for instance, have to work with examples of communication, which, when publicized, could compromise persons in the company. In this case, the students must consider whether these examples have been sufficiently anonymized, or whether they should be omitted from their study. Perhaps their work uncovers conflicts or disputes in the company. In this situation, they must consider whether these conflicts should be part of their study. Here, they face the problem of their explications strengthening conflicts, which could lead to confrontations that might have been avoided. In answering these and other ethical questions, they can draw on the theories examined above.

Questions

1. Explain the principles of utilitarianism.
2. According to Kant, what characterizes a moral action?
3. How are we to understand Kant's categorical imperative?
4. How are we to understand Kant's practical imperative?
5. According to the virtue ethicists, what characterizes morality?
6. Explain Aristotle's concept of the "golden mean".
7. According to Aristotle, what constitutes "the good life"?
8. Which ethical issues can you think of that pertain to your own field of study?
9. What is your opinion of the ethical dilemmas concerning Viktor and Cheminova?
10. In your opinion, what are the strengths and weaknesses of each of the three moral philosophies presented in this chapter?

Which Key Concepts Have We Examined?

In the third part of this book, we first explored the question of what society and social science is and ought to be. According to the French sociologist Durkheim, scientists are meant to study *social facts* not individuals. Social facts are those phenomena that govern the behaviour of the individual, but which exist independently of individuals and manifest themselves in what he calls *collective consciousness*; for example, religion, morals, and language.

For Marx, it is of fundamental importance that we understand the world according to the way we live and work in practice. According to him, the concept *ideology* describes our worldview as being a reflection of social practices. The significance of this concept comes from Marx's analysis of modern society's organization of production, *capitalism*. This concept encompasses three aspects: society's production is controlled by the capital owners; it is based on the purchase of labour; and products are made to be sold on the market. This means that society is a *class society*; i.e., divided into a number of social *classes* of which one or more monopolize the means of production and thus also the profit created. The ideology of the upper class dominates society because the financial power of this class is "translated" into cultural dominance.

The task of social science is therefore to criticize ideological prejudice found, for example, in texts. Marx calls this the *critique of ideology*.

Max Weber believes that the point of departure for sociology is the interpretation of individual behaviour. This view is called *methodological individualism*. Another feature of his theory is the concept of *ideal types*. These encapsulate the characteristic features of, for example, power or Christianity, and the way in which these phenomena have manifested themselves at different times. Weber uses the ideal types to put forward hypotheses, which can subsequently be examined by social science. One of Weber's most important ideal types is *bureaucracy*, which is the predominant form of government in modern society and is characterized by its purposeful, rational way of functioning.

In the chapter about society and the sciences, we first considered the university as an institution. We outlined *the five basic principles of the university*, which state that universities must provide research-based teaching; that researchers must have freedom to research and teach; that universities are self-governing; and that all sciences, in principle, are represented in the university institution. The beginning of the modern university can be traced back to the *Enlightenment* in the eighteenth century. During this period, the dominant view among philosophers was that society must be improved by the enlightenment of the population, and that all of society must be organized rationally. The Enlightenment paved the way for *Humboldt's university*. The university Humboldt founded in Berlin in 1810 inspired and served as the model for modern universities around the world. Humboldt's university is where the above-mentioned principles were first upheld.

Should scientists be critical of the role of their research in society? The right-wing view that the sciences must be objective and neutral is supported by the positivists, by Weber and by the idea of *the naturalistic fallacy*. Hume and Moore believed that it is impossible to derive *ought* from *is*; i.e., to derive how the world ought to be from how it is. The sciences must therefore limit themselves to uncovering how the world is in reality. Politicians, on the other hand, should make laws based on scientific insights. This is the principle of *evidence-based policymaking*.

We first encountered the left-wing view of this question in the shape of *critical theory,* a philosophical school of thought critical of society and civilization, inspired by Marx and Freud. The critical theorists believe that the scientification of society leads to *alienation.* According to this theory, the way society is organized may conflict with human nature. When this happens, man experiences the world as an alien power, which he is not a natural part of and which he does not belong in. By means of his concept, *cognitive interests,* the critical theorist Habermas describes how the sciences are never neutral, but are always supported by concrete interests.

An additional left-wing view can be found in the discussion of the role of *the intellectuals* in society. "Intellectuals" is the classic collective name for knowledge workers. According to Sartre, the knowledge worker becomes an intellectual when he breaks with the injustice of society. In contrast, Jørgensen believes that the intellectuals' political importance is due to their visionary thinking; something bureaucrats are not capable of.

In the chapter about research ethics, we first looked at three different ethical theories. *Utilitarianism* is the understanding that the morally good action is the one that results in the greatest possible happiness for the greatest number of people. For this reason, utilitarianism is also known as *consequentialism* because the moral quality of an action is solely determined on the basis of its consequences.

Kant, on the other hand, represents an *ethics of disposition,* which is the view that an action must be judged on the basis of the underlying intentions. An action is good if it is motivated by the good will, and the good will is defined by *the categorical imperative,* Kant's moral law: we must always act in such a way that we would be able to accept it, as rational beings, if all other people acted in the same manner. This point is also expressed in what Kant called *the practical imperative:* when acting, one must be sure to respect other people, not merely treat them as a means to one's goals.

Finally, we considered *virtue ethics.* This moral philosophy focuses on the character traits or virtues of the moral agent rather than isolated actions. In other words, emphasis is placed on a person's actions and dispositions observed over a longer period of time. Lastly, we contemplated some of the ethical issues found in the sciences, which these different moral philosophies can help to solve.

Some Important Features of the Selected Themes in the Philosophy of the Social Sciences

Although they differ, the themes of the three previous chapters are connected. For instance, following Durkheim's view that social science must be objective and neutral when studying social life also requires the rejection of the idea that scientists can or should be critical of the role their research plays in society. According to this view, the sciences must also be ethically neutral, so although scientists must comply with the fundamental guidelines of research ethics (because they constitute a precondition for good science), they do not have to take ethics into account in any other way. Their job is exclusively to uncover truth and present it to the public.

However, if one follows Marx and his view that social science must be critical to avoid being ideological, the scientists must necessarily be critical of the societal role their work plays, and they must investigate which cognitive interests govern the sciences. Being critical of the ethical consequences of science is a natural extension of this view, although this is not the focus of Marx himself.

The considerations that are at the centre of these three chapters (i.e., the consideration of knowledge in social science, of the role of research in society, and of its ethical correctness) do not only implicate each other, but in many cases also collide.

The Danish professor of developmental psychology Helmuth Nyborg (born 1937) is an example of this. Because of his controversial research, he has found himself in the media's spotlight on several occasions. On the basis of his studies, he claims, among other things, that men generally have a higher IQ than women (Nyborg 2005). This is a controversial view, also amongst his peers; however, if we hypothetically accept that Nyborg is right, it illustrates well the clash between the different concerns of science. On one hand, we are dealing with an important finding in social science. On the other hand, most people will distance themselves from the political and ethical implications of these findings. If it becomes universally accepted that men are generally more intelligent than women, it could, for instance, lead to political demands that men be prioritized in the educational system. In general, it would prove ethically problematic to argue that men and women are equal and therefore have the same fundamental rights. Just because a claim is true does not necessarily make it socially acceptable.

The development of the atomic bomb, which we considered in the chapter about science, politics, and society, is another, no less dramatic, example of how successful scientific projects are not always in society's best political and ethical interests.

Finally, in the previous chapter, we briefly touched upon the account of the climate researchers who had manipulated their results. In this case, it would be possible to argue that the political concerns of making research directly politically applicable is more important than scientific accuracy. Once again, it shows how the different roles of science do not necessarily harmonize.

The Knowledge Worker and the Three Themes in the Philosophy of the Social Sciences

How can the knowledge worker make use of the three themes discussed above? We have already seen how he can apply Durkheim's, Marx's, and Weber's approaches when attempting to understand an organization. The knowledge worker can also combine their perspectives to illuminate different aspects of the organization. While Durkheim's concept of, for instance, social facts can aid in understanding corporate culture, Marx turns his attention to the conflicts of interest between owner and employee, and how these conflicts are directly, and especially indirectly (ideologically), expressed. Finally, Weber can help the knowledge worker focus on the employees' motives for acting in the way they do, just as his concept of ideal types provides a useful tool in understanding behaviour in both the company and its surroundings.

Understanding the question of science, politics, and society can make the knowledge worker aware that knowledge is never just theoretical, but always plays a concrete role in society. He will be able to directly apply this political and social insight to organizations, which similarly influence their surroundings. Keeping in mind the discussion of the researchers' responsibility, the knowledge worker should decide for himself to what extent he believes knowledge workers ought to be critical of the way the company they work for influences society.

Finally, ethical considerations are no less relevant in businesses and organizations than in the sciences. The knowledge worker can make use of his insight into the different moral philosophies and schools of thought to articulate the company's work with business ethical problems. This work is relevant to the company itself (How does management treat employees and how do employees treat each other?) as well as in relation to its surroundings (the "corporate social responsibility" of companies to contribute to society in a positive way).

Questions

1. In your opinion, what is the most important thing to focus on when studying a social context, for example, an organization?
2. In your opinion, should researchers seek to remain neutral in their field of science, or ought they be critical of the social, ethical, and political consequences of research?
3. Choose an (imaginary or real) exam question from your own field of study. Explain how you would approach the assignment differently, depending on whether your work is inspired by Durkheim, Marx, or Weber.
4. Make some suggestions as to how you imagine ethical and political questions can become relevant to your future life as a knowledge worker.
5. Return to the questions from chapter 1. Discuss them again, but this time in light of the three previous chapters. How would representatives of the different positions answer the questions?

Chapter 15

Conclusion

In chapter 1, the imagined reader of this book was identified as a future knowledge worker. The question is, what has he learned by now?

First of all, he has been introduced to some of the many schools of thought and theorists that in diverse ways have reflected on the sciences and their different roles in society; thus, he has not merely become better at being critical of his own and other's knowledge, he has also become better equipped to delve deeper into the many theorists and problems that, unfortunately, had to be left out of this book. However, whether the reader intends to continue his journey into the philosophy of science will most likely depend on whether he considers it to have a practical purpose, so which concrete, applicable insights should he, preferably, have drawn from this book?

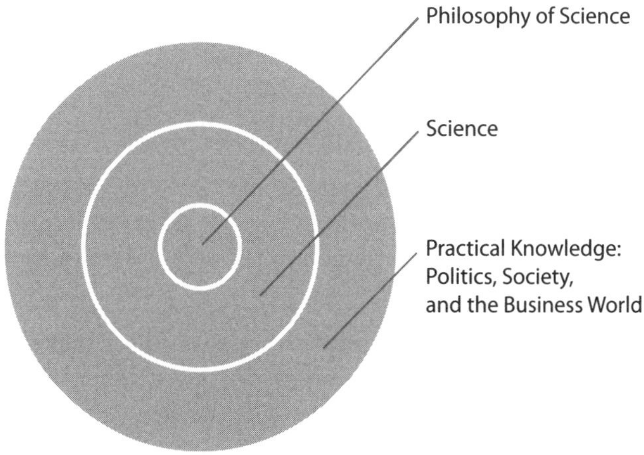

Figure 15.1. Society's Levels of Knowledge

In chapter 1, we applied the above figure to thematize the way in which society's three levels of knowledge are interlinked. Let us now, for the last time, leave the knowledge level of philosophy of science to sum up how this book has strengthened the reader's work on the two remaining levels.

As a student and as a knowledge worker, one needs methodological understanding when approaching one's subject. For this reason our first stop is the scientific level of knowledge. We noted how the predominant methodological understandings of the business sciences are drawn from the ideas of positivism, critical rationalism, structuralism, Kuhn's theory of paradigms, and social constructivism. Methodological understanding therefore requires insight into these theories of science. Furthermore, the examples in each chapter have illustrated how these philosophical insights can be applied to everything from communication to economics, management, and marketing.

Our second stop is the practical level of knowledge. In the summarizing chapters we have presented examples of how philosophical insights can be applied to the knowledge worker's everyday life in businesses and organizations.

Through working with the different theoretical positions, the students will have had opportunity to consider the complexity of the world, for it appears very different according to which philosophical perspective is applied to it. When gazing out of the window, the positivist and the social constructivist will see completely different things. This insight is not merely important for the practical work in businesses and organizations, where different groups with different horizons of understanding must cooperate daily, it also strengthens the knowledge worker's awareness as a citizen in a democratic society where there is not one single truth, but many different perspectives and interests. This was also illustrated in the chapters about ethics and politics.

To sum up, the objective of *Philosophy of Science – An Introduction for Future Knowledge Workers* has been to turn the reader into a more theoretically founded student and a more critically reflective knowledge worker. This classic ambition of philosophy of science can be traced all the way back to the Greek philosopher Plato (ca. 428–348 B.C.), the father of western rationality and science. He is the first philosopher who systematically considered our understanding: What is knowledge and how do we acquire it? In a famous parable, Plato claims that our everyday life is like living in a dark cave where seeing clearly is impossible. Philosophy helps us out of the cave and into the light, where we are able to see the true nature of things; however, Plato's point is that we cannot stay in the sun engaging in purely theoretical knowledge. Possessing knowledge obligates us to share it with others. Therefore, the person who has acquired theoretical insight must return to the cave to lead and help the people who have never escaped it. Once his eyes have re-accustomed themselves to the dark, he will find it much easier to orientate himself because he now knows the true nature of the world.

This book is intended to be just such an ascent from the practical level of knowledge to the philosophical level of knowledge, but as Plato emphasizes, this ascension is not a goal in itself. Instead, the hope is that the student, after having reached the light of philosophy of science, will be much better equipped to use the actual sciences on his return to everyday life in the cave.

Significant Theorists: An Overview

Adorno, Theodor (1903–1969): German-American philosopher, co-founder of Critical Theory. See chapter 12.

Althusser, Louis (1918–1990): French Marxist political philosopher, often associated with structuralism. See chapter 8.

Aristotle (384–322 B.C.): Greek natural philosopher and virtue ethicist. See chapters 2 and 13.

Bentham, Jeremy (1748–1832): British philosopher, co-founder of utilitarianism. See chapter 13.

Bourdieu, Pierre (1930–2002): French social constructivist sociologist and philosopher of science. See chapter 9.

Christensen, Anne-Marie Søndergaard (born 1972): Danish philosopher of virtue ethics. See chapter 13.

Comte, Auguste (1798–1857): French philosopher and founder of positivism. See chapter 2.

Derrida, Jacques (1930–2004): French poststructuralist philosopher, inventor of the analysis strategy known as deconstruction. See chapter 8.

Descartes, René (1596–1650): French rationalist philosopher. See chapter 2.

Dewey, John (1859–1952): American scientist and pragmatist philosopher. See chapter 4.

Dilthey, Wilhelm (1833–1911): German historian and hermeneutic philosopher. See chapter 7.

Durkheim, Emile (1858–1917): French sociologist and one of the founders of sociology. See chapter 11.

Fink, Hans (born 1944): Danish philosopher. See chapter 12 (on the basic principles of the university).

Gadamer, Hans-Georg (1900–2002): German hermeneutic philosopher. See chapter 7.

Habermas, Jürgen (born 1929): German philosopher and representative of critical theory. See chapter 12.

Horkheimer, Max (1895–1973): German-American philosopher and co-founder of critical theory. See chapter 12.

Humboldt, Wilhelm von (1767–1835): German statesman and scientist who is recognized as being the originator of the modern concept of the university. See chapter 12.

Hume, David (1711–1776): British, empiricist philosopher, who problematized the "naturalistic fallacy". See chapter 12.

James, William (1842–1910): American scientist and co-founder of pragmatism. See chapter 4.

Jørgensen, Dorthe (born 1959): Danish intellectual historian who, among other things, has written about the role of the intellectuals. See chapter 12.

Kant, Immanuel (1724–1804): German philosopher of great importance to both epistemology and deontology. See chapters 2 and 13.

Kuhn, Thomas S. (1922–1996): American philosopher of science and progenitor of the concept of paradigm. See chapters 5 and 9.

Lakatos, Imre (1922–1974): Hungarian philosopher of science trying to find a middle ground between Popper and Kuhn. See chapter 5.

Latour, Bruno (born 1947): French philosopher, inspired social constructivism. See chapter 9.

Lévi-Strauss, Claude (1908–2009): French anthropologist and structuralist theorist. See chapter 8.

Locke, John (1632-1704): British empiricist and liberal political philosopher. See chapters 2 and 12.

Marx, Karl (1818–1883): German politician and philosopher, one of the founders of sociology. See chapters 11 and 12.

Milgram, Stanley (1933–1981): American psychologist, known for the Milgram experiment, which raised questions about research ethics in scientific experimentation. See chapter 13.

Mill, John Stuart (1806–1873): British politician and philosopher, and co-founder of utilitarianism. See chapter 13

Pierce, Charles Sanders (1839–1914): American scientist and co-founder of pragmatism. See chapter 4.

Plato (app. 428–348 B.C.): Greek philosopher and founder of European philosophy. See chapter 15.

Popper, Karl (1902–1994): Austrian-British philosopher and leading figure of critical rationalism. See chapter 3.

Rorty, Richard (1931–2007): American pragmatist philosopher. See chapter 4.

Sartre, Jean-Paul (1905–1980): French philosopher who, among other things, wrote about the role of the intellectuals. See chapter 12.

Saussure, Ferdinand de (1857–1913): Swiss linguist and founder of structuralism. See chapter 8.

Schleiermacher, Friedrich Daniel Ernst (1768–1834): German theologian and hermeneutic philosopher. See chapter 7.

Weber, Max (1864–1920): German sociologist and one of the founders of sociology. See chapters 11 and 12.

Wittgenstein, Ludwig (1889–1951): Austrian-British philosopher who inspired social constructivism. See chapter 9.

Woolgar, Steve (born 1950): British sociologist who inspired social constructivism. See chapter 9.

PHILOSOPHIES OF SCIENCE

MORAL PHILOSOPHIES

400 B.C.

Antiquity

500 A.D.

The Middle Ages (ca. 500-1500)

1500

The Renaissance

1600

1700

The Enlightenment

1800

Industrialization (ca. 1770-1900)

1900

1950

2000

Aristotle
The first formulations
of virtue ethics

Empiricism
Locke
Hume

Rationalism
Descartes

Ethics of disposition
Kant

Positivism
Comte

Hermeneutics
Schleiermacher
Dilthey
Gadamer

Utilitarianism
Bentham
Mill

Breakthrough of the social sciences
Marx
Durkheim
Weber

Pragmatism
Pierce
James
Dewey

Discussions of the (role of the) intellectuals
Sartre
Jørgensen

Critical rationalism
Popper

Critical theory
Adorno
Horkheimer
Habermas

Structuralism
Saussure
Althusser
Lévi-Strauss

Theory of paradigms
Kuhn

Social constructivism
Wittgenstein
Bourdieu
Latour

Rorty

Bibliography

Adorno, T. and M. Horkheimer (1995). *Oplysningens dialektik. Filosofiske fragmenter.* Copenhagen: Gyldendal.

Althusser, L. (1976). *Positions.* Paris: Editions Sociales.

Althusser, L. (1996). *Lire le Capital.* Paris: PUF.

Althusser, L. (1996b). *Pour Marx.* Paris: La Découverte.

Andersen, N.Å., C.B. Laustsen and A. Esmark (eds.) (2005). *Socialkonstruktivistiske analysestrategier.* Frederiksberg: Roskilde Universitetsforlag.

Andersen, H. and J. Faye (eds.) (2006). *Arven efter Kuhn.* Frederiksberg: Samfundslitteratur.

Arbnor, I. and B. Bjerke (2009). *Methodology for Creating Business Knowledge.* London: Sage Publications.

Aristotle (1976). *Ethics.* London: Penguin Books.

Baden-Fuller, C., J. Porac and H. Thomas (1986). Competitive Groups as Cognitive Communities: The Case of the Scottish Knitwear Manufacturers. *Journal of Management Studies,* 26: 397–416.

Balibar, E. (1997). *La crainte des masses – Politique et philosophie avant et après Marx.* Paris: Éditions Galilée.

Barnes, T.J. (2006). American pragmatism: Towards a geographical introduction. *Geoforum,* 39: 1542–1554.

Beckert, J. (2007). The Social Order of Markets. *Max-Planck-Institut für Gesellschaftsforschung, Discussion Paper,* 07/15.

Bohr, N. (1950). *Open Letter to the United Nations.* Copenhagen: J.H. Schultz Forlag.

Bourdieu, P. (2003). *Pascalian Meditations.* Oxford: Polity Press.

Bourdieu, P. (2004). *Science of Science and Reflexivity.* Cambridge: Polity Press.

Bukdahl, J.K. (1980). *Kritiske tolkninger. Videnskabsteoretiske essays.* Copenhagen: Gyldendal.

Burks, A.W. (1946). Pierce's Theory of Abduction. *Philosophy of Science,* 13(4): 301–306.

Carnap, R. (1931/1932). Überwindung der Metaphysik durch logische Analyse der Sprache. *Erkenntnis,* 2: 219–241.

Christensen, A.M.S. (2008). *Moderne dydsetik. Arven fra Aristoteles.* Aarhus: Aarhus Universitetsforlag.

Comte, A. (1974). *The Essential Comte.* New York: Barnes and Noble.

Craig, R.T. (2007). Pragmatism in the Field of Communication Theory. *Communication Theory,* 17: 125–145.

Derrida, J. (1992). *De la grammatologie.* Paris: Les éditions de minuit.

Descartes, R. (2002). *Meditationer over den første filosofi.* Frederiksberg: Det lille Forlag.

Dewey, J. (1998). *The Essential Dewey,* vol. 1. Bloomington/Indianapolis: Indiana University Press.

Dilthey, W. (1999). "Udkast til en kritik af den historiske fornuft". In J. Gulddal and M. Møller (eds.). *Hermeneutik – en antologi om forståelse.* Copenhagen: Gyldendal.

Durkheim, E. (1972). *Den sociologiske metode.* Copenhagen: Fremad.

Durkheim, E. (1972b). *Selected Writings.* London: Cambridge University Press.

Fink, H., P.C. Kjærgaard, J.E. Kristensen and H. Kragh (2003). *Universitet og videnskab. Universitetets idehistorie, videnskabsteori og etik.* Copenhagen: Hans Reitzels Forlag.

Foxall, G.R. (1974). Sociology and the Study of Consumer Behavior. *American Journal of Economics and Sociology,* 33: 127–135.

Frandsen, F., H. Halkier and W. Johansen (2007). *Netværk – introduktion til international erhvervskommunikation.* Aarhus: Academica.

Gadamer, H.-G. (1999). "Forståelsens historicitet som det hermeneutiske princip". In J. Gulddal and M. Møller (eds.). *Hermeneutik – en antologi om forståelse.* Copenhagen: Gyldendal.

Gergen, K.J. (1999). *An Invitation to Social Construction.* London: Sage Publications.

Gulddal, J. and M. Møller (eds.) (1999). *Hermeneutik – en antologi om forståelse.* Copenhagen: Gyldendal.

Habermas, J. (2005). *Teknik og videnskab som "ideologi".* Frederiksberg: Det lille Forlag.

Hanfling, O. (1996). "Logical Positivism". In S. Shanker. *Philosophy of Science, Logic, and Mathematics in the Twentieth Century.* London: Routledge: 193–213.

Hansen, H.F. and Rieper, O. (2010). The Politics of Evidence-Based Policy-Making: The Case of Denmark. *German Policy Studies*, 6(2).

Hempel, C.G. (1965). *Aspects of Scientific Explanation and Other Essays in the Philosophy of Science.* New York: The Free Press.

Hempel, C.G. (1983). "The Logical Analysis of Psychology". In N. Block (ed.). *Readings in Philosophy of Psychology,* 1. Cambridge: Harvard University Press: 14–23.

Hume, D. (1985). *A Treatise of Human Nature.* Harmondsworth: Penguin.

James, W. (1907). Pragmatism's Conception of Truth. *The Journal of Philosophy, Psychology, and Scientific Methods*, 4(6): 141–155.

Jameson, K.P. (1986). Latin American Structuralism: A Methodological Perspective. *World Development,* 14: 223–232.

Joravsky, D. (1986). *The Lysenko Affair.* Chicago: University of Chicago Press.

Jørgensen, D. (2002). *Viden og visdom.* Frederiksberg: Det lille Forlag.

Kant, I. (1993). *Grundlæggelse af moralens metafysik.* Copenhagen: Hans Reitzels Forlag.

Kant, I. (2012). *Groundworks of the Metaphysics of Morals.* New York: Cambridge University Press.

Koppl, R. and Whitman, D.G. (2004). Rational Choice Hermeneutics. *Journal of Economic Behavior and Organization,* 55: 295–317.

Korhonen, J. (2002). The Dominant Economics Paradigm and Corporate Social Responsibility. *Corporate Social Responsibility and Environmental Management,* 9: 66–79.

Kriel, J. (1994). *Matter, Mind, and Medicine. Transforming the Clinical Method.* Amsterdam: Editions Rodopi.

Kuhn, T.S. (1973). *The Structure of Scientific Revolutions.* Chicago: Chicago University Press.

Kuhn, T.S. (1977). "Second Thoughts on Paradigms". In F. Suppe (ed.). *The Structure of Scientific Theories.* Chicago: University of Illinois Press: 459–482.

Laclau, E. and Mouffe, C. (2001). *Hegemony and Socialist Strategy.* London: Verso.

Lakatos, I. (1970). "History of Science and its Rational Reconstructions". *Proceedings of the Biennial Meeting of the Philosophy of Science Association*, 91–136.

Latour, B. and Woolgar, S. (1986). *Laboratory Life. The Construction of Scientific Facts.* Princeton: Princeton University Press.

Lee, Y.-J. and Ku, Y.-W. (2007). East Asian Welfare Regimes: Testing the Hypothesis of the Developmental Welfare State. *Social Policy and Administration,* 41: 197–212.

Lévi-Strauss, C. (1958). *Anthropologie Structurale.* Paris: Plon.

Lévi-Strauss, C. (1994). *Den vilde tanke.* Copenhagen: Gyldendal.

Locander, W.B., H.R. Pollio and C.J. Thompson (1994). The Spoken and the Unspoken: A Hermeneutic Approach to Understanding the Cultural Viewpoints that Underlie Consumers' Expressed Meanings. *The Journal of Consumer Research,* 21: 432–452.

Locke, J. (2006). *An Essay Concerning Human Understanding, Volume 1, Books 1 and 2.* Teddington: The Echo Library.

Lyotard, Jean-François (1988). *La condition postmoderne.* Paris: Les éditions de minuit.

Mach, E. (1959). *The Analysis of Sensations and the Relation of the Physical to the Psychical.* New York: Dover.

Martin, R.M. (2000). *Scientific Thinking.* Peterborough: Broadview Press.

Marx, K. (1953). *Die Deutsche Ideologie.* Berlin: Dietz Verlag.

Marx, K. (1968). *Økonomi og filosofi.* Copenhagen: Gyldendal.

Marx, K. (1970). *Kapitalen, Første bog.* Copenhagen: Rhodos.

Marx, K. (1993). *Det kommunistiske manifest.* Frederiksberg: Det lille Forlag.

Marx, K. (1994). *Selected Writings.* Indianapolis. Hackett Publishing Company.

Milgram, S. (2009). *Obedience to Authority. An Experimental View.* London: HarperCollins.

Mill, J.S. (1995). *Utilitarisme.* Frederiksberg: Det lille Forlag.

Mill, J.S. (1998). *On Liberty and Other Essays.* Oxford: Oxford University Press.

Moore, G.E. (2005). *Principia Ethica.* London: Barnes and Noble.

Mouffe, C. (2000). *The Democratic Paradox.* London: Verso.

Nyborg, H. (2005). Sex-Related Differences in General Intelligence, Brain Size, and Social Status. *Personality and Individual Differences,* 39: 497–509.

Ormerod, R. (2006). The history and Ideas of pragmatism. *Journal of the Operational Research Society,* 57: 892–909.

Pierce, C.S. (1878). How to Make Our Ideas Clear. *Popular Science Monthly,* 12: 286–302.

Pierce, C.S. (1905). What Pragmatism Is. *The Monist,* 15(2): 161–181.

Plato (1992). *Skrifter, bind 5.* Copenhagen: Hans Reitzels Forlag.

Popper, K.R. (1974). *Conjectures and Refutations: The Growth of Scientific Knowledge.* London: Routledge and Kegan Paul.

Popper, K.R. (1975). *Objective Knowledge: An Evolutionary Approach.* Oxford: Clarendon.

Proctor, R.N. (1991). *Value-Free Science? Purity and Power in Modern Knowledge.* Harvard: Harvard University Press.

Rendtorff, J.D. (2003). *Videnskabsetik.* Frederiksberg: Roskilde Universitetsforlag.

Rodríguez, C.J.F. (2005). "The Figure of the 'Hero Manager' in Management Books: A Structuralist Approach". In F. Gustafsson, A. Rehn and D. Sköld (eds.). *Excess and Organization.* Stockholm: The Department of Industrial Management and Organization, The Royal Institute of Technology.

Rowland, I.D. (2008). *Giordano Bruno – Philosopher/Heretic.* Chicago: Chicago University Press.

Rorty, R. (1993). *Philosophy and the Mirror of Nature.* Chippenham: Blackwell.

Russill, C. (2005). "The road not taken: William James's radical empiricism and communication theory". *Communication Review*, 8: 277–305.

Sartre, J.-P. (1979). *Forsvar for de intellektuelle.* Copenhagen: Rhodos.

Saussure, F. de (2000). *Course in General Linguistics.* London: Duckworth.

Schleiermacher, F. (1999). "Om begrebet hermeneutic – med stadigt hensyn til F.A. Wolfs antydninger og Asts lærebog". In J. Gulddal and M. Møller (eds.). *Hermeneutik – en antologi om forståelse.* Copenhagen: Gyldendal.

Skytte, H. (2005). *Kend dig selv – og dine omgivelser.* Aarhus: MAPP working paper 86.

Smart, J.J.C. and B. Williams (1973) *Utilitarianism. For and Against.* Cambridge: Cambridge University Press.

Stiglitz, J.E. (2002). Information and the Change in the Paradigm in Economics. *The American Economic Review*, 92: 472–540.

Summers, L.H. (1986). Does the Stock Market Rationally Reflect Fundamental Values? *The Journal of Finance*, XLI: 591-603.

Szöllösi-Janze, M. (ed.) (2001). *Science in the Third Reich.* Oxford: Berg.

Vohnsen, N.H. (2012). *Absurdity and the Sensible Decision. Implementation of Danish Labour Market Policy.* Aarhus: Aarhus University.

Ward, I. (2008). Bricolage and Low Cunning: Rorty on Pragmatism, Politics and Poetic Justice. *Legal Studies*, 2: 281–305.

Taylor, F.W. (2008). *The Principles of Scientific Management.* San Diego: Icon Classics.

Weber, M. (2003). *Udvalgte tekster, bind 1.* Copenhagen: Hans Reitzels Forlag.

Weber, M. (2003b). *Udvalgte tekster, bind 2.* Copenhagen: Hans Reitzels Forlag.

Wittgenstein, L. (1993). *Tractatus Logico-Philosophicus.* Copenhagen: Gyldendal.

Zimbardo, P.G. (2008). *The Lucifer Effect: Understanding How Good People Turn Evil.* London: Random House.

S

T

U

V

W

Z